TORNADO!
84 Minutes, 94 Lives

TORNADO!
84 Minutes, 94 Lives

For Dick,

With warmest regards

John M. O'Toole

The eyewitness story of the June 9, 1953 tornado that killed 94 people and left 15,000 homeless in it's devastating 84 minute journey through Central Massachusetts.

by John M. O'Toole

Published by

DATABOOKS®
335 Chandler Street
Worcester, MA 01602-3402

First Edition
Library of Congress Catalog Card Number: 93-70976
ISBN 0-9636277-0-8

Book Design: Marianne Brady Bergenholtz
Cover Design: Janet Amorello
Typesetting, Electronic Prepress Production: Brady & Berg, Inc
Edited by: Gloria Abramoff
Cover Photo: Aerial view of devastation on upper Burncoat Street. Three people lost their lives within view of this photo. Courtesy of the Worcester Telegram & Gazette and Mrs. Alexander Talbot.
A special thanks to the Worcester Telegram & Gazette and Lafayette Graphics/Davis Press for the use of their photos.

To order additional quantities of this book:
DATABOOKS®
Mail Order & Sales Desk
335 Chandler Street
Worcester, MA 01602-3402
FAX 508-756-9425
1-800-642-6657 (USA)
1-800-262-6657 (MA)

Also available: *Tornado in New England*
by Marvin Richmond, a 20 minute newsreel
documenting the tornado's aftermath.

The paper used in this publication meets the minimum requirements of American National Standard for Information Sciences–Permanence of Paper for Printed Library Materials. ANSI Z39.48-1984.™

Dedication

To all the victims of the June 9, 1953 tornado, especially to the memory of the ninety-four who lost their lives, and to the countless individuals who reached out helping hands, this book is respectfully dedicated.

Dedication

For Phyllis

Acknowledgements

Among the hundreds of individuals who contributed in some way to this narrative, there are a number whose contributions were especially significant, and it is a pleasure to recognize them here.

For background information on tornadoes in general, and for U.S. Weather Bureau maps of June 8, 9 and 10, 1953, Thomas Holmes, chief meteorologist at the Worcester airport.

On Petersham, Mr. and Mrs. Gilbert King, Sr., and Earl Olson; on the two fatalities in Barre, Mr. and Mrs. Donald White, who are brother and sister, respectively of Eddie White and Beverly Strong.

Priscilla Briggs was tremendously helpful with Rutland; Rita Canney's photo of the tornado and that of the funnel in Holden were provided by Jim Duncanson.

Holden's ordeal was most vividly portrayed by Mrs. Alvera Faucher and Mr. and Mrs. Steven Grant of the Brentwood development; Steve Grant also loaned the aerial photo of their neighborhood.

Without the enthusiastic help of Wendell Cheney, describing the ordeal of the Norton Company and its employees would have been much more difficult; Frank Doherty at Norton Headquarters made copies of the Norton Spirit available to me, of great value in identifying and contacting survivors.

Dozens of persons described the funnel's passage across West Boylston Street and up the densely-populated slope of Burncoat Hill. Russell and Agnes Oliver, Simeon Fortin, Anna Rebert, Wallace Myers, Michael Falcone, Richard Girard for both information and photos, Tim and Ruth Connors, Francis Walsh, Fred Underwood, and special appreciation to Pat Cahill for her lengthy letter and to "Bobby" Frankian - a real "survivor".

Assumption College's experience is a story in itself; with the help of Rev. Gregory Boisvert, A.A. and Rev. Louis Dion, A.A. in particular, I did not lack for eyewitness information. Among many others who rounded out the Assumption story were Richard Dion, Edward Kennedy (not the senior U.S. Senator from Massachusetts), William Ormond, who also furnished a striking photo, and Charles Bibaud.

Driane Leland, one of the "two Mrs. Lelands", gave invaluable help with a detailed account of "upper" Burncoat Street in the first moments after the tornado's passage; "Sandy" Naylor and his daughter Lorraine gave a fascinating "ground zero" account, as did Mrs. Alexander Talbot, who lived diagonally across the street.

Paul Webster loaned a booklet published six months after the tornado; many of the illustrations therein greatly aided my research.

The Lee Bartletts, Senior and Junior, the latter now a Catholic priest and a parish pastor, Ethel Gow, Mary Mulhern, Carl Carlson, Barbara Williams, Nancy Connors and Edna Fitzmaurice, Annie Balitis, John Gray and Mary Hehir were among the many who described the conditions in the Clark Street neighborhood (my present residence); the accounts of Helen Phillips and Mary Gagnon were especially vivid, as were those of Sadye Steiman and "Scotty" Benedict.

It is impossible to overstate the value of help provided by Jack and Jeanette Hildreth and their daughter Janie, and that of Kay Jackson. Ted and Alice Mateiko and Paul and Kay Dolan also readily shared their personal stories; so did David Connors, in my only tape-recorded interview.

Clarence Clement and Malcolm Hannah spoke of a day in which their lives were forever changed, when the tornado erased their neighborhood. Irene Howe, Mary Boucher, Mary Dixon and Yvonne Brunell were also most helpful; so were Kathleen Loosemore and Steven Williston telling of St. Nicholas Avenue.

It is with good reason that Chapter Eight is entitled "Diane". Diane Bisnette (nee' DeFosse), who survived the loss of both legs, became a symbolic rallying point in the aftermath of the tornado. [Readers will be pleased to know that the unsinkable Diane never allowed her loss to dampen her zest for life. Happily married for many years, she's fully ambulatory on prosthetic lower legs. She has several grown children and a career managing a group of condominiums in Shrewsbury, Massachusetts. On June 9, 1988, she was the guest of honor at the thirty-fifth tornado anniversary remembrance breakfast sponsored by Worcester's Chamber of Commerce and held on the site of the razed Assumption College science building, in a building belonging to Quinsigamond Community College, present occupant of the campus.

Francis "Bud" Senior and his wife Rita were also very helpful on the funnel's passage through the two new veterans' housing projects in Worcester's Great Brook Valley. Annette Bolduc, who also furnished a photo, was extremely informative as well.

Mrs. Marian Dagostino furnished a gripping account of the funnel's passage across the Humes-Yukon-Pasadena Parkway residential neighborhood. Michael Falcone's patience in showing me who lived where among the cellar holes and foundations now overgrown with tall weeds is deeply appreciated, as is "Franny" Forhan's vivid account of his home's demolition over his head.

Edward Kennedy's lengthy interview helped to convey the tragedy at the Home Farm; Annie Holm's experience at the Lincolnwood housing project was typical of many.

Chapter Nine deals with the funnel's passage through the towns of Shrewsbury, Westboro and Southboro. Robert Claflin, Jr., and Dorothy Allen were especially helpful for Shrewsbury; John Flaherty's account injected a lighter note into the narrative and Steve Donohue, Catherine Monahan, Marjorie Anderson and Emily Weagle provided detailed accounts, as well. Dorothy Allen of Shrewsbury gave a lengthy and valuable interview at a rather difficult time for her, and I am especially grateful.

Among my sources in the town of Westboro, Bob Harvey's help was unparalleled. He retraced the tornado's path through the town with me and gave a detailed account of the instances in which lives were lost and of his own family's remarkable deliverance. John Personis's vivid account of his brush with potential violent death was not exceeded in sheer drama by any other interviewee.

The initial Red Cross response was described in detail by Eleanor Connelly who set the wheels in motion, Cheryl Uhlinger of the Worcester Red Cross office provided a wealth of that agency's records from 1953, complete with photos; documentation to gladden the heart of any researcher.

Francis Logan and Harold Rossi filled me in on Civil Defense emergency response measures and Francis Moy provided an absorbing account of the contribution of area ham radio operators.

Bishop Timothy Harrington spent an hour and a half with me one afternoon describing how his then tiny Catholic Charities organization struggled to meet the demands thrust upon it by a sudden avalanche of homeless and destitute.

Agnes Blomgren collected information for me from other Salvation Army members and volunteers who served during the 1953 emergency. Without her assistance, no meaningful account of that organization's efforts would have been possible.

A number of physicians furnished information which helped me better understand how Worcester hospitals managed to cope with an unparalleled influx of dead and injured. Most helpful were two Memorial Hospital physicians, Robert Dunlop and Ivan Spear. Dr. Robert Johnson a Hahnemann Hospital neurosurgeon gave me a sense of the enormous overcrowding at the smallest of the city's hospitals. Another neurosurgeon, Dr. John T.B. Carmody, described the situation at City Hospital. Philip Finn of Hahnemann's public relations department furnished me with a list of physicians on staff there in 1953 which was most helpful.

I was able to locate and interview a substantial number of other physicians but surprisingly few nurses. One of these, Eva Jones, on duty in Memorial's pediatric ward was by far the most helpful.

If nurse eyewitnesses were in short supply, former National Guardsmen who had been mobilized for up to twelve days service patrolling the devastated areas were plentiful and easily located once Mr. James Fahey, founder and curator of Massachusetts military archives in Natick helped me locate muster lists, by company, of the units activated for the emergency.

Most helpful among the former Guardsmen interviewed were Walt Whitney, John Pakula, Harvey Ball, Grover "Buddy" Wittig, Norm Atterstrom, Paul Doherty, Andy Munter, George Welch, Jack Ronayne and the late Clarence "Skip" Quillia. Taken together, these and many other citizen-soldiers who spoke with me formed a picture of an operation which at least at first was neither a smoothly functioning machine nor a collection of puzzled civilians in fatigues, but of men who, through improvisation and sustained effort, got better rather quickly at their unusual task.

I'm doubly indebted to the Worcester Telegram & Gazette, firstly for its fine reportorial coverage of the 1953 disaster, including interesting color pieces, which form a connective tissue throughout this book, and also for permission to use a number of its most graphic photographs.

For word-processing the manuscript into final form on an Apple IIc, he calls wholly inadequate to the task, my thanks to Dan Tanner, whose many helpful suggestions have made him the "Godfather" of the work, and Ruth Tanner for her efforts in captioning the photo layouts.

Thank you to Caron C. Merrill for her technical help.

Table of Contents

About the Author

John M. O'Toole is a resident of Worcester, Massachusetts. He holds B.A. and M.A. degrees in history, and for the past twenty-five years has taught U.S. History in the Worcester Public Schools. Presently he is also an instructor in the History Department of Worcester State College.

He is married to the former Joan Curé of Worcester and is the father of three grown children.

In addition to TORNADO, Mr. O'Toole is the author of an historical novel entitled *Return to Zion.*

1

The Setting

Like the water-filled footprint of an immense, three-toed dinosaur, Quabbin Reservoir stretches for eighteen miles, north to south, along the western edge of Worcester County. Created in 1938 to meet the ever-increasing demands for water of a growing metropolitan Boston, Quabbin is surrounded by thousands of acres of forest; it lay wrapped in the solitude of wilderness.

On this sultry June day, the surface of the reservoir was dappled by wavelets from a warm breeze blowing from the south. Beginning the previous year, and subject to stringent regulation, motorboats had been allowed on the reservoir. On this afternoon, here and there, a boat could be seen moving slowly across the vast surface as hopeful fisherman trolled deep, hoping to entice a late-season trout. In the shallow coves, other fishermen cast surface plugs or shallow-running lures among the lilypads in quest of a brawny large-mouth bass.

First one, then another and another of these fishermen looked up curiously at the dark, boiling cloud forming above the northern reaches of Quabbin. A peculiar tumbling movement within the cloud began to be discernable, becoming better defined with each passing second, taking on the appearance of an enormous, revolving, horizontal cylinder, rolling eastward across the sky.

A menacing cloud formation slid over the shoreline, passing above a corner of the heavily forested town of New Salem. Moments later, the rolling mass was over the northwestern edge of Petersham. The watchers on the water saw one end of the asymmetrical cylinder reach down like an enormous tapered finger, until it touched the ground. Without pause, the whirling cloud began its eastward march across the forested hills of central Massachusetts, only the looming upper part of the spinning vortex still visible to those who had witnessed its birth.

Worcester, Massachusetts, is a medium-sized city in the central part of the state, roughly centered in the county of the same name. Like Rome, it is a city of seven hills, with little level land between them. Unlike Rome, many of its sloping streets are lined with three-tenement wood-frame homes of a type of construction known as "balloon frame". These "three deckers" are common in the older urban communities of Massachusetts such as Lowell, New Bedford and Fall River. Most were built between the 1880's and World War I.

In 1953, Worcester's population was about 200,000. A combination of post-war prosperity and the burgeoning baby-boom was causing a demographic expansion, especially to the northwest of the city, into the relatively undeveloped tracts of land off Holden, Salisbury and Brattle Streets, in the direction of the town of Holden.

Single-family ranch houses, many with attached garages, were springing up off these major thoroughfares. Other Worcesterites, especially professionals or the increasingly common two-income couples, were relocating from the city into the town of Holden itself, attracted by a desire for privacy, for more spacious surroundings, and, sometimes, for a more favorable property tax situation.

Three years earlier, the same year as Worcester's population edged past the 200,000 mark, the municipal government had undergone a drastic restructuring. Worcester had adopted the city manager form of government. Gone were the old-style autocratic mayor and his aldermen who "ran" the city.

Worcester now had a city manager, Francis McGrath, 41 years of age in 1953, overseeing the operations of every municipal department except the public schools, and exercising a well-defined fiscal authority even in that area.

Worcester in 1953 had a diversified industrial base, just as it has today, and was never a one-industry city. Yet its largest single employer for many years had been the Norton Company, the world's largest manufacturer of abrasives and grinding wheels. A company with plants in numerous countries worldwide, Norton's Worcester facility sprawls for about three-quarters of a mile alongside state route 12 in the northern part of the city.

Its many different plants within the Worcester complex employed a total of 5,700 persons in 1953. An enormous new machine tool plant, built at a cost of $6 million with a modern, commodious cafeteria had been formally dedicated on April 1.

The leading story which greeted readers of the Worcester Telegram on the morning of Tuesday, June 9, was an optimistic assessment of the status of the peace talks at Panmunjom, a town situated astride the 38th parallel in Korea, the postwar boundary between South Korea and its Communist neighbor to the north. The Korean Conflict, an undeclared war, had been raging for nearly three years and had cost about 45,000 American lives. Now, after many months of bitter and heretofore fruitless negotiation, a cease-fire appeared to be imminent.

"An armistice could be signed this week", the Associated Press dispatch confidently announced. "All policy issues, including the voluntary repatriation of prisoners...settled"; only "minor technical matters" remained to be ironed out.

Vying for the reader's attention, however, was another large headline in the upper left-hand corner of the front page. Another AP story, dateline Flint, Michigan, told of several tornadoes which had plowed through northern Ohio, central and southern Michigan the previous evening. With an accurate count of the dead and missing far from complete, the estimate for the Flint area alone was 83, with another 50 fatalities in the southern part of the state. Possibly thirty had perished in northwestern Ohio.

The U.S. Weather Bureau's Buffalo, New York, office was predicting unsettled conditions, including scattered thundershowers, with occasional wind gusts reaching 65 mph in western New York. It also warned area residents of the possibility that a "tornado may occur". The Coast Guard in Buffalo, in its daily notice to mariners, was warning all shipping and boating interests to stay off Lake Erie because of the tornado activity in Cleveland and elsewhere along the lake's western shore.

Locally, some six hundred Holy Cross alumni, from all parts of the country, had gathered on campus for two days of annual homecoming festivities. The alumni were jubilant that "their" baseball team had beaten arch-rival Boston College the previous afternoon, on BC's home field, just outside Boston.

Some of the more adventuresome members of that Boston College class had lured Holy Cross's star pitcher, Ronnie Perry, into taking a ride in a vintage automobile an hour or so before the game, whereupon he was informed that he was a "prisoner". An appeal to good sportsmanship prevailed. Perry was released a few minutes before game time.

None the worse for his short-lived captivity, Perry proceeded to hold BC to a total of four hits. Holy Cross scored eight runs, seven more than their opponents could manage, including the first Crusader home run of the season, a 454-foot blast off the bat of Tony Parisi, Holy Cross's right fielder. The one-sided victory was seen by some as a graduation present to the class of 1953, whose members would be receiving their degrees on the following day in the college's field house.

TORNADO!

For the numerous Worcester area fans of the Boston Red Sox, Monday, June 8, was disappointing. After riding the crest of a 13-game winning streak, the Red Sox lost to the Tigers by a score of 6 to 3. In the absence of their star player, Ted Williams, a Marine pilot in Korea, and despite their recent winning streak, Boston was still 11 games out of first place in the American League in the still-young baseball season of 1953. Boston fans eagerly awaited the end of Korean hostilities, now seemingly so near, and the return of their popular left-fielder to the Red Sox lineup.

Local and area investors in the stock market had seen a lackluster trading day on Monday, with the Dow Jones 30-stock composite index slipping slightly to close off fractionally at 267.91. Many Wall Streeters, it was reported, were saying that the currently drifting stock market was only awaiting the signing of a Korean truce to begin another upward climb.

A popular annual event in the city, the Stadium Festival, a Catholic Charities benefit held at Fitton Field, was just five days off. Along with Julius LaRosa, vocalist on the Arthur Godfrey television program, the guitarist/singer duo Les Paul and Mary Ford would perform, accompanied by the Ted Herbert Orchestra of Boston. The Boston Pops Orchestra, Arthur Fiedler conducting, would perform as well.

Worcester's police chief, William Finneran, the Telegram reported, had just announced that the city's police patrol boat on five-mile long Lake Quinsigamond would be manned for use on a 24-hour basis beginning Monday, June 15, as the local swimming and boating season began in earnest.

On page 15 of the newspaper, it was announced that the local Red Cross chapter would be honoring its volunteers for their work at a program to be held the next evening, Wednesday. Members were to be awarded citations for their volunteer work in a number of service areas. Among these were nursing services, the blood program, and public information.

Members of the city's North High School senior class anticipated class day activities scheduled for later in the day, including a picnic and games. With graduation close at hand, it was the last social activity involving all members of the class.

Monday had been warm and muggy and no immediate relief was in sight for Worcester County. The U. S. Weather Bureau office at Logan Airport in Boston predicted even warmer temperatures than on the preceding day, with inland highs expected to exceed ninety degrees. There was a likelihood of a thundershower in the afternoon.

For New England generally, the warm, unstable air was expected to spawn locally severe thunderstorms from northern Vermont and New Hampshire southward to Long Island Sound. By the calendar, summer was twelve days away; in point of fact, in central Massachusetts, it seemed to have already arrived.

TORNADO!

2

First Victims

At about 4:30 that oppressive afternoon, George Jones, a Petersham farmer living on Hardwick Road, saw the huge black funnel-shaped cloud spinning its way toward the back of his home. Jones ran into the kitchen, collected his wife and ran with her to the cellar. The rumble of the advancing tornado became a roar, shaking the house. In seconds it began to die away.

The Joneses climbed from the cellar into their still-intact first floor, relieved that they had escaped the tornado's fury. Not quite. Across the yard they saw a concrete rectangle upon which until a few moments earlier, had stood a barn. Now the structure has vanished; gone as completely as the wind which had erased it from the landscape.

The couple next discovered that the front half of their home's attic had been torn away as had been parts of the second story walls. These boards had been put in place with wooden pegs when the house was built, one hundred seventy-eight years earlier.

+++

Earl Olson, a Petersham teacher, was working at the general store in the center of town that afternoon, as he often did after school. Standing outside the store, Olson could see the looming black cloud to the west, apparently heading in his general direction. Even as he watched, he saw the tornado change course to its right, angling now to the southeast and passing by nearly a mile to the south of the spot where he stood.

About three-quarters of a mile southwest of the town common, the tornado was churning along a course which would take it across South Street. Set back from the road was the home of the King family. The four young children were home alone. The frightened children gathered around the kitchen window, watching the giant funnel roll toward them. The eldest, Gilbert Jr., 13, had studied about tornadoes in school the day before and he told his two sisters and brother what it was they were seeing. Tree limbs and boards could be seen whirling around in the spinning cloud. Young Gilbert turned off the oil burner at the valve near the stove, then crowded under the kitchen table with his three terrified siblings.

The tornado tore the roof off the King home, as well as much of the second-story walls, creating an enormous updraft. Clothing, books, papers, even some of the lighter furniture were sucked up the stairwell, joining other garments and blankets from the wide-open second story, spiraling upward and outward. The heavy dining room table was somehow dragged into the living room. A fresh egg, about to be cooked by the children, had been lying atop the kitchen counter. In the sudden updraft and plunging atmospheric pressure, the egg wafted across the room, through the dining room and into the living room, alighting on the piano, the shell completely intact.

As the tornado was passing across a portion of the Kings' extensive acreage, it came upon a huge, ancient, red oak tree, with a trunk nearly four feet in diameter. In an early demonstration of its enormous power, the tornado tore the heavy and well-anchored tree from the ground, roots and all, and spun it away, never to be seen by the Kings again.

Next door to the King family lived the Siddons. They had left the house a short while before, going to a dairy bar for some cooling ice cream. It was well that they had, since their home, unlike that of the Kings, was not merely damaged or emptied of its contents, it was reduced to matchwood in a few seconds.

+++

Earl Olson and others still watching from the center of town saw the black funnel moving almost directly away from them, edging toward Route 122, which ran southeastward through the adjoining town of Barre, and on to Worcester.

The tornado pushed across Russell Road and enveloped the home of a Mrs. Larson, an elderly widow. Windows popping, the woman was sucked bodily through one of these openings and dropped, more frightened than hurt, on the lawn. Considering the fact that she and her home had been directly in the storm's path, neither paid a particularly heavy price.

+++

The roaring funnel, its course now paralleling Route 122, chewed its way down the side of a long well-wooded hill and across Connors Pond, a small, manmade body of water. Sucking up some of the pond water and vegetation, it virtually destroyed a small island in the pond.

The picturesque island was a local beauty spot, favorite subject of many area artists and photographers, especially in the fall with its bright reds and yellows. The tornado tore up the island so thoroughly that its esthetic appeal was destroyed forever. Additionally, for years thereafter, the pond would be almost devoid life.

On the far side of the pond, the tornado clawed its way up a steep hillside, apparently bouncing into the air from the ridge-top, not to return to earth until alighting in Barre, more than a mile away. The tornado had been steadily augmenting in size and destructive power in its transit of Petersham, but it had yet to claim a human life.

+++

Slamming back to earth in Barre, it plowed across Old Stage Road. Beverly Strong, an eighteen-year-old high school senior, due to graduate in a week's time, was in her family's large colonial farmhouse, as was eleven-year-old Edward White, whose family occupied the second floor.

The cyclonic winds were now revolving at a speed which may have exceeded 300 mph. They collapsed the building, strewing pieces of the structure downwind for hundreds of yards. Before either could grasp what was happening, Beverly and Eddie were either sucked or blown from the collapsing farmhouse, their bodies arcing 300 feet through the air and passing through the branches of trees, to which small shreds of their clothing clung, before being slammed back to earth, to instantaneous death.

An older sister of Eddie White's had been opening a door to an interior room, and was about to speak to her mother when the funnel hit. As the house exploded around her, the girl somehow landed atop the door, and on it she floated down to the yard, dazed but unhurt. Mrs. White however, would spend a long painful summer of hospitalization and home recuperation.

+++

At quarter to five, the tornado, which had lifted from the ground a few minutes earlier in Barre, returned to earth again in Rutland, still heading in a southeasterly direction. Moments later, Rita Canney, a Rutland resident, snapped a picture of what she thought was merely an unusual cloud formation, across a meadow, a half-mile distant. So far as the author has been able to determine, this is one of only five pictures taken of the tornado during its seventy-five minute progress of destruction. The Canney photo, and one taken a few minutes later in Holden, show a generalized tapering of the tornado cloud.

Rutland in 1953 was a rural community with an extremely small population, part of which was concentrated along quiet, well-shaded Main Street, with the remainder mostly living with-

TORNADO!

in a mile or so of the center, along one of the side streets. One of the buildings directly in the tornado's path was the Main Street home of Donald Marsh, principal of the town's elementary school. The 31-year-old Marsh, his wife Margaret and their two children, Linda, 5, and Dwight, 2, were just sitting down to supper when the tornado hit.

In a nightmare of roaring wind and flying debris, the tornado smashed the home apart and battered the occupants with huge, heavy pieces of the collapsing building. Mrs. Marsh sustained a spinal fracture; her daughter Linda was flung against a nearby tree and was impaled on the stub of a broken branch. The branch went completely through her chest and protruded from her back; she hung there, feet off the ground.

When rescuers arrived a few minutes later, they carefully cut the branch on which the young girl was impaled, as other willing hands supported her weight. Then still impaled upon the branch, Linda was rushed to the nearly Rutland Heights Veterans Administration Hospital.

Donald Marsh's body was found sprawled in his yard, near the foundation where his home had stood. There were no vital signs. As Loring Briggs, one of the neighbors who had rushed to assist, turned away from Marsh's body, he thought he heard the muffled cry of a child. Turning back to the corpse, Briggs carefully rolled it over onto its back. As he did so there appeared tiny Dwight, Marsh's young son, who had been cradled in the arms of his dead father. The infant proved to be unhurt. Possibly Donald Marsh had given his own life in protecting that of his son; no one will ever know for certain.

+++

Margaret Harding and her son Robert - who went by the nickname "Pete" - had recently moved into a new home. Mrs. Harding had lived in Rutland since her son was a year old and had been widowed when Pete was small. By contemporary accounts, Pete was a popular, well-rounded young man, known and liked by many in the town.

On June 9, 1953, Pete Harding's hopes and dreams, and a mother's pride and love in her growing son were dashed in a few horrifying seconds of roaring blackness. When the dazed woman regained consciousness, she was lying on the ground near where their home had stood. Near her lay the motionless body of her son. She was certain he was dead and in her grief at the loss of her only child, the pain of her own injuries was momentarily forgotten.

Demolition of the Harding home was so complete, and remains of the dwelling scattered so far and wide, that the foundation appeared newly-poured.

+++

On Pommegussett Road stood a three-story, 90-foot-long henhouse. The tornado thoroughly demolished the structure and killed between three thousand and four thousand hens roosting there.

+++

Next door to Don and "Midge" Marsh's home was the house of Albert and Phyllis Scales. The two younger Scales children were home, playing with two other neighborhood children. Mrs. Scales had been doing some hand sewing, putting it aside when the Evening Gazette was delivered in late afternoon. Her eye fell upon the front-page headline. It described the tornado devastation which had occurred in Flint and in northern Ohio the previous day. The death toll was known to be at least 135, and there was a picture of an uninjured man emerging from the cellar hole of his ruined home.

At about five minutes before five, Mrs. Scales could hear a rumbling sound which quickly grew in volume. The children said they thought it was thunder, but Phyllis knew better. The noise grew to a roar, the house began to shake and a brownish haze seemed to fill the room.

Thoughts of the Gazette front page flashed through her mind as Phyllis quickly rounded up the four children and hustled them down to the basement. Although some of the roof carried away, walls were buckled and one ell shoved 18 inches off its foundation, the building stayed in place over the heads of the frightened woman and the four children clustered around her.

When the roaring died away, the five climbed the stairs to the first floor. The tornado had blown in the north windows and the glass had pocked and pitted the opposite wall, some shards still embedded there.

+++

Some distance away, on Main Street, Maurice and Peggy Gordon had also sought refuge in their basement, but in this case the wind reduced the structure to a heap of rubble, much of which fell into the basement, pinning Mr. Gordon beneath several heavy timbers. Try as he would, he could not extricate himself.

Peggy tugged vainly at the timbers pinning her husband. In desperation, she crawled up the sloping debris and out through a gap in the rubble, beneath the ruined house. Looking frantically around for someone who could help her trapped husband, she could see no one within hailing distance. She wriggled back through the tiny opening.

She again approached the timbers immobilizing her prone husband. Seizing one, she found to her surprise that she was able to move one end. She heaved it aside, grabbed the end of a second timber and repeated the process freeing her bruised husband.

+++

At her home on Memorial Drive, Mrs. Phyllis Currier gathered her aunt and her five children around her and huddled in the living room with them. As the tornado tore at the house, it was deroofed, windows were blown out and an entire bedroom wing was blown away. By choosing to ride out the storm in the south side of the house rather than the heavily damaged western portion, all seven came through uninjured.

There were only the two fatalities in Rutland, thanks in part to its small and well-dispersed population. A number of homes were flattened, however, and others badly damaged. In the process some of the residents were injured, a few seriously. When the home of Alfred Fish and his wife was demolished, he escaped unharmed, as did the couple's two young sons. Mrs. Fish, however, was badly injured, suffering the loss of an arm and the sight of an eye.

Another Rutland resident's home, that of Charles Martin, was swept from its foundation as cleanly as that of Mrs. Harding and her son. The Martin automobile came to rest upended and protruding from the gaping cellar hole. In the whirlwind of destruction, Mr. Martin suffered the loss of an ear. He was admitted to the Rutland Veterans Administration Hospital, bleeding profusely.

In all, seventeen Rutland residents were admitted to the local Veterans Administration Hospital for treatment, while nine others with lesser injuries were treated as outpatients. With the normal flow of electricity to the hospital interrupted by the tornado, Grenier Brothers of North Rutland, a construction company, provided the emergency power needed to enable the hospital to deliver its vital services.

In one of the more unusual effects of the wind, the poured concrete front steps in front of one ruined home, a single, immensely heavy unit, was pushed ten feet forward, away from the foundation. In the cellar when the tornado struck, had been a large bucket containing a considerable quantity of white paint. When the dazed owner happened to look for the pail after his home had been virtually blown away, he was surprised to see that the paint had been neatly sucked out by the cyclonic winds and whirled away, without spilling a drop on the cellar floor.

+++

Just before 5 p.m., the tornado swept into Holden, plowing first through the Jefferson section, in the western part of town. It struck the poultry farm of Oscar Nygard on Newell Street, leveling the farmhouse as well as the henhouses, containing a total of about four thousand chickens. Some of the birds were blown outwards in all directions by the tornado; hundreds of others disappeared into the whirling funnel.

+++

On a baseball diamond near the center of town, Charles Samborski Jr., 14, stood with his baseball glove covering the top of his head. It was the best way he could think of to protect himself from the walnut-sized hailstones falling all around.

+++

At two minutes past five, the funnel charged diagonally across Salisbury Street fragmenting the home of the Hakala family. Arne Hakala, 37, died instantly, as did his daughter Liisa, 6. Mrs. Hakala and the couple's ten-year-old son Alan were critically injured, but both would eventually make complete recoveries.

A quarter mile further south along Salisbury Street, the tornado blasted the home of William Martilla, He and his son were injured in the sudden demolition of their home; Mrs. Virginia Martilla was killed.

+++

Worcester resident Norman Atterstrom had left the Reed Rolled Thread Company just a minute or two after 5 p.m. and had driven only about a third of a mile down Route 122 into the Chaffins Village section of Holden when his car was engulfed by the tornado and shoved completely off the road, still in an upright position.

When the roiling black wall just ahead had passed, Atterstrom could see that the road was impassable. He was at least temporarily prevented from turning his car around by having a car pushed by the tornado's winds against the rear of his own. He got out and discovered that the car resting against his was that of a woman employee of the Reed Company. Like Atterstrom, she had escaped injury, but she was visibly distraught.

Atterstrom could see a cluster of homes nearby which had been pounded by the tornado, so he set off on foot to see whether anyone was trapped or seriously injured. None of the residents were in desperate condition, and he returned to his vehicle.

TORNADO!

Like so many other vehicles scoured by the cyclonic winds, the wiper armatures had torn completely away, the finish was down to bare metal over most of the vehicle's surface and there were dings and dents all over the body. Less fortunate was the owner of a Buick parked not far away.

The heavy automobile, fortunately unoccupied, was lifted high in the air, upended, and dropped front end downward into the waiting embrace of a trifurcated tree trunk.

+++

Henry Zottoli, a Holden lumber and building materials dealer had been talking that afternoon to local real estate developer Jack Fairchild. They stood in the midst of Fairchild's recently completed and occupied tract of single-family homes known as Brentwood. Zottoli remembers half-jokingly saying to Fairchild that he supposed the developer would soon be breaking ground for another collection of homes.

Casting an eye on the lowering sky, Zottoli bid Fairchild goodbye and headed back to his lumberyard. Back only a few minutes, Zottoli heard a deep-throated roaring sound approaching from the west. When the funnel struck, it peeled off most of the roof of one of the large storage buildings, but that was the worst damage to the lumberyard that Henry Zottoli can recall.

The center of the funnel passed several hundred yards south of the lumberyard and the adjacent Chevrolet dealership belonging to his brothers, Joseph and Ernest. The funnel appears to have maintained continuous contact with the ground as it churned eastward through this part of Holden.

+++

Just to the southward of the Zottoli businesses, across Main Street, lay shallow, weedy Chaffins Pond. Only about 15 acres in size, its surface area and volume of water suddenly and dramatically decreased as the tornado passed over it. The enormous funnel sucked up water, mud, weeds, fish and frogs indiscriminately like an enormous vacuum cleaner, and became at least momentarily, something of a waterspout.

+++

Mrs. Charles Oslund, panicking at the approach of the roaring funnel, ran from her Main Street home, her two-week-old son, Charles Jr., clutched tightly in her arms. The tornado lifted mother and baby high into the air and carried them together for a distance of 400 feet before dropping them back to earth. Slamming into the ground badly injured Mrs. Oslund she involuntarily released her hold on the baby, whose tiny form was spun away by the wind.

+++

After crossing Main Street about a mile and a half northwest of the Worcester city line, the tornado pounced on the new Winthrop Oaks development, an extensive private circular street, lined with seventy-five modern, well-constructed Cape Cod and ranch style homes. Within the space of a minute, sixty of the seventy-five homes in the development were either destroyed or damaged to some extent. Some were completely pulverized and the debris blown from the slab foundations, leaving many as bare as an empty dance floor.

One young couple, John and Bernice Walsh, married two months, were scarcely settled in their new home. When the roaring of the wind convinced the couple that this was no ordinary storm, they sought shelter in their utility room, crawling behind the refrigerator. Their house was deroofed, but the structure itself was left more or less intact. Their new, maroon convertible was instantly reduced to an undriveable wreck. Compared to many of their neighbors, whose homes were simply crushed and blown away, the Walshes were lucky.

+++

Edward St. Andre, a Norton Company employee, was at home with his wife Loretta and two small sons; two-year-old Francis and Kevin, five months. The St. Andres saw the blackness descend and heard the roar of the winds. Within seconds the picture window and the outer storm pane shattered inward, the flying glass missing the frightened family.

Ed threw the children none too gently onto the living room sofa, his wife as well, then lay atop them shielding them from harm with his own body, even as the winds demolished the home above and around them. None of the flying debris struck them; all, including baby Kevin, emerged unscathed.

+++

Among the more fortunate Winthrop Oaks residents were the members of the Kemp family. Howard Kemp's arrival home barely preceded that of the tornado. With no time to plan measures to increase the family's chances of survival, Mr.Kemp hurried his wife and 26 month-old daughter into their ranch-style home's utility room.

Jean Kemp suffered a broken leg in the battering from flying pieces of her totally demolished home. The baby sustained a slight concussion, while Mr. Kemp escaped with only a cut on his scalp.

+++

TORNADO!

A few minutes before five, Mrs. Dorothy Hurd had looked out a front window of her home on Mayflower Drive, in the Winthrop Oaks development, wondering at the commotion in the street outside. The Bacon boy, who lived next door, and another neighborhood boy were trying to catch some of the outsized hailstones that were falling. They were picking up the ice balls and flinging them at each other. They had never seen such hailstones, and they seemed to Mrs. Hurd to be having the time of their young lives.

The short-lived fall of such large hail struck an ominous chord in the back of Mrs. Hurd's mind, and she called sharply to them to come into the house. A few minutes later from the kitchen window at the rear of the house she saw the dark funnel approaching. Dorothy Hurd and the two boys reached the comparative safety of the cellar. The Hurd home was one of the few in the neighborhood with a basement beneath it.

The damage to the Hurd home was light; it sat just to one side of the tornado's path, to the left of the advancing funnel. Beginning a hundred feet to the eastward, however, and continuing for hundreds of yards, were bare concrete slabs surrounded by debris, destruction as complete as that directly beneath the explosion of an atomic bomb.

As the Oslund child was being hurled to his death, the broad front of the tornado smashed into a gasoline station a hundred yard or so further east. The son of the owner was on duty inside the small cinderblock structure. He was badly injured by a flying block, as roof and part of the walls were carried instantly away.

Nearby a horse was standing placidly in its stall as the tornado blasted the barn apart. A scant three minutes later, as human survivors were crawling from the rubble or cautiously emerging from homes, like the Hurds', located just outside the swath of destruction, they were surprised to see the horse grazing peacefully between two of the foundation slabs alongside Colonial Road, 250 yards from its barn.

Although none of the survivors can say positively that the animal did not emerge from its flattened barn, then pick its way through several hundred yard of thickly-strewn debris, it is far more likely to have been carried through the air and dropped near where it was found standing unsteadily.

Examination of the horse by a veterinarian soon afterward, disclosed severe injury to the animal's forequarters, so serious in fact that the animal had to be "put down". This disabling injury to what had been a strong, healthy animal, is further indication that the horse did not get to the spot where it was found, of its own volition or under its own power.

+++

Crossing Main Street from the demolished stable and gasoline station, the right side of th. broad-based funnel churned up Oakwood Street which ran off Main Street parallel to Winthrop Oaks', one hundred fifty yards to the west. The tornado slammed into Ernest Zottoli's chicken coop, killing scores of chickens and defeathering and scattering scores more of the frightened fowl. Many of the birds landed in the backyard of abutting property, upon which sat the 3-year-old home of Guy Jones. The chickens were blown beneath and between a number of toppling trees in the rear of the Jones lot.

Mr. Jones had been making an early supper for his son and daughter, Guy Jr, and Annie. Suspecting that a major thunderstorm was imminent, he sent Annie into the bedroom to close a window. She called back to her father that she was trying, but wasn't able to. Her father then quickly gathered up the two children and ran down to the cellar with them. Telling them to crouch in a corner beneath a large horizontal soil pipe, Mr. Jones ran back upstairs, grabbed two bath towels, then returned quickly to the cellar. He had the two children wrap them quickly around their heads, just as the tornado hit.

When the roaring died away, Guy Jones and his children, like hundreds of others along the tornado's path, warily climbed back to the cellar stairs, wondering what sight awaited them. In the case of this family, it might have been worse - a lot worse. The garage and breezeway had succumbed to the battering winds, but the house proper was still intact.

The doors of the kitchen cabinets had been driven straight up through the ceiling and the refrigerator had been shoved across the kitchen, and there were chicken droppings everywhere. They covered the floor, the countertops and shelves as well; they were plastered against the walls. All thoughts of supper were forgotten.

+++

William R. Johnston was on his way home from his job in Worcester at the State Mutual Life Assurance Company. Shortly before 5 p.m., while still on Holden Street, a quarter-mile or so from his home, Johnston saw a familiar-looking dog racing down the road toward him. Recognizing his dog, Jishian, Johnston braked to a stop.

The dog wheeled around, bounded back to his master's car and jumped in. When the two arrived home a minute later, Johnston parked his car in the driveway in front of the garage, got out and headed for his front door. Loping beside and slightly forward of Johnston, Jishian kept bumping him, apparently trying to persuade his master to return to the car. The dog pranced back to the car and jumped in, through a door which Johnston had left open.

Johnston pulled the car into the garage, got out and started walking toward the garage's house door, a few feet away. Jishian again tried insistently to stop him. Johnston, hearing now the roar of the approaching tornado, looked out a garage window.

Seeing the looming blackness overshadowing Brentwood, Johnston jumped into the car beside Jishian and slammed the door. Man and dog lay down on the front seat, almost burrowing into the upholstery in their common eagerness to get as low as possible.

+++

Once during the interminable few minutes which followed, Johnston felt the shuddering automobile jolt, as a wall of the heaving garage slammed against it. He gingerly raised his head, long enough to see that where the house had been attached to the garage was now a gaping hole. The cellarhole overlain with debris, just beyond.

Mr. Johnson's wife, Phyllis, was in Worcester's City Hospital recovering from surgery. Had she been convalescing at home, she would have been in a bed that was flattened by the caved-in roof.

+++

Down the street a couple of hundred feet and on the opposite side, was the Cape Cod style home of Richard and Esther Smith. The couple had the presence of mind to run to the basement as the tornado was about to hit. They rode out the funnel's short-lived fury there, and when they climbed back to the first floor, found the structure basically intact, although windows were blown in and the interior was somewhat the worse for the scouring wind.

The tornado apparently had exerted a high degree of torsion on the home, with the result that the front door wouldn't budge when they tried to open it, forcing the Smiths to exit the damaged building through a living room window.

Once outside, they could see that a house almost directly opposite them had been blown to bits, as had several others up the street, which would have been partially screened from the Smiths' view by small shade trees. These trees, having been reduced to gaunt skeletons or splintered stubs, Esther Smith's view was unimpeded, and what she saw appalled her.

+++

Alvera Faucher, of 18 Brentwood Drive, had picked up her daughter from her junior high baseball game, at around 4 p.m. Mrs. Faucher and her husband, Charles, had been working in the yard of their year-old home for much of the day, and when the young mother arrived home with her daughter she resumed her outside work. It had been a hot, muggy, airless day, but suddenly the temperature began to drop and a roiling mass of low gray clouds began passing overhead.

Assuming that rain was about to follow, the Fauchers ceased their yard work and went inside. Just before 5, young Alvera came running in, describing to her parents the huge hailstones which had begun falling. Mrs. Faucher was astounded at the size of these monstrous ice chunks, describing them as being "...big as baked potatoes..." This comparison was doubtless an overstatement, but she grabbed several, putting them in her freezer to show any future skeptic.

Within a few minutes, the tornado's advance winds struck Brentwood and the Fauchers saw and heard shingles being torn loose from their roof and whirled away. Outside in the street, they saw Mr. Faucher's twelve-year- old nephew, Larry, trying gamely to push his bicycle toward his nearby home. They would never see him alive again.

Just as Mr. Faucher reached for the handle of the door at the top of the cellar stairs, the tornado struck. The wind's force exerted tremendous torsion, buckling walls and jamming shut the door to the basement.

Mrs. Faucher remembers standing uncertainly in the room, opposite the fireplace. Her husband and daughter were nearby. A blow to the head by an unseen object sent her sprawling to the floor; she recalls sinking into unconsciousness while experiencing neither pain nor fear.

When she came to, Mrs. Faucher was lying on the lawn outside her home. The tornado had passed; it was very still and from somewhere she could hear what sounded like her husband's voice calling to her. "I'm here," she replied, wondering why her husband's voice had a faraway, hollow quality to it. Looking around, she realized that the voice was coming from beneath the overturned bathtub, which also lay on the lawn, a short distance away.

When extricated from beneath the tub, Mr. Faucher was found to have a deeply lacerated back, with several nails embedded in his flesh. Both he and his wife would require several days of hospitalization; his daughter an even longer period. Before being taken to Hahnemann Hospital in Worcester, Mrs. Faucher looked into her rubble-clogged cellar hole. The northwest corner, where they had intended to seek refuge before the buckling caused the cellar door to jam, was, she noted, full of heavy debris.

Across the street, the home of Gerald Davey survived at least partially intact. The Daveys had a barometer mounted on a wall. In attempting to measure the plunging atmospheric pressure the plummeting needle gauge had broken.

+++

Young Charlotte Grant had been released early from her piano lesson in Worcester and she and her father arrived home at about 5 p.m. No sooner had father and daughter come through the door of their home at 6 Fairchild Drive, than Marian Grant rushed up to her husband, visibly agitated.

She was certain that there would be a terrible tornado. She had heard no forecast to that effect, although like many Worcester County residents, she knew of the killer tornado in Flint a day earlier. With Mrs. Grant it was more than a hunch or a premonition - it was a dreadful certainty.

Stephen Grant tried to calm her. Despite her urgings, he refused to accompany her to the basement. Charlotte seemed to take her mother's words more seriously; she followed her mother to the basement without protest.

As Mr. Grant cast an approving eye on the cherry pie that his wife had baked for dessert and which was now cooling on the kitchen counter in front of an open window, he heard a strange growling roar. The window faced westward and through it he could see a mass of whirling blackness studded with parts of trees, buildings and household articles. He headed for the door at the top of the steps leading to the basement.

He grabbed the knob and pulled the door. but the eerie vacuum noted by so many others under the funnel, was in effect and the door resisted his attempts to pull it open. With wife and daughter pushing from the opposite side, he pulled harder, and their combined efforts overcame the suction long enough for Steve to push through the door and bound down the stairs, wife and child at his heels.

Although they knew beyond doubt what the storm was, and they expected to hear the house coming apart over their heads, this did not occur. Instead, after a minute or two, the basso roar of the wind died and the three returned cautiously to the first floor.

The kitchen was the worst-hit of all the rooms. The large window, from in front of which Steve Grant had hastily removed himself as he sprinted for the basement, had imploded violently. The inward blast had been with such force that glass shards by the dozen, large and small, had embedded themselves in the plaster wall opposite.

What was left of the carefully-baked cherry pie was smeared across the same wall, the filling dripping down to the floor. The whole effect of the damage was to make the room appear like the scene of a very angry - and very strong - toddler's temper tantrum.

Looking past his garage to the home of his next-door neighbor, Bill Birge, Steve Grant can still remember the expression on Birge's face when he looked out on the scene, right after the tornado's passage. Birge's jaw dropped, and his eyes, according to Grant, "got as big as half-dollars." What Greeted Birge was the sight of the Grant automobile, which was lying in his own front yard. His own vehicle had been lifted and tossed across the street. If he noticed his battered car at all, Mr. Birge probably paid it scant attention, since it lay against a backdrop of vacant foundations, from which every home had been completely blasted. Without conscious thought, the fortunate residents along the south side of Fairchild Drive crossed the street to offer what assistance they could to their ravaged neighbors.

+++

Directly across from the Birge home, Mr. and Mrs. Regan were deeply buried in the rubble of their home. When he went to investigate, Steve Grant neither saw nor heard any sign of life. Soon, however, someone heard moaning coming from the rubble pile, and the digging, already underway, was redoubled. Both Regans were soon recovered; Mr. Regan would recover from his injuries, but his wife Alice died en route to the hospital.

Three houses away, at the corner of Fairchild and Brentwood, Alice Beek, 59, was blown from her fragmenting home and landed in the back yard, one leg nearly torn off. Blood pouring from a ruptured femoral artery, Mrs. Beek was dead within minutes.

Edward Butler and his wife, who lived beside Mrs. Beek at 1 Fairchild Drive, had just driven away from their home when the tornado engulfed their automobile. The car was flung into the air and tumbled into the yard of Charles and Alvera Faucher, where it came to rest on its roof. Mr. Butler was crushed to death in the compacted vehicle. His wife was flung out of the vehicle, her body travelling past the the disintegrating Faucher home and coming to rest in a basement walkout stairwell at 20 Brentwood Drive, the home

TORNADO!

of Jack Fairchild, the real estate developer who had built the entire Brentwood neighborhood of homes.

+++

Paul Hedlund and his wife Alice owned a good-sized lot of land which sloped up from the rear of their home at 344 Holden Street, a stone's throw from the Worcester line. Mr. Hedlund had been feeding the couple's saddle horse after exercising it in its corral, but at about 5 p.m., the ominous blackness in the western sky made him decide to return to the house.

He joined his wife in the living room, but she felt even more strongly than her husband that something powerful and dangerous was bearing down on them. From her position on the sofa beside her husband she could neither see nor hear what she feared, but she had a feeling...

"It's coming! It's coming!" she burst out, jumping to her feet. "Let's go!" she called to her husband, taking his arm. Where she intended to go with him, she did not know, but she could not bear to sit still a moment longer. And now, "it" had arrived; not the funnel's full punch, but still a wind like the Hedlunds had never heard before, strong enough to shake the house.

Running to the kitchen they could see that the door to the narrow breezeway and garage just beyond was being assaulted by the wind. It seemed about to blow in, so the pair used their combined weight in a successful effort to keep this from happening.

Somehow, the windows remained intact, but they could hear a creaking sound, as though a giant was prying boards apart. It was the breezeway and garage, in the process of being pulled several inches away from the house.

As this separation was occurring, the garage of the Handy family next door was blown upslope, dashing itself to pieces. However, the barn in which Mr. Hedlund kept his horse was not in the tornado's well-defined path, and so after the storm had passed, the couple was relieved to find the animal standing placidly in its stall.

3

Norton Company

After punishing Brentwood, the front wall of the tornado pushed across the city line into Worcester. Within a minute it was cutting through the homes lining the northern end of Brattle Street, a neighborhood containing some of the most expensive homes in the city. The home of the Gustafson family at 107 Brattle was demolished. Clara Gustafson, seriously injured, was given first-aid by Bill Bow, a neighbor, before she and daughter Ann, 15, who was less seriously injured, were evacuated to Worcester's Memorial Hospital. Another daughter, 12-year-old Sandra, was taken in by a neighbor, Mrs. Hollis, who treated the girl's cuts and bruises.

Across the street from the site of the Gustafson home was a just-completed house, the pride of A. Alfred Marcello, Worcester Telegram day city editor. Marcello and a friend of his, Larry Cure', assistant foreman of the newspaper's composing room had spent many hours that spring landscaping around the setting of the new home to make it as attractive as possible.

The busy city editor had been occupied receiving initial telephone reports of tornado damage and organizing staff coverage of the breaking story. He would not be aware that his home and those of his neighbors, tucked away in the northwest part of the city had been directly in the path of the tornado until he went home early in the evening. Unable to drive up Brattle Street past the intersection of Ararat, Marcello would be frantic for his wife's safety as he ran up the street, the houses on either side in various stages of demolition. A fellow reporter would hail him with the news that Mrs. Marcello had not been injured when the funnel completely demolished their home. She had not been at home at 5:08 p.m. that fateful afternoon, but had been visiting friends.

+++

All along upper Brattle Street the storm's passage left houses demolished, such as that of Rev. Eskil G. Englund, that of Frederick J. Underwood and the nearby farmhouse of the Estabrook family. Other homes had whole walls sheared away, giving them the appearance of gigantic dollhouses, like that of Roland Proctor at 79 Brattle.

More "fortunate" residents of the neighborhood, such as John Swenson and Helge Lindquist lost only their roofs, or at least large sections thereof in this grim lottery of destruction in which the tornado itself was the only winner.

+++

Mrs. Harriet Sears thought her home at 198 Brattle Street had just been buzzed by a daredevil jet pilot. Looking out the den window at the rear of the house, she saw large trees in the back yard, trunks and all, canted over at a bizarre angle. Perhaps, she thought, it was not a jet engine after all.

Down the street, young Gerald Sears, 14, had just finished his afternoon paper route. When a sudden windstorm blew up, Gerry, his best friend Peter Carlson, and a couple of other neighborhood boys who were with them, sought shelter in the nearest structure, a barn which had been recently converted into a garage.

As the boys were struggling to close the large doors against the roaring wind, Gerry was struck in the back of the head so hard it made his ears ring and sent him sprawling. His first angry thought was that Peter had thrown a playful punch which had landed harder than intended, while in fact it had been the swinging edge of the mate to the door with which he had been struggling. Before he had time to react, the tornado hit.

Even though spared the funnel's fullest impact, the fringe winds which hit the boys blew them from the converted garage, scattering them across an adjacent field and shredding their clothing.

Minutes later Harriet Sears saw her son being helped toward their home by a neighbor. At first horrified glance she thought he'd been impaled on something, then realized he'd been hastily wrapped in someone's kitchen curtain, over what little remained of his clothing, and the person doing the wrapping had simply forgotten to remove the curtain rod.

Gerry had deep cuts on his face and body and his head ached terribly. Upon being removed to Holden District Hospital, X-rays revealed "green" fractures of the skull. He was transferred to Memorial hospital soon after, kept under observation for several days, then discharged and allowed to return home.

+++

Parallel to Brattle, just to the east, was a short, curving street, Chevy Chase Avenue, lined with impressive new homes, attractively designed and carefully constructed. Conspicuous among them was the home of the Harrison family at number 46. The largest supplier of building materials in the city, Sawyer Lumber Company, had just chosen this home as "House of the Year". It had cost $25,000 to build, a considerable sum for the day, and had received national publicity in Better Homes and Gardens.

The tornado sheared into this showplace, fragmenting the house and scattering the pieces from the concrete slab foundation upon which it had stood. Mrs. Harrison was killed instantly as her house virtually exploded about her.

+++

At about nine minutes past five, Elmer "Al" Hurd, who had just said good-by to his co-worker, Harold Erikson, emerged from "C" Street, a Norton Company street, and swung left, up sloping Ararat Street en route to his home in Holden. Before he had covered two hundred yards, Mr. Hurd had the odd sensation that his normal forward motion had ceased, and that his vehicle was for some inexplicable reason, moving backwards.

A glance out the side window of the car confirmed this. Without attempting to deduce a reason for this puzzling situation, Al stepped hard on his footbrake and engaged the car's handbrake as well. Both braking systems fully engaged, his vehicle continued to slide backward, down the hill.

Seeing any distance was difficult because of an odd haze or gloom. From out of this murkiness, however, emerged something that made his blood run cold. Rolling straight at him was a large tree, a hardwood of some kind. The tree had been torn from the ground and was rolling down the hill toward him, root system supporting the tree's weight at one end, its crown of branches the other, with its trunk off the ground.

With the tree rolling toward him faster than his car was sliding backwards, Al braced himself for the jar of impact. Having rolled to within a few yards of the front of the car, the huge tree suddenly swerved to its left and rolled past the vehicle on the passenger side. Hurd breathed a deep sigh of relief.

Within seconds, whatever it had been was past and over with. The shaken Mr. Hurd, without stopping to inspect the now-dulled finish of his sandblasted car, continued toward Holden and home. Forced by a dense debris field to park his car at the town line and continue on foot, he would find that his home had been spared the tornado's worst fury, and that his wife Dorothy had her own story to tell.

+++

Dr. Karl Benedict, contract physician to the Norton Company, had been to a Community Chest meeting earlier that hot afternoon.

He left the company offices just after five, dropping his boss, Harvey Howard, at the parking garage just off New Bond Street, then turning right onto "C" Street which would take him to Ararat Street and the short drive to his Holden home.

The wind suddenly rose to hurricane strength and the doctor saw one car in front of him spun around in a half circle. Another automobile was turned over by the blasting wind. Dr. Benedict pulled over to the side of the company street, switched off the ignition and grabbed a pillow that was lying on the back seat. Lying across the front seat, he covered his head, listening to the deep roar of the wind and the higher-pitched counterpoint of sand and small pebbles, travelling at several hundred miles an hour, sandblasting his rocking vehicle.

After perhaps a minute and a half, the noise and wind died away and Benedict got out of his car. Seeing heavy damage ahead, he slung a camera which had been on the car seat over his shoulder and headed in the direction of the Machine Tool Division plant. By the time he turned from the end of "C" Street into Ararat, he had entered the path of tornado devastation. Appalled at the destruction, he began taking photographs almost reflexively, including one of a woman sitting in front of her home, from which the front wall had completely torn away, allowing much of the household contents to be whisked away by the scouring wind. The same scene of desolation and despair would impress Norton's Roger Perry a few minutes later, and he would also photograph it.

+++

At ten minutes after five, just as the tornado had begun chewing its way through the northern part of the sprawling Norton Company abrasives plant complex, Wendell Cheney and his wife stood in the Publicity Department, half a mile away on the second floor of Mill 7. With the Cheneys were three or four other Norton employees. Cheney, managing editor of the company's monthly newsletter, the Norton Spirit, had observed a birthday the previous day. In observance, Cheney and his wife would be guests at a cookout hosted by Roger Perry, a fellow employee, who stood with the Cheneys and a few other invited guests, waiting expectantly for the sudden torrential rain to pass, so they could drive the short distance to Perry's home in Holden.

Screened by the rain from this relaxed little group, the tornado was moving relentlessly forward, moving easterly along Ararat Street, shattering plant windows by the hundreds in the plant's buildings along "C" Street and casually blowing freight cars off the spur track which ran alongside the company street. This was the work of the right (southern) wall of the moving funnel.

+++

Directly in the tornado's path was the new six million dollar Machine Tool Division. The building had been formally dedicated a little more than two months earlier. Its spacious cafeteria was well-lighted, tastefully decorated and efficiently designed. It had already won an honors prize for these qualities from Institutions Magazine.

Andrew Peterson, a security guard, was on duty in the guard shack near the new plant. His post afforded an unobstructed view of the funnel cloud as it bore down on his post from the west, and he recognized it for what it was. A plant nurse and four other Norton employees whose workday had just ended were passing the guard shack en route to the plant parking lot, and Mr. Peterson yelled at them to get inside the new brick security post with him as quickly as they could.

The group instantly complied, and Mr. Peterson stood just inside the doorway as the tornado bore down on them. Philip White, one of this group, remembers that another man, whom he recalls only as "George", shouted to the others to lie flat on the floor, which all immediately did. A second later the front wall of the wind blasted the shack's window into flying fragments and blew the door off, sucking Mr. Peterson out of the small building and slamming him to the pavement.

Mr. Peterson sustained severe head and kidney injuries and was rushed to Holden District Hospital. His wife, who would not be notified of her husband's whereabouts or condition until 10 p.m., believes that he was the first Norton casualty to be rushed to that hospital.

Sid Copeland, another of those who sought shelter in the guard shack with Peterson, emerged with a deep gash in one arm, which a doctor stitched closed at the scene.

Although all six occupants of the wind-blasted security shack were rendered unconscious, according to Philip White, another of the emerging occupants, the fact that there were no deaths, and that he as well as Marian Lovell, the secretary to the Machine Tool Division's chief engineer and another unidentified man escaped virtually unscathed, was due, in White's opinion, to "George", whose barked command to "hit the deck", was instantly obeyed by all present.

A stretcher which had been affixed to an inside wall of the guard shack would be found ten days later, several hundred feet away, on the opposite side of Brooks Street.

TORNADO!

The second shift in the Grinding Machine plant was working 3 p.m. to midnight in June of 1953. Since the workers in the shop would not be heading for the cafeteria and a supper break for a few more minutes, all were busy at their work stations. There was absolutely no advance warning when the windows on the west side of the plant shattered and blew inward, and much of the roof peeled away.

Like a rabbit streaking for its hole, a foreman, Ed Ledoux headed straight for a pair of support columns in the center of the enormous plant floor. A big man, he was nonetheless seen to wriggle between the posts, set nine or ten inches apart, and disappear.

Richard Boucher, who had been working in the machine shop for three years, saw the fluorescent light fixtures plummeting toward him and instinctively covered his head with his hands and forearms. He felt the tubular bulbs shatter on his hands and the glass penetrate his skin and flesh, driven by the weight of the fixtures.

Nearby, the overhead crane had been operating near the paint shop; it was lifted off its tracks and dropped down again at a slight angle. All power, of course, had been knocked out, including the means by which the operator could have lowered himself to the floor. Dick Boucher remembers that the face of the operator, whose massively heavy machine had just been heaved upward, was a mask of terror. The man vaulted from his seat, grabbed the two sides of the steel ladder welded to the side of the crane, and slid to the ground, without his feet ever touching a rung.

Dick's friend Bob Moody had been working beside him and when Dick turned to check on his condition, he found Moody still on his feet, but with blood coming from the whole top of his bald head and pouring down on all sides. Dick took him by the arm and led him to the dispensary upstairs, there the profuse bleeding could be staunched, and his own deeply-gashed hands could be treated.

Just as the two men arrived at the dispensary, another worker was carried in, suffering from a broken leg, sustained when the heavy side-planer he'd been operating was pushed over, crushing one of his legs. Boucher helped lift the man on to a cot.

When he turned back to Bob Moody again, he saw that the blood had been wiped from his face, neck and shining pate. The only remaining trace was the source, a small cut on the top of his head.

Arthur Henry, from his work station in the tool crib, heard the express-train roar heralding the approach of the tornado. When the roof stripped away with a shrieking howl, he saw machines weighing many thousands of pounds heave into the air, topple over, or move across the concrete floor of the plant, as though being shoved by the hand of an invisible giant.

He saw a steel beam, perhaps part of the disintegrating roof, sail across the plant without striking anyone. He was struck from behind by a far smaller piece of metal, but so absorbed was he in the sight before him, he hardly noticed the shock of its impact.

Stuart Bailey, whose home and family in Shrewsbury lay directly in the tornado's path, was uninjured in the initial impact of the tornado upon the plant. In the interest of remaining thus, he began running for shelter. Suddenly realizing that the men around him were all headed in another direction, he turned around and headed after them.

+++

Thomas Kivlan was one of the more fortunate men in the plant that afternoon, coming through the gamut of imploding windows and falling fixtures unscathed. He left the plant determined to get to a working telephone, from which to call his family on Pleasant Street, to see whether they had been hit also.

In the plant parking lot, which could now easily pass for a junkyard, he finally spotted his car. It now rested at the far end of the lot from where he'd parked it. Windshield and side windows had been fragmented, and the shards of glass driven into the upholstery. The finish had been sandblasted down to the primer, or in some places to bare metal.

The rags lying in the back seat went unnoticed for the moment. Upon examination later, several of the items would be found to have identification labels, by means of which they would be traced to a Holden family, from whose clothesline the tornado had blown them.

The car started easily. More surprising still, it proved to be driveable, so Mr. Kivlan headed off on a seven or eight-minute obstacle course, which ended at a West Boylston Street pharmacy. The drug store was on the southern fringe of the tornado swath and its pay phone was in perfect working order.

The Kivlan family was in an area unaffected by the tornado, and learned of it only from his phone call. Mr. Kivlan's son, Thomas, had been sitting on the porch of their home at about 5 p.m. and had seen the fall of hail earlier, as well as a rain shower, with at least one lightning flash and rumble of thunder. What had really struck him as peculiar, however, was having seen a flock of small birds in the yard try to take off in flight, struggling vainly to get into the air, almost as though they were invisibly tethered to the earth.

+++

Although the tornado ripped three-quarters of the roof from the huge new Norton plant and shattered nearly every pane of glass in the building, the strong brick walls had remained intact, which accounts for the fact that there was no loss of life in the building and only a handful of relatively serious injuries, caused by the cyclonic winds which howled down into the plant the instant the roof tore away. Doctor Benedict, who arrived on foot just before 5:30 p.m. recalls treating a man with a shoulder injury, another who had suffered a head trauma, and a third man who had sustained a back injury. It is possible, even probable, however, that one or more of these cases was a survivor of the guardshack.

+++

At 5:09, the tornado slammed into the triple-decker at 108 Ararat Street, owned by Ronald Borjeson, Sr., whose family occupied the first floor. Mr. Borjeson ran out to the hallway and threw the main power switch, cutting electricity to the entire building and reducing the chance of fire.

He could hear some of the tenants above him pounding down the stairs toward the first floor. As the two young boys who lived on the third floor reached the second floor landing, the force of the wind twisted the building part way around, unseating it from its foundation and simultaneously shearing off a large part of one wall. What had been a stairway became, in an instant, a yawning chute, down which slid the two terrified boys, past Mr. Borjeson and into the basement below.

The pair landed on the basement floor more frightened than hurt. Reaching up, they were pulled to safety by their landlord scant seconds before heavy debris tumbled into the corner of the cellar from which they had been extricated. Mr. Borjeson's son, Howard, was cut by flying debris during these few traumatic moments, but his injuries were not serious.

+++

At about the same moment the tornado blasted the machine tool guardshack and its frightened occupants, at Norton Company, its winds curled around the home of one of the guard shack refugees, Philip White. His home was located a short distance to the north. It did not lift the cottage off its foundation, but the upward stress exerted by the tornado was sufficiently strong, that when it was released, at the funnel's passing, the house settled back forcefully enough to crack the main beam.

In a freak phenomenon that seems almost whimsical, a house near the White's cottage had its roof lifted off long enough for the ends of the second story window curtains to curl upward inside the house and flare out over the top of the house wall, whereupon the roof settled back into place, leaving the tip ends of the curtains protruding from beneath the eaves.

+++

Just south of where Andrew Peterson spotted the advancing funnel, along the same side of Brooks Street, stood half a dozen duplex homes, built soon after World War II and occupied in 1953 for the most part by young couples with children. One of these children, Susan Casale, age 5, had climbed into the lower branches of a small pear tree, behind her home at 93 Brooks Street.

Mrs. Casale looked out in annoyance at her daughter perched in the tree. Susan had taken a spill the previous day from a playmate's go-cart, and had required several stitches at the hospital emergency ward. Such strenuous activity on Susan's part before the previous injury had begun to heal might cause the stitches to part, Mrs. Casale felt, and the deep gash to reopen.

She walked toward Susan, scolding her as she went, then she saw the sky and heard a roaring sound, as of a freight train, but with a different resonance. The blackness looming above them to the west was unlike any thunderstorm she had ever seen - and she had heard and seen many. She was running by the time she reached the tree and Susan.

Plucking the little girl from her perch and clasping her tightly, Mrs. Casale, wind rising quickly about her, ran with her daughter into the house. Setting the little girl down, she shut the back door, then ran through dining and living rooms to the front of the house, Susan at her heels.

The little girl watched as her mother struggled in an effort to close the heavy front door against the force of the wind. An instant's lull between blasts of wind, and the door was shut.

Mrs. Casale lay atop Susan to protect her, just inside the front door, at the foot of the steps leading up to the second floor. During the ensuing seconds of roaring wind, the west-facing windows at the rear of the house blew in, the glass spraying the unoccupied kitchen. It is likely that the roof, at least along the back of the house, lifted off of the house proper before settling back in place again, as had happened with Philip White's home on the far side of the

Norton plant. "Likely", because it is the only rational explanation for the debris which entered the attic of the still-intact house.

A plywood sheet covering the square hole in the second floor ceiling which gave access to the attic, was blown aside by the wind. The debris falling across the open attic access hole, caused Susan and her mother to fear that their own roof had gone and that the attic was open to the sky, and to any objects falling from the swirling blackness.

Alone of the numerous tornado survivors with whom the author has spoken, Susan remembers a brief lull, when the winds abated sufficiently to allow Mr. Olson, who lived in the adjoining duplex unit to dart across the four feet of porch from his front door to the Casale's. He then shepherded the frightened mother and daughter back to his own apartment.

"Lull", it should be noted, is a relative term in the context of this tornado. Susan, carried by Mr. Olson, remembers seeing several of the small back porches which were attached to the rear of each duplex apartment, being bounced along by the wind, along with whole trees. Had this house not faced east, leeward with respect to the tornado's direction of travel, and had these homes not been spared the full brunt of its impact, then the thoughtfulness and neighborly concern which prompted Mr. Olson's selfless act would have resulted in his death.

+++

Two houses closer to the Norton plant lived the family of John Nylander. They were sitting down to supper at the moment the tornado arrived at their back doorstep. The couple, their daughter and a young friend from nearby Mount Avenue ran for the cellar.

Once there, they found it essential to lean against the door leading to the back yard to prevent its being blown open by the roaring winds. In this they were successful; however, the cellar windows, as with most of their neighbors', had shattered. The wind blast thus admitted blew some of the coal, which had been stored in a cellar bin to await the start of the heating season, around the basement. The flying lumps caused no injury worthy of mention, but far more of a nuisance was the coal dust that had been raised by the scouring winds. They could taste it, smell it, and it stung their eyes. It was moving with such velocity and was driven into the skin with such force that later it would require repeated scrubbings over several days before the complexions of the family members regained their normal hue.

Barely audible through the tornado's roaring was a metallic scraping and banging against the rear wall of the house. With the passage of the tornado, the Nylanders and their young guest discovered the source of the odd noise. Metal molding which had extended around the top of the walls of the adjacent Norton plant to form a tight seal to the edge of the roof, had been detached by the wind as easily as one might strip away the metal vacuum seal around the rim of a coffee can. Huge strips of this metal molding had been blown at high speed into the rear of the Nylanders' house.

Shortly, the little girl who was spending a few hours with the Nylanders, rather than be alone for that time, while her parents were elsewhere, was escorted home. Her home, empty when the tornado struck, had been demolished.

When the tornado passed Brooks Street, it left in its wake a stillness that was profound. Birds and insects did not resume their chirping, humming and buzzing for the simple reason that here, as along the entire route of the funnel, the local population of these creatures had been obliterated; other populations would take time to filter in. What had been an unnoticed part of the landscape, now in its sudden total absence, strengthened the eerie sense of unreality felt by those who cautiously emerged from their homes.

Sue Casale remembers the mud which was pressure-driven into the back wall of their house and those of their neighbors. To her it was just an ugly curiosity; to the adults it would be difficult to scrub away. Even the most pessimistic grownups would underestimate this mud. Complete removal to a clean surface would prove impossible.

Sue looked to see whether the pear tree in which she'd been climbing had been damaged by the tornado. It had been uprooted and blown away, leaving a ragged hole in the ground to indicate where it had stood.

The tornado, after sideswiping the Brooks Street duplexes, climbed the hill to the east and smashed into the single-family homes along parallel Mount Avenue, deroofing some, demolishing others and inflicting many injuries from flying glass and splintered wood, but taking no lives.

The enormous Sunnyside Greenhouse complex, the city's largest, collapsed like a house of cards. The glass cascaded around an elderly woman employee who was seated beneath one of the fragile structures. She was cut by the falling fragments; they were not wind driven missiles, which may have saved her life.

The woman appeared to be in a state of shock, as she continued sitting placidly on her kitchen chair. A couple of men lifted her, still seated in the chair, broke the chair's legs off, then carried it and the woman upon it, to a waiting vehicle.

+++

At the Vellumoid Company not far away, personnel on the second floor hurried downstairs as the blackness descended and the buffeting winds began to shake the building, blowing out windows in rapid succession. The secretaries and some of the other office personnel had left at 5 p.m., others had completed the day's work but had not yet left.

As the last of the workers hurried downstairs, the roof ripped away with a roar. Most of the remaining window panes were blasted to fragments and the metal frames of several twisted grotesquely as the walls suddenly were subjected to torsion of a sort the builders never envisioned. Portions of the walls pulled away at the level of the floor, but the second story did not carry away, as was happening at Norton's Moule Labs.

Alexander Gordon, an engineer at Vellumoid, remembers that the electric clocks stopped at 5:09, marking a moment which saw many people, including some senior company officials, scramble for cover. Instinctively, those seeking protection tried to get as low as possible and to squirm or crawl beneath something substantial, such as a desk or heavy table. The ceiling above these offices stayed overhead for the most part, and there were only two minor injuries, both of which received first aid on the spot.

+++

Mrs. Dolan had been scurrying from room to room of her second-floor apartment at 33 Rockdale Street, hastily closing windows before the approaching storm broke. Her sister, on the first floor, was busying herself in the same fashion. Christine Dolan had heard the strange roaring from the sky, had seen the hazy sunlight quickly dim to a nocturnal gloom. Now, glancing out a back window, she saw something else.

The house that had sat firmly anchored to its foundation two doors away from the Dolans, was now moving across the yard, like an oversized cardboard box being blown by the wind. The windows which Mrs, Dolan had just closed tightly had begun to burst, popping like a string of Chinese firecrackers when the wayward house piled into the Dolan home and came to a shuddering halt. The Dolan garage, missed by the moving structure and spared the worst of the rotating winds, was undamaged.

Perhaps even more surprising was the fate of the home located between the colliding buildings. It was a Quonset hut, looking like half of a tin can; a type of structure widely built in World War II, able to deflect high winds. This particular version, now employed as a family home, passed a wind test on this day such as its designers never envisioned, and remained intact and in place.

What is most remarkable is that the owner had leaned several wood- frame storm windows against the curving side of his home earlier that day. They were leaning thus when the tornado struck and were there when it passed, still lightly propped against the wall, panes unbroken.

+++

Holger Ahlstrom was a standards engineer at the Norton Machine Tool plant. One of his additional duties was to chauffeur Norton executives visiting from out of town, who were in need of transportation while in Worcester. Late on that Tuesday afternoon, Ahlstrom went to the Bancroft Hotel, picked up one such executive, and drove him to the Worcester airport.

It was during the hour or so that Ahlstrom was away from the plant that another out-of-town visitor arrived at the plant, an unanticipated and most unwelcome one. When Mr. Ahlstrom returned, the altered state of the plant and parking lot occurring during his brief absence, made a deep and lasting impression.

+++

Roy Erikson, another plant engineer, was ready to leave at 5 o'clock, but feeling that a storm - probably a bad one - was imminent, he delayed his departure five or six minutes, after which he decided to take his chances, and left. A minute or so later, having driven south on Brooks Street to the point where it begins to curve east toward West Boylston Street, and Ararat forks off in the opposite direction toward Holden, Erikson found himself sitting in his car in the middle of the most violent windstorm he'd ever experienced.

Tree limbs were whirling through the air and entire trees were being toppled. Facing the greenhouse of Holmes Florists, just across the intersection of Ararat, Erikson saw the wind dissolve the greenhouse into thousands of shards of flying glass. Parked only thirty yards from the fragmented structure, Roy heard the cracking and pinging sounds of shards striking and ricocheting from the car's windshield and metal surfaces.

There was a greater concern to Erikson, however, than either the flying glass or the distinct possibility that the roaring wind might, at any moment, overturn his vehicle. A utility pole near his car was leaning toward it. An electric transformer had been installed near the top of the pole, and, even as Erikson watched, the pole was pushed further and further from the vertical, bringing the high-voltage transformer steadily closer to his car.

Then the wind-blast subsided, dying away almost to a flat calm in what seemed to Erikson less than a minute's time. His car restarted easily, then he continued along Brooks Street, detouring into adjacent Kendrick Field, since rubble at the mouths of Mount Avenue and Rockdale Street rendered Brooks Street impassable at these two points.

Passing through the railroad underpass and turning right onto West Boylston Street, Erikson emerged from the damage fringe along the south side of the tornado's swath. The sun shone overhead, and Roy Erikson could almost believe it had all been a dream. Only the cracked and pitted windshield and the front and right side of his car, looking as though sandblasted, served to remind him that the nightmare had been real.

+++

As Roger Perry, Wendell Cheney and their friends had been confidently expecting, the rain stopped at about 5:15. As they were about to leave for the cookout at Perry's the Publicity Department got word of storm damage - unbelievably severe - in the northern part of the sprawling complex.

All thoughts of the social gathering now forgotten, and sensing the extent of the disaster, Roger Perry broke into the locked company darkroom to get the camera used by the official Norton photographer, Norman Flink, who had gone to Boston that day. Together Cheney and Perry, the journalist and the pro tempore photographer, hurried to the tornado-blighted area a third of a mile to the northward.

Their passage along "D" Street, another of the several company streets, was impeded by a scattering of debris from the winds along the storm's southern fringe. Trees, damaged or overturned cars and torn roofing, coupled with countless shards of glass, even entire windows underfoot, posed a challenge to the two men. The damage became progressively heavier as the pair hurried along. Perry had already begun taking pictures and would use an entire roll of film before the sun set, three hours later.

Arriving at the Machine Tool plant, Cheney's first impression of the large adjoining parking lot, which had been filled with scores of automobiles belonging to the second-shift employees and parked in neat rows, was of a sprawling junkyard.

Vehicles lay scattered about, upright, on their sides, on their roofs, in every position and condition imaginable, from those with scratches and small dents to total wrecks, unrecognizable as to make or model. As would later be noted by dozens of automobile owners along the tornado's route, the windward side of those vehicles which had escaped being thrown about by the winds, gave the appearance of having been treated by a careless sandblaster, the inevitable result of the abrasion from countless small pebbles and millions of grains of sand moving at several hundred miles an hour. Even the fringes of the parking lot looked to Cheney like the "floor of a theater after a busy Saturday matinee".

Nearby, also on Brooks Street, Cheney and Perry saw a middle-aged woman, a Mrs. Hedlund, sitting despondently on the front steps of her home. The entire front wall had been sheared off; what remained resembled an enormous dollhouse, affording a bizarre side view of floors and walls, with all the rooms in the front of the house completely open to the elements and to the view of anyone passing by. Roger Perry snapped a picture of the scene, and considers it a classic, illustrating wordlessly both the brute power of the tornado and the total helplessness of anyone who has seen and felt that power.

+++

The full brunt of the tornado struck Norton's Moule Laboratories, just off Rockdale Street, deroofing it and destroying as well, most of the second-story walls, leaving the building "looking like a large modern ranch home", according to an account in the Norton Spirit. The nearby Frank L. Adams Company, one of a number of smaller businesses in this heavily industrialized area adjacent to West Boylston Street, had somehow caught fire in the wake of being struck by the tornado. Despite the Norton firefighting team's best efforts, the Adams building was completely gutted.

TORNADO!

4

Mother Will Be Worried

At 5:10, the air was filled with flying lumber as the tornado tore into the Diamond National Company's lumberyard, located beside West Boylston Street, a busy thoroughfare which appeared on road maps as state route 12. The whirling planks, moving almost at the speed of the winds which carried them aloft, became lethal objects. A National Guard truck, returning to the city armory from Fort Devens was moving south on the highway, and had nearly pulled opposite the lumberyard. Before the driver, Sergeant Edwin Larson, or the man in the cab with him, Warrant Officer Henry Wolosz, knew what was happening, the wind lifted the 7-ton truck off the road and set it down in the opposite lane. It also sent a piece of lumber lancing through the windshield into the cab, striking the driver a glancing blow on the back.

A short distance behind the truck and also headed south, was an automobile driven by Mrs. Josephine Lee. Beside her sat her son Robert, 14. Like the heavy truck just ahead, they were just outside the tornado's "left wall" of cyclonic wind as the funnel plowed across West Boylston Street. The Lee vehicle was not overturned, nor was it struck by lumber or other heavy objects whirling just ahead, but young Bob Lee and his mother had just witnessed a fall of heavy hailstones, bouncing from the hood of their car, now they saw pieces of straw sift down, followed by several dead frogs, late of Chaffins Pond, which splatted into the vehicle and prompted young Bob to remark to his mother that it seemed to be "raining frogs."

The tornado had appeared so suddenly and violently that both Mrs. Lee and her son thought there had been an explosion at the near-by Vellumoid Company. They knew Vellumoid was doing some semi-secret work under contract to the government, and they thought this might have been the source of an accidental blast.

Less lucky was another motorist, Bruno Holmstrom, who was driving in the opposite direction. A windborne sign, wrenched from its moorings by the funnel slammed into his car, demolishing it and badly injuring Mr. Holmstrom.

Less fortunate still were three occupants of another car heading in the same direction as Holmstrom. Ann Lovell of Norton's Routing Department had left work an hour earlier. With her sister, Joan Karras, and Joan's husband Peter, she had stopped at Fortin's Market in Greendale, for some grocery shopping. At eight minutes after five, the three left the market and headed north on Route 12, en route home to the Oakdale section of West Boylston, six miles away. A minute later they were opposite the Diamond National lumberyard, when the tornado hit them broadside.

Wind and wood smashed into the car simultaneously. The vehicle was lifted and flung hundreds of feet, landing atop a house, which was also in the process of collapse. Death, for the two sisters was almost instantaneous. Joan Karras's identity was tentatively made by means of her husband's driver's license, found on her person. So extensively mutilated was Ann's body that she could only be identified by her family's physician, who recognized a scar on one of her hands, the result of minor surgery which he had performed. He was doubly certain when he recognized an unusual ring which Ann always wore on the same hand.

+++

Simeon Fortin, manager of Greendale's only supermarket, was in the meatroom of the two-year-old frame building at 550 West Boylston Street when the first of the five large plate glass windows which extended across the front of the store blew in. Thinking that perhaps a truck had rammed into the front of the building, Mr. Fortin ran out of the meat room and into the main store.

Before he'd covered half the distance to the front of the store, a second window, adjacent to the first, was blown in by the force of the wind. Mr. Fortin yelled for the cashiers and the small number of patrons to go through an interior door on one side of the building and down the stairs to the basement beneath. This space was not illuminated, and people were hesitant to follow this directive, so Fortin immediately shepherded them into the meatroom, furthest from the flying glass, as a third window burst.

Running back to the front of the store to be certain that everyone had cleared the area, Fortin glanced around quickly, noting that the three heavy cash registers had been flung to the floor and that the main door at one front corner of the store had blown completely off its hinges.

Just inside the door and directly in front of one of the two remaining plate glass windows was a circular table, placed there for the convenience of adults who wished to rest. It also functioned as an inanimate baby-sitter for shopping mothers, with its magazines and simple games.

At this moment, with the fringe winds of the tornado shrieking through the broken windows and door, and howling through the aisles, Fortin spotted two small children, obviously terrified, but sitting obediently and quietly where their mother had left them before beginning her shopping. Mr. Fortin grabbed the two children and half-dragged, half-carried them as quickly as he could, to the safety of the back room.

Busy as he was trying to see to the safety of his customers and employees, Simeon Fortin probably did not take the time to ponder the fate of customers who had left his store just before the tornado struck. Later, however, he would recall that Ann Lovell and Joan Karras had finished their shopping and were ready to depart shortly after 5.

Mr. Fortin, apprehensive because of the looming blackness in the west visible through the front windows, had urged the sisters to remain in the store until it could be determined if a storm was about to break. The two women had voiced concerns about their mother, alone at home, who, they felt would be worried should their arrival home be delayed. And so, with Joan's husband, and against Simeon Fortin's advice, they had departed.

+++

On short, unpaved Hyde Street, which ran along the western slope of Burncoat Hill, parallel with West Boylston Street and overlooking it, stood the home of the Rebert family. Mrs. Rebert had hosted a bridge party at her home that afternoon. Just after 5 p.m., the son of one of the women arrived to drive his mother and the other two women home.

Wallace Myers, a law student in his early twenties, was home from college for summer vacation. He had been painting wooden lawn furniture that afternoon when he climbed into his big 1942 Oldsmobile and drove to the Rebert home.

With his mother on the front seat beside him and the other women in back, Wallace turned right onto Randall Street, coasted down the hill and turned right onto West Boylston Street, heading north, to begin delivering his mother's friends to their homes.

As he passed the mouth of Trottier Street, having driven only one block on the highway, the leading edge of the tornado caught his vehicle, rocking the heavy car. Up ahead, Myers could see the billboard atop the Pullman Standard building fold down like a box-top, so he pulled over to the curb, half-consciously positioning

TORNADO!

himself midway between two tall and dangerously swaying light poles. Just as he applied the emergency brake and switched off the engine, the funnel hit full force.

Instantly, both windshields and all side windows vanished as Myers yelled: "Watch out for glass...get down!" He and the three women crouched down and protected their heads as best they could. Wallace felt the left side of the vehicle rise as the car was lifted into the air. The sensation reminded him of one of the rides at nearby White City amusement park.

The vehicle came to rest some seventy-five yards to the northeast, halfway up Assumption College's long, sloping, front lawn. Wallace Myers was uninjured; his mother, Priscilla, and Mabel Phillips were bruised and cut, shards of glass from the vehicle's shattered windows driven under their skin.

The fourth occupant of the vehicle, Mrs. Blanche Lesage, sustained a number of serious injuries. The others, after squirming from the overturned auto, tried to make her as comfortable as possible while she awaited removal to Hahnemann Hospital.

Wallace saw what was left of another wrecked automobile lying not far away. He approached and saw the battered, blood-smeared bodies lying near it. In spite of himself he had to turn away from the bodies of Ann Lovell and her sister. Peter Karras, Joan's husband, lay nearby. Few of the onlookers could tell that the young man still clung to life; fewer would have given him any chance of survival.

+++

Mrs. Agnes Oliver stood looking out a west-facing window of her second-floor apartment at 25 Randall Street. The two-story house stood on the lower slope of Burncoat Hill, almost in front of the Rebert dwelling and nearer West Boylston Street.

"Come look at this, Russ," she called to her husband; "it's a tornado, just like the one we read about in the paper this morning!"

Agnes could see the looming black funnel, only a few hundred yards away and seemingly headed straight for them. She could make out barrels and fuel tanks being whirled around in the spinning maelstrom, objects picked up either in the Vellumoid plant or from Jon's Railroad Salvage, both diagonally across West Boylston Street from where she stood staring in horrified fascination.

+++

Just a hundred yards or so downhill from Agnes Oliver's vantage point stood the Shell gasoline station of Harland Tupper, at 600 West Boylston Street. The tornado exploded the station's large plate glass window and several smaller ones, but the outward-flying glass fortunately struck no one. The wind's roaring reminded Mr. Tupper of a squadron of World War II bombers.

When the funnel had passed, Mr. Tupper made several runs in his panel truck, taking injured neighbors to City and Memorial hospitals. He then spent several hours helping to extricate a Mrs. Daley from the ruins of her home. When freed she was found to be virtually uninjured.

+++

Three houses uphill from Agnes Oliver's vantage point, Douglas Anderson, 18, had been taking a late-afternoon nap when he was awakened by the rising wind, with an underlying rumble that grew steadily louder. He had just gotten out of bed and reached the bedroom door, when the window opposite imploded. Pieces of glass flew across the room faster than the eye could follow, some to pulverize against the wall, other shards driven into it like spearheads by a wind such as Douglas had never before experienced.

Directly across the street, at number 40 Randall Street, young Bobby Frankian had been watching the funnel's approach through the west-facing kitchen window of his family's third-floor apartment. The twelve-year-old had seen a Movietone newsreel at the Greendale theater the previous Saturday in which tornadoes, that had been punishing the Midwest and plains states this spring of 1953, were shown. They had been both unusually frequent and especially destructive this spring.

Bobby had heard what he thought was a train passing on the tracks just across West Boylston Street about 250 yards from their home. Mrs. Frankian called to her son from the bathroom, wondering aloud why the noise didn't fade as the train passed and moved away. Looking down at the tracks, the youngster could see no train, but instead saw sizeable objects, which he couldn't identify, flying through the air. Then it was coming toward him, a looming, churning, black cloud half a mile or less across the tracks and headed his way.

Bobby called to his mother, still in the bathroom. "There is no train, Mom...it's a tornado! Let's get out!"

His mother called back in disbelief, telling him that he was crazy; we simply didn't have tornadoes in this part of the country.

Bobby didn't bother calling back to his mother, to try to reason with her; instead he ran into the bathroom. His mother was no longer there. By now the house had started to shake.

He found his mother at a dining room window in the front of the house. It was not a good vantage point from which to see the approaching tornado; trees and the three-decker across the street blocked most of the view to the northwest.

"Please, Mom...let's get out!" Bobby yelled, grabbing his mother around her waist. The house was rocking in the windblast; now windows on the north and northwest sides of the apartment began to blow out.

Bobby grabbed his mother and began pulling her into the kitchen. The two could hear the snapping of timbers and feel the house begin to settle beneath their feet. Within seconds the remaining window panes were gone, admitting a blast of wind which acted on the furniture and other articles like water from a high-pressure hose, smashing them to pieces and whirling the fragments through the air, to be sucked out through one of the gaping holes where moments before there had been a window.

Mother and son started down the stairs at the back of the house, descending almost to the second floor when the buckling and settling of the house seemed to accelerate. Bobby pulled his mother up to the top of the staircase, setting her down on the second step. He sat on the top step, above and behind her, wrapping his arms around his mother and pressing his face into her back, while telling her to lean forward and try to put her face between her legs. This type of self-protection he remembered from recent Boy Scout training.

At the same moment, across the street, Douglas on the top floor, had retreated with his mother and grandmother to the comparative safety of the enclosed back hall. The house settled rapidly, possibly as the tornado's eye passed over. In the stairwell, Douglas and the two women felt as though they were riding a cushion of air, or were on a descending escalator, as the stairs upon which they stood neared the ground.

The Frankians, mother and son, were likewise nearing the ground, although they still crouched at the top of the stairs, nearly at the level of the third floor. Had they stayed on the stairs near the second floor level, they would have been crushed as the building folded inward at this point, west-side windows on the second floor now pointing upwards like skylights, while the first floor and its occupants, the Aslanians, slid downward into the basement.

The whole back wall had torn away as the house was collapsing and now, suddenly, it was over. The sun shone brightly in the silence. Bobby and his mother crawled down from where they had sat on the steps, now only 8 or 10 feet from the ground.

Mrs. Frankian was nearly hysterical. She was sure the neighborhood had been hit by an atomic bomb, and thought at first that she and her son were the only survivors. The two climbed over the debris and came around to what had been the front of the house. Within a minute or two, other voices began to be heard. Bobby and his mother walked a few hundred feet north, in the direction of Assumption College, then, moving just as aimlessly, returned to where their own home had stood.

They saw Bobby's cousins, the ten-year-old Karagosian twins, crawl up through the crazily-canted second-floor windows, helped to safety by Richard Paretti, a neighbor from Fales Street, whose back yard abutted that of the collapsed three-decker. The twins said that they had crawled under the kitchen table when the house seemed to be falling apart. They were not sure of their mother's whereabouts. She would shortly be found in the basement, crushed beneath rubble deposited by the jackknifing floors.

Bobby's aunt, Betty Aslanian, lived on the first floor with her husband, daughters Nancy and Marilyn, and her mother-in-law, Mary Aslanian. Mr. Aslanian was not yet home from work. While pinned in the rubble, awaiting rescue, Betty Aslanian's arms were badly burned by electric wires. Her daughter Marilyn lay in the rubble with a broken leg.

Rescue efforts involved digging down, tunnel-fashion, to the trapped family. After six hours, the two women and little Marilyn were finally extricated. The body of five-year-old Nancy Aslanian was found under a radiator.

Diagonally across the street, the two-decker at 43 Randall Street was flattened in the opposite direction, uphill. Mrs. Sigrid Johnson, owner and first floor occupant was killed in the collapse. Her daughter-in-law, who lived upstairs, escaped through a trap door that opened onto the roof, but the elder Mrs. Johnson's body would not be recovered for many hours, finally located as digging proceeded under the glare of portable searchlights.

+++

Downhill only a few hundred feet from where Mrs. Oliver had called her husband to see the approaching funnel; elderly Mrs. Lettie Smalley was killed in the collapse of the multi-family dwelling in which she made her home. She did not have Agnes Oliver's view of the approaching funnel, if she had it is questionable whether she could have taken any action which might have saved her life.

+++

A block south of the toppled Johnson home at 43 Randall Street the tornado had rampaged up parallel Fales Street. At number 9, Mrs. Charette's windows blew in, admitting a small blizzard of Norton Company invoices. Next door, uphill, the wooden steps fronting number 11 were torn from the front of the house, despite being anchored by wrought-iron railings and were bounced or blown one hundred yards further uphill, coming to rest on the front lawn of Our Lady of the Rosary church. The large sheet of plate glass in the storm door of number 11 escaped breakage and was not even cracked.

Across the street it was a different story. The funnel spared the home of elderly Mrs. Fortin, whose grocer son was at that moment assuring the safety of his customers in his market at the foot of Fales Street. At the building adjacent to Mrs. Fortin's, the wind showed its power once again by hammering the large three-decker into the ground and tilting the remnant uphill, its eave slamming into the building next door. The corner of the roof, which had been about thirty-five feet in the air a few seconds earlier now angled down to within six feet of the ground.

Despite the sudden and dramatic compression of their home, members of the Richards family on the first floor survived without serious injury. The downward telescoping of the top floor into the second, however, instantly killed Mrs. Tillie Pettigrew, a second floor tenant.

Elderly Mr. Johnson, the top floor tenant, suffered a severe head wound. Willing hands extricated him from the rubble; two women wrapped a bath towel around his head in an effort to stanch the worst of the blood flow. They then led him down the hill to West Boylston Street and hospital evacuation.

+++

Some of those who survived the horror in that part of Greendale later recalled Herbert Oberg's remark made in the Greendale Spa, a neighborhood luncheonette. At about ten minutes before five that afternoon, he had said that a tornado would be coming that afternoon. Mr. Oberg, who lived on nearby Airlie Street, had lived in the Midwest and had seen tornadoes spawned and moving across the land. Today, he felt certain, it would be Worcester's turn.

Just a block up West Boylston Street from the Greendale Spa, and just beyond where Mrs. Smalley met her death, was a large ten-apartment building on the corner of Trottier Street, a short, unpaved side street. This unusual building was known in the neighborhood by the colorful sobriquet, "the beehive".

A Jamaican immigrant, working on the windows that day, abruptly stopped work at noon, saying as he packed up his tools that there would be a storm, terrible beyond belief, passing through the neighborhood later that day. When interviewed several days afterward, the man said that the heaviness in the air and the appearance of the sky were almost identical to those which invariably preceded a hurricane in his native island.

+++

In the midst of sudden death, hideous injury and mind-numbing devastation, there occurred several incidents, fraught with potential hazard, but with such amusing overtones, that each brought smiles to the begrimed, tear-stained faces of impromptu rescuers.

In one instance, a man came picking his way on foot down rubble-choked Randall Street, clothes, face and hands liberally spattered with blood. A solicitous neighbor approached, wanting to clean the blood from the man and perhaps bandage the cuts he had suffered. The "victim" then told of having reached into the cupboard for a bottle of ketchup when the tornado slammed into his home, causing him to drop the bottle which shattered and splashed him with its scarlet contents.

Nearer West Boylston Street, a woman was using the toilet in her home when the tornado demolished the house. Still seated thereon, the woman saw and heard the building being destroyed around her. Within seconds she was pinned, unable to move, although unhurt; she was likewise in utter darkness and total silence.

A few minutes later, she heard her frantic husband calling to her. In embarrassment at her predicament, she did not answer his repeated calls. She could hear his voice and those of others as they strained to move huge sections of roof and walls from above the the tiny space in which she sat. It would be several desperate hours before she was rescued and pulled, blushing furiously, from her temporary prison.

When her husband's initial wave of relief at finding his wife unhurt had somewhat subsided, he asked her in puzzled exasperation why she hadn't immediately answered his first yell. She told him she had been too mortified at her state of undress to welcome rescue by a group of strange males.

Not far from the Beehive, on Trottier Street, stood a house that had been bombarded by stalks of grass and straw at several hundred miles per hour. The wind velocity drove the stalks and stems into the clapboard siding of the house in such quantity that the building appeared to be sprouting the vegetation. For weeks thereafter, this odd-looking building would be called the "hair house".

+++

Michael Falcone and other members of Engine II at the Greendale Fire Station had watched the roiling black cloud cross West Boylston Street only a few hundred yards north of the station. The men felt the rising winds and quickly brought their chairs inside, closing the massive roll-down doors as they did so.

Buffeting winds so strained the doors inward, that Falcone started the engine inside and carefully inched it forward until it was touching the door and adding the strength of its massive weight.

Moments later an alarm rang in from Norton's machine tool plant a mile away. The engine responding had covered only a quarter of the distance, swinging off West Boylston Street, under the railroad overpass and onto Ararat Street, when it found the way ahead blocked by several crushed and fragmented buildings.

By this time, roiling smoke was visible to the eastward, somewhere near the upper part of Fairhaven Road, where it crossed Burncoat at right angles. Turning around, the engine recrossed West Boylston Street and managed to make its way a third of a mile up Fairhaven. Now it could be seen that several three-decker homes on Francis Street, parallel to Fairhaven a block away and inaccessible to the engine, were fully ablaze.

Hoses were quickly attached and run from Fairhaven through backyards and driveways two hundred feet to Francis. While busy at this task, Michael Falcone saw a woman run back into her home. The home backed up to one of the blazing buildings on Francis Street and was itself beginning to smolder. The young firefighter reached the woman just as she started up the stairs for the second floor. He tackled her down and began dragging her toward the door, while she screamed to retrieve some valuable item of personal property. Wrestling the woman to the street, Falcone ran to help his panting fellow firefighters once again. By the time the hoses could be brought to bear, the three-deckers at 122, 118 and 114 Francis were fully engulfed in flames and the story-and-a-half cottage of Valmore Gaucher, next in line downslope, was also ablaze.

The cottage, entirely consumed in flames, collapsed. At the same moment, a few minutes after 6:00 p.m., Michael Falcone, exhausted, dehydrated and affected by both the furnace-like heat and smoke inhalation collapsed, losing consciousness as he struck the ground.

+++

Almost beside the fire station from which Michael Falcone and the others had watched the funnel's approach, stood a three-decker, the second floor apartment of which was occupied by Francis Swenson and his wife, Evelyn.

Her husband Francis, whose Norton shift ended at 3:00 p.m., was taking an afternoon nap. She woke him before starting supper. These preparations were suspended a few minutes later when she looked across West Boylston Street and the parallel railroad tracks beyond, to see a small structure lifted from Kendrick Field and whirled through the air in her general direction.

The small building smacked back to earth without striking the three-decker from which the Swensons watched the strange storm. Later they would learn that they were just south of the fringe winds along the south side of the funnel. Serious damage commenced three blocks northward; one block further and the buildings were obliterated; utterly destroyed. The extent of the damage to the Swenson's three-decker home was the loss of a television aerial.

In the wake of the tornado's passage, Mr. Swenson, located as he was on the edge of the damage swath, found himself directing traffic on busy West Boylston Street, trying to facilitate the departure of makeshift ambulances exiting the area and entry of official and emergency vehicles.

A friend of Mrs. Swenson's who lived a third of a mile further up West Boylston Street arrived, ragged and disheveled, at the Swensons' door. Her home on Assumption Avenue had been on "ground zero" when the funnel rolled over it, and, along with most neighboring structures, had been demolished. She wondered if Mrs. Swenson would drive her to her mother's home, located in the city's undamaged west side. Evelyn immediately agreed to do so and the pair set off.

Returning soon afterward from this errand of mercy, Mrs. Swenson would be stopped by a police roadblock just before reaching her home. It would take forceful arguing on her part, as well as proof of residence in an undamaged home before she would finally be allowed through.

+++

Carl Soderberg, a Norton Machine Tool Division employee, was in his second-floor apartment at 10 Assumption Avenue, where he lived with his wife and three sons. Mrs. Soderberg was at work and the youngest son was out delivering the Evening Gazette.

At about five o'clock, the youngster had finished his route and was excitedly telling his father to look out a window at the enormous hailstones that had just fallen. The ceiling he was busy whitewashing commanded Mr. Soderberg's full attention at the moment, so he only half- listened to the excited boy.

At about ten or eleven minutes after five, Mr. Soderberg's efforts were abruptly terminated as the tornado slammed into the building. Before he and his three sons could contemplate taking shelter in the basement, two flights of stairs below, not only was the house deroofed, but the entire third floor, fortunately unoccupied at that moment, was demolished and blown away. The walls of the Soderberg apartment bowed out and major portions exploded outward, landing in the neighboring yard and points beyond.

Mr. Soderberg sustained a cut on his arm, possibly from flying glass. So savage was the force of the wind in the half-enclosed apartment that both his shoes were torn off and blown away. One of his sons suffered a cut shoulder, neither a deep wound nor a serious one.

Considering the enormous sail-like surface presented by this and similar structures to the advancing funnel, and considering the position of this house, squarely in the center of the broad funnel's advancing track, the Soderbergs were extremely fortunate.

On the floor below, Soderberg's brother-in-law, Edward Harris, ran with several members of his family to the building's basement, where they rode out the blast unscathed.

+++

Twenty-three year old Patricia Senior of 33 Fales Street worked in the payroll department of the Riley Stoker Company at the southern end of the city's Greendale section. Leaving work as usual at 5:00 p.m., Pat caught a bus and rode the short one-mile stretch of West Boylston Street to the foot of Fales.

As Pat alighted from the vehicle that afternoon, she was nearly blown off her feet. The time was 5:09 p.m. She quickly ducked into the Greendale Spa, better known in the neighborhood as "Mike the Greek's" - located in the first floor of a three-decker on the corner of Burncoat and Fales. Her home was only a quarter-mile up the hill, but something told her to take cover instead.

No sooner had she entered the store than its large, west-facing windows began blowing in. An authoritative voice was heard telling everyone to lie down on the floor; nearly everyone, including the frightened Miss Senior, quickly complied.

Pat felt the building shuddering and watched the square ceiling tiles, loosened by the wind blasting through the broken windows, pull away and begin falling to the floor. Uppermost in her mind at that moment was the thought that she was scheduled to be married on July 4 in San Antonio, Texas, and she wondered if she'd still be alive on her wedding day. She was engaged to Airman Roger Cahill of Whitinsville, who was stationed at Lackland Air Force Base.

Michael Sefakis, the spa's owner, and several other men were struggling to cover the blown-out plate-glass windows, through which a host of objects were flying into the store. Pat remembers clearly the bravery of these men, who risked injury, even possible decapitation, and recalls that the most valiant among them was a man generally regarded as the neighborhood drunk, one whom she had seldom seen draw a sober breath. He was now fighting hardest of those who were attempting, vainly, to reclaim the store's interior from the howling wind.

Someone pushed Pat into the store's enclosed phone booth, along with another woman and her two small children. Someone else - Pat does not remember who - began reciting the Lord's Prayer out loud, and was spontaneously joined by most of the adults present.

Even more quickly than it had arisen, the howling tempest subsided. Pat went outside and looked up Fales Street hill. Three-deckers marched up the hill on both sides of the street and it seemed to her that two-thirds of them had been flattened or toppled.

As she started up the street, not able to see past the Catholic church on the shoulder of the hill to her family's home through houses beyond, she was intercepted by a neighbor, Russell Oliver, who had watched the tornado's approach with his wife from their Randall Street apartment window for some reason he physically restrained her from proceeding further.

Not thinking very rationally, Pat quickly returned to the Greendale Spa and tried to telephone her mother. The instrument in the booth where she had spent the last moments of the tornado was, not surprisingly, dead. Telephone service in the damaged swath across Greendale and Burncoat Hill was nonexistent.

Pat hurried out of the store once again, but not before assuring the men that she was all right, and that she would be particularly careful to give any downed wires a wide berth. Such wires seemed to be everywhere, it seemed to Pat, except safely overhead.

Looking ahead as she once again began to climb Fales Street, it seemed as though she was ascending a giant corridor into which rubbish had been carelessly thrown, the severed wires curving down from battered utility poles like strands produced by an enormous spider.

After having carefully covered perhaps half the distance to her home, she saw her father running toward her. When he reached and embraced her, he began crying from the wave of joyful relief that washed over him at finding his daughter unharmed. It was the first time in her life Pat had ever seen him cry.

Mr. Senior told Pat that her mother, who had been at home, was unharmed. So was her brother, Paul, who had gone in search of his sister, Kay. Kay worked at Norton Company, just down the hill and across West Boylston Street. Knowing that she would have left work at 5:00 and walked the half-mile or so to her home, the family feared she might have been caught in the open by the tornado, as Pat had been, but without the opportunity to take immediate shelter.

Moments later, the object of their concern came into sight. When she came up to her father and sister she told them that she had been offered a ride home that afternoon, which, because of the black sky in the west, she had gladly accepted.

The car in which the two were riding crossed West Boylston St. almost at the exact moment as the tornado. The funnel was just to the north of them and on a parallel course, so close that the powerful and extensive fringe winds on the southern side of the tornado rocked the car violently. The driver pulled over to the side of the road and waited for the buffeting to pass.

When the funnel had completely passed and sunshine, calm air and blue sky suddenly appeared, Kay's friend decided to drive home via the shortest possible route. Leaving him to determine what that route might be, Kay got out of the car, thanked her friend and began to pick her way toward home.

Kay was moving deeper into the debris field as she went; damage had now become outright destruction. Fearing now for her parents and siblings, she was relieved to meet her father and sister and to learn that her brother Paul and her mother were unhurt.

+++

After saying goodbye to her bridge partners, Anna Rebert had begun walking down the hill toward nearby Fortin's Market. Within a minute she had turned the corner onto Randall and the winds seemed about to sweep her off her feet, so she decided to seek shelter at the Greendale Spa, only a hundred yards down the street, at the corner of Burncoat. A few more seconds, and she realized she couldn't cover even this short distance.

As she reached Pruneau's barbershop, she grasped the handle, but was unable to open the door. With the tornado now fully upon them, Mr. Pruneau pulled open the door to his shop from the inside, and the desperate woman practically fell into his shop.

The barbershop was sheltered to some degree by adjoining buildings from the worst of the tornado's fury, and so those inside, including the fortunate Mrs. Rebert, escaped injury. She saw, however, a large sign from a nearby business establishment, which had torn loose and blew past the shop.

Climbing back up Randall Street once again, which involved threading her way between huge sections of downed homes lying partly across the street, Mrs. Rebert reached her own house. The wind had deroofed it, part of the walls had been torn away and it was apparent that what remained would have to be razed.

Sigrid Johnson, who had lived next door and who now lay entombed in the collapsed home, had just had her car delivered to her driveway by a mechanic who had been working on it. Now the vehicle, still upright, rested on the Rebert's front lawn, or rather what had been the lawn. A hatbox had been blown from a shelf in one of Mrs. Rebert's closets and had sailed through a shattered window of the Johnson car, coming to rest on the back seat.

+++

At the Norton Company picnic grove in Princeton, Richard Girard, an instructor in the company's pistol club, was getting ready to start grilling some steaks as soon as the other members of the club arrived for the late-afternoon outing. His teenage son and another Norton employee had volunteered to help. They had set up their makeshift kitchen and were waiting expectantly for the hungry shooters to arrive.

Four-thirty came and went and no one appeared, then five o'clock passed. A few minutes after five, realizing that something untoward must have happened to explain the failure of any of the club's members to arrive, but not having any notion of what the explanation might be, and not being near a telephone, the three got into Girard's car and began the twelve-mile drive back to Worcester.

Two-thirds of the way home they were suddenly stopped in the middle of West Boylston by a police officer who told them that a "hurricane" had passed through northern Worcester, and that they would find a roadblock ahead, near the city line, preventing all traffic from continuing on that part of Route 12, known as West Boylston Street, as it ran through the northern part of the city. Thus cautioned, the trio continued toward Worcester. A half-mile before the city line they turned right on Prospect Street, which would take them through Holden.

Certain that this "end run", which would permit them to approach the city from the west, would allow them to skirt whatever area of damage there might be, they were surprised to come upon a roadblock well before reaching Holden center. As they were turned back, someone mentioned that a tornado had torn through both Holden and the northern part of neighboring Worcester.

Reversing direction, they drove as close as they were able to the edge of the damage swath, through what is known as "the Summit", the northernmost major intersection in Worcester, where Mountain Street crosses West Boylston Street. They were stopped at a police roadblock, questioned, and when it was learned that they were Greendale residents, allowed to proceed on foot.

Dick's son started to run when the three first saw ahead of them the lumber and other debris which was being cleared away to allow free passage to emergency vehicles. The two adults were unable to keep up with the sprinting teenager, and after a hundred yards or so, gave up the attempt. Slowing his pace when he passed a police officer, Mr. Girard asked whether King Philip Road had been hit. The officer's reply was not encouraging; he told Dick it had been "wiped out".

The two men moved across the zone of maximum destruction, which extended for about six hundred yards, but seemed to diminish in severity when they passed the foot of Fairhaven Road. Still further on, they met a man at the corner of Summerhill Avenue. They again asked how badly King Philip Road had been hit and were told that it had escaped with minor damage. Moments later, Dick approached his home and found that the dwelling, which was not near the lower, or West Boylston Street end of King Philip, was practically untouched. Further up the street, as it climbed toward Burncoat, falling limbs and even whole trees had damaged homes - and the hood of Harold Williston's car - but no houses blew down despite "fringe" winds of perhaps ninety to one hundred miles per hour as the funnel quartered closer to the upper end of the street.

+++

At about ten minutes before five, Ruth Connors looked toward Holden from the kitchen window of her home at 5 Olin Street. Seeing the blackness in the west, she went to the telephone to call her husband at the U.S. Envelope Company to tell him to try to get a ride home with a co-worker so that she would not be caught in the approaching thunderstorm. She removed an earring and reached for the phone, then changed her mind. She replaced the receiver and left the house to drive the three miles to her husband's place of work.

When she picked him up the two drove a short distance to where Mrs. Connors' father worked, intending to drive him to his home in Holden. On Ararat Street, near "D" Street, one of the Norton Company's private streets, they encountered major tornado damage from the funnel's passage fifteen minutes earlier. The also saw something that made their blood run cold.

A young boy of perhaps thirteen was sitting motionless in the middle of the street while downed electric wires snaked around him, their severed ends snapping and crackling. The boy was visibly nervous, so to calm him down, the Connors started talking to him quietly and reassuringly, stressing the importance of his staying motionless and not trying not trying to find his way out of the danger surrounding him until someone cut the power.

Able to do nothing further for the boy, and with Ararat Street impassable, the three attempted to drive the mile and a half to Ruth and Tim's home. The three parked on Burncoat Street, south of the funnel's swath, and began making their way on foot along it, then down Fales Street.

Both Tim and his wife had served in Europe during the recent war, Tim as an infantryman and Ruth as an army nurse. They had seen cities which had been reduced to rubble. Somehow, though, this totally unexpected carnage in their own quiet residential neighborhood was even harder to comprehend and accept.

Part-way down the hill, before reaching the corner of Olin Street, they saw coming up the hill toward them, a curate of Our Lady of the Rosary Church. Father Edward Dyer wasted no words when he came up to them. "Don't give a thought to your home," he said, "it's gone. Try to help your neighbors as best you can." Then he continued on his way.

Gone it was, indeed, along with most of its neighbors on the short, dead-end street. The three-decker which had stood diagonally across the street had collapsed to the northward, parallel to the street on which it had stood. Mr. Milano, the owner and first floor resident, lay injured in his backyard, his wife holding an umbrella above him to protect him from the few drops of rain that had started to fall.

Mr. Milano was conscious and lucid but in pain. Ruth quickly determined that one of his arms was fractured. The man commented wryly that this was a terrible way to die; lying in the grass with someone holding an umbrella over your head.

Ruth assured him that people did not die from broken arms and shortly thereafter Mr. Milano was evacuated to Worcester City Hospital. There, he would succumb several days later to a combination of internal injuries.

Leaving Mr. Milano's side, Ruth joined several men at what had been the third floor level of the toppled building; the apartment of John Sheerin, Jr., and his wife. From someone, Ruth learned that Mr. Sheerin had been taking a bath when the funnel hit and either he or his corpse was positively known to be under a fallen wall section of the flattened home.

No sound could be heard from within the wreckage; its removal was progressing slowly and there was the ever-present danger of fire breaking out before the trapped man could be extricated. None of the men present could wriggle beneath the heavy wall section, but the petite Mrs. Connors volunteered to try. Soon she had squirmed to a spot where she could see a foot before her. She stretched to touch it and found it warm, with a pulse beating in the ankle.

She spoke to the frightened Mr. Sheerin, and to her relief he answered her. Being in the tub as the building toppled had been an unnerving experience but may have saved his life. The victim's chief worry now was the outbreak of fire while he still lay helpless in his wooden prison. Ruth assured him that the nearest fires were on Francis Street, more than a block away and that he would soon be free now that his exact position and location were known. Then the nurse slowly inched her way backward the way she had come.

With only their own physical strength, Tim Connors, Rocco Pizzula, and a couple of other men from the immediate neighborhood managed to free John Sheerin and he was soon on route to a hospital.

When Tim and Ruth Connors looked at the ruins of their former two- story home, they saw their refrigerator standing upright in the backyard. Opening the door, they found that most of their food inside was undisturbed. The appliance looked as if it would have functioned perfectly, if there had been an outlet anywhere around into which it could be plugged.

Ruth had earlier removed her diamond engagement ring from her finger and carefully put it atop the hand soap dispenser over the kitchen sink. In the waning hours of daylight, she and her husband searched vainly through the nearby wreckage in the desperate hope of finding it.

The next day, Mr. Connors' brother was helping to determine what might be salvageable when a gleam of light caught his eye. Bending over, he picked up the ring.

+++

Francis and Mary Walsh had moved into their brand-new ranch-style home at 90 Randall Street only six months earlier. They were a family of six, which included three young children and a baby. The Walshes had begun landscaping efforts around the house earlier in the spring, and on this hot afternoon had been spreading loam in their large back yard, as the first step toward establishing a lawn.

Their work was briefly interrupted by a shower at 4:30 that afternoon, then, right afterward, by a fall of large hailstones. These entranced the children; Steven, 6, and his younger brother Peter kept running to their parents eagerly showing them the walnut-sized balls of ice.

At about five o'clock, Jane Montgomery, a widow who lived next door, pulled into the driveway. Returning the Walshes' greeting, she commented that the darkness in the west doubtless meant they were in for a storm, and she didn't want her dog to be alone, since thunderstorms frightened him badly.

A few minutes after five o'clock the Walshes could see the row of poplars adjacent to the Assumption College tennis courts swaying wildly in the wind. In addition, and in the opposite direction, the tall elm which overlooked the far end of the Walshes' back yard was creaking and groaning in the high wind which seemed to have come out of nowhere. There was a roaring sound, deeper than the whistling of the wind, which seemed to come from the northwest, where the sky was inky black. The Walshes ran for their cellar.

At eleven minutes after five, the tornado struck. Just down the slope of Randall Street from the Walshes, the tornado shoved the two-family home of a Mr. Johnson - not the same Mr. Johnson as that in which Sigrid Johnson would be buried, further down the street - a couple of feet to the eastward, moving it partially off its foundation. This lateral movement of the building was arrested by its coming in contact with a large tree, which resisted pressure of both building and wind and acted as a backstop to the sliding house.

The Walshes' home was instantly deroofed, with windows shattered and the west wall shoved inward, buckling to an angle of about forty-five degrees. Mr. Walsh noted a fleeting glimmer of light above him as the tornado lifted the home from its foundation, allowing it to move eastward a few inches, then setting it down once again.

The house had a door set in the basement wall on the west side where the land sloped away, which afforded direct access to the yard. Although this door held fast against the blasting wind, a piece of corrugated steel roof flashing from the Norton plant a mile-and-a-half to windward, somehow made its way under the door and slithered across the floor to where the Walshes sat huddled together, giving the baby, David, a small cut on his hand.

The Giguere family's home, directly across the street from the Walshes', was leveled; so too was that of Mrs. Montgomery. Across from the Montgomery home, a three-decker belonging to the Tashjian family looked as though it had been sledgehammered into the ground, while a two-story home behind the Walshes' on Gunnarson Road had been shoved a dozen feet eastward, where it perched half on and half off its foundation. The house behind it was lifted and turned thirty degrees before being dropped back onto its foundation. Then, as suddenly as it had arisen, the tempest was over.

Mrs. Giguere lay in the cellar of her demolished home, assuring her husband that she was all right, but with her legs pinned behind a fallen beam. Her distraught husband found a length of pipe lying nearby, which he used as a lever, lifting the timber off his wife's legs, allowing her to wiggle free. As Mr. Giguere was hurriedly completing the work of freeing his pinioned wife, the end of the pipe which he was holding suddenly whipsawed, catching him in the throat and injuring his larynx.

Across the street, curious young Steven Walsh scampered up the cellar stairs when quiet returned, his father only a step behind him. The pair stopped in amazement at the sight which greeted them. Instead of a ceiling above their heads, father and son were staring up at a blue sky. Not a fragment of the house's roof or ceiling remained.

Frank Walsh saw the pile of rubble that had been Jane Montgomery's home and immediately feared the worst. His attention was diverted to the Gigueres across the street, so he headed over to where their house had stood. Mrs. Giguere had by now been freed from the restraining timber and would require medical examination and treatment.

When she told Mr. Walsh what had befallen her husband as he was struggling to free her, Frank led him through the devastation of lower Randall Street, carefully avoiding the downed electric wires which crackled and buzzed around them. Mr. Walsh, a city letter carrier, brought his injured neighbor into the post office substation at the corner of West Boylston Street. There, he and Cornelius Collins, the branch manager, lay the man down, cushioning his head on folded mail sacks. Leaving Mr. Collins to arrange evacuation of the injured man to a hospital, Mr. Walsh hurried back up the hill.

He could see a fireman's ladder at a side window at the second floor of the wrecked Tashjian home, just uphill from the Gigueres. The firemen were lifting a small child out through the window and down the ladder.

+++

Fred Underwood, advertising manager of Heald Machine Company, and editor of the company's newspaper, The Craftsman, had returned that afternoon to the company office on New Bond Street, from an out-of-state business trip. He had phoned his wife, who had the family car at home, and she agreed to pick him up at about 5:15.

Very shortly after five, Underwood noticed strong winds outside the office window, but did not become unduly alarmed. In the parking lot at 5:15, he noticed that high winds had torn some of the rigid metal awnings from the engineering side of the office. Fred waited for his usually prompt wife for ten minutes or so, but she failed to appear. Now slightly apprehensive, he returned to his office and called home. There was no answer.

Returning to the parking lot, he was offered a ride home by a fellow employee who lived in Princeton. The pair drove west on Ararat Street towards the intersection of Brattle Street, on which the Underwood home was located. To their right, along the northern side of Ararat, they noticed many roofs with loose or missing shingles.

At the end of Ararat, where Brattle crosses at right angles, Underwood looked uphill in the direction of his home. The road was completely blocked by uprooted elm trees. Large trees with trunks two feet or more in diameter. Beginning to appreciate the magnitude of the disaster, Fred thanked his friend and advised him to get home as quickly as he could to see to the welfare of his own family.

Moving around and over the fallen elms as quickly as he could, Mr. Underwood rounded a curve in Brattle Street from which his home and the other large colonial homes on both sides of the road, were visible. On this fateful afternoon, however, in Fred Underwood's own words, "I saw utter disaster ahead. I could not identify the location of my home. Some of the houses had exploded, leaving only a cellar hole and mounds of twisted boards, broken furniture and much broken glass."

From the corner of Chevy Chase Road and Brattle, diagonally across from Underwood's house lot at number 105, across from the Marcellos, Bill Bow, a neighbor, called over to Fred. "Your family is OK," he shouted; "they're down at my home!" After hearing these words, the most reassuring of his life, Mr. Underwood suddenly recognized what was left of his home, a large three-bedroom colonial. Blown completely off the foundation, it had been deroofed and the only room with four walls still standing was the dining room.

Bill told Fred about having done what little he could to make Clara Gustafson as comfortable as possible until she could be evacuated by trained medical personnel.

Having been reassured by his friend that his wife and children were safe and had not been seriously hurt, Mr. Underwood decided to help extricate and evacuate whomever might still be lying injured in the rubble. It was now just a half-hour since the tornado's onslaught.

Fred saw a knot of people at what had been the Estabrook home, a couple of lots beyond the Gustafsons', so he ran over. With two other men, he managed to free one of the Estabrook sons, a teenaged boy who had been trapped in the ruins of the collapsed home.

Employing a door as a stretcher, the boy was carried down gently- sloping Brattle Street. Fred spotted a car at the side of the road with the front windshield almost completely blown out. The keys were still in the ignition and the car started instantly, so Underwood and the others carefully eased the injured boy through the gaping hole where the windshield had been, supporting it as it was pushed rearward until the further end came to rest on the top of the rear seat, the middle of the stretcher supported by the front seat back and the front end by the dashboard.

Fred got behind the wheel of the vehicle and by a tortuous route through back yards and gardens and around fallen trees managed to work his way south parallel to Brattle Street to a point below the intersection of Ararat Street where the Brattle Street Market stood, just beyond the damage zone. He then proceeded in a more normal manner the five miles or so across the city to Memorial Hospital, being thankful that he was wearing safety glasses with shatterproof lenses, since an occasional loose shard of glass worked loose from the edge of the shattered windshield and flew rearward, into the passenger compartment.

Returning to the devastated neighborhood again, Fred hurried to Bill Bow's to check on members of his own family. The three Underwood youngsters were unscathed, but he learned that his wife, Mary Frances, had been pinned between the dining room table and a wall during the blow, and had been taken to a hospital for X-rays.

Mr. Underwood borrowed another car, this time with the owner's permission, and drove to the hospital. His wife's x-rays disclosed no broken bones, so she was released, and with husband and children finished the eventful evening at the home of Mr. Underwood's parents where they spent the night.

5

Agony at Assumption

The Greendale Elementary School baseball team had been having a practice session on the Assumption College baseball diamond, located above and behind the college, adjacent to Burncoat Street. The session had been interrupted earlier by a fall of huge hailstones. Baseball gloves held over players' heads had prevented any injuries and by five o'clock the workout had resumed.

A few minutes after five the coach looked to the westward, across the rooftop of the college building and was alarmed by what he saw. Ordinarily, the "horizon" in that direction was a ridgeline to the west of Indian Lake, a spot about four miles from where he stood. At this moment, an angry black cloud, roiling and apparently in contact with the ground, rolled toward him.

He had heard no muttering of thunder, nor felt the freshening breeze which usually signaled the approach of a storm. Fearing the worst, the coach quickly terminated the team's workout; some of the boys grabbed their bikes and scooted for home; those who lived closest began running for their homes.

Assumption College had been founded a half-century earlier by the Assumptionist Brothers, a French-Canadian religious order. In 1953 it was still small, with an all-male student body; many, if not most of whom were of French-Canadian descent. French, rather than English, was the primary language of instruction at the college.

Classes at both Assumption College and Assumption Preparatory School had been originally scheduled to run through June twelfth, but in examining the books of the two schools at the beginning of June, Rev. Henry Moquin noticed that the state's minimum teaching period had already been satisfied. He accordingly recommended to the dean, Rev. Louis Dion, that considerable cost savings would result if classes were to end early. His suggestion was adopted, and graduation was moved to Monday, June 8, following which most students departed the campus for the summer.

Assumption was holding a provincial retreat for members of the religious community from Quebec and the New England - New York area. On this, the third evening of the retreat, the usual

5:00 p.m. vesper service had been cancelled due to the oppressive heat and the predicted likelihood of a severe thunderstorm. Thus, the Reverend Louis Dion, A.A., Dean of Assumption College, was not in the larger of Assumption's two chapels where the evening prayers would have been said.

Instead, Father Dion was occupied in a purely secular task. He was moving through the so-called "college section" of Assumption's main building, closing the windows on the second floor. He was being assisted by a prep school student. The pair had finished closing the windows in the rooms and in the corridor along the eastern side of that floor. In moving into the connecting main building, they met eighty-one year old Father Francisco. Since it was getting darker by the second, Father Dion told the elderly priest that he'd close his windows for him, in the course of his rounds.

At 5:10, Fr. Dion, alone now, walked through a dormitory and into a large lavatory-shower room in the northeast corner of the building and began closing the several open windows.

At the same instant, ten minutes after five, Father Thomas Hebert rushed through the main entrance of Assumption's main building yelling hysterically: "Tornado's coming!" A part of this building served to house the priests and brothers who comprised the faculty, but some of those who heard the shouted alarm knew Father Hebert to be something of a worrier and occasionally prone to overreaction, so they paid scant attention.

One who discounted the warning was a young Assumptionist, Brother Gregory Boisvert, whose eyewitness recollections, set down at the time in a letter to his parents, form the basis of much of what is known to have transpired during the following unforgettable few minutes.

The roaring funnel, having blasted across West Boylston Street, carried tons of lumber aloft, as well as a huge fuel tank, possibly plucked from the grounds of Jon's Railroad Salvage, located near the Diamond Match lumberyard. The tornado churned up the gentle slope upon which Assumption stood, tossing the Karras and Myers automobiles onto the lawn.

Within thirty seconds of the shouted warning, any private doubts were dispelled as quickly as the rising of the wind. The west-facing main building, built in 1904, with major additions added in subsequent decades, took the brunt of the tornado, head-on. The airborne fuel tank slammed into the brick facade of the "college wing" where Fr. Dion had been closing windows three minutes earlier, punching an enormous hole in the wall between the second and third floor levels.

After closing and locking his room's window, Bro. Boisvert ran toward the "little" chapel, located in the building's interior. He was narrowly missed by falling masonry, as were others, although a Father Clermont was knocked unconscious. Above them, much of the slate roof tore away and sections of the walls collapsed, with the upper two floors of the large four-story structure falling in upon themselves.

Father Englebert Devincq, Assumption professor and director of the French Summer School, was in his second-floor room when the tornado struck. He was immediately immobilized, and then crushed, by an avalanche of granite and brick. The floor of his room gave way and he fell into the sitting room below, in the midst of the avalanche of rubble, coming to rest with only one hand protruding from the debris.

Richard Dion, younger brother of the cleric who had been so conscientiously closing windows in the college wing, had just completed his sophomore year at the prep school and was working at the college that summer.

He and his roommate, Richard Harnois, were in their third-floor room facing West Boylston Street when the tornado arrived. The two boys saw a huge tree limb sail past. Young Dion suggested that the two take refuge in the room's closet. His roommate reached it; then, before Dion could join him, something massive crashed through the window, tearing out the entire sash and slamming it into the closet door, banging it back and pinioning Richard Dion behind it.

As the boy was pushed against the wall, he was shoved from the path of the flying shards of glass which buried themselves in the door to the hall, directly in front of which he had been standing.

Presuming correctly that his roommate was as sheltered from harm as circumstances permitted, Dion wrestled open the door to the hall and was immediately swept from his feet. Blown-out windows and doors blasted from their hinges made a wind tunnel of the third-floor hallway. As Richard was being blown and bounced along, he managed to grab one of the vertical heating pipes which connected one of the radiators along the hall with another on the floor above. Richard maintained his deathgrip on the pipe and rode out the remaining seconds of the tornado.

Richard Dion's older brother, Fr. Louis, emerged from the lavatory where he had been closing windows, bleeding profusely from a cut on the back of his head and another on his left elbow.

Hurrying down to the first floor, he spotted the protruding arm of Fr, Devincq and clasped the hand of the buried man. He identified himself and told the entombed priest he would give him absolution. The hand squeezed his in acknowledgement.

Absolution given, Father Dion, quickly joined by three other priests, worked to free their trapped friend. Someone shouted to them that fire had broken out in the furnace room behind and below them. They were urged to leave, in case the flames spread. They refused, and redoubled their digging efforts.

+++

Among those who gathered in an attempt to extinguish the blaze, or at least retard its spread, were the two Richards, Dion and Harnois, reunited once again. They had grabbed a carbon tetrachloride fire extinguisher, approached the flames as closely as they could and activated the device. There was no emission; the fluid had been drained from the extinguisher. The two young men quickly obtained a second extinguisher of the same type. It, too, proved to be empty of chemical.

In disgust and frustration, Dion threw the empty extinguisher into the flames. These extinguishers, the young man knew, had long been used by the students as a handy source of cleaning fluid; many a spot and stain had been treated with fluid surreptitiously siphoned from these canisters.

All telephone service having been severed by the tornado, someone had run the half-mile down West Boylston Street to the Greendale Fire Station to summon help in extinguishing the boiler room fire. That station's units were already fully involved in fighting the string of three-decker fires on Francis Street.

A truck from another station was summoned, but found approach by road to the college impossible. The driver was forced to drive cross-country, between houses and across back yards, then negotiating debris from the college itself, before arriving at the boiler room. The fire was quickly attacked and speedily extinguished.

The quartet of courageous priests working to exhume Fr. Devincq discovered Fr. Louis Brassard similarly entombed in the debris nearby. The four priests now divided their efforts. Father Brassard, they discovered, had sustained a horribly mangled leg and numerous lesser injuries, but, against the odds, would somehow survive. Fr. Devincq succumbed before efforts to free him had been completed.

The wooden convent, home to a number of sisters of the Antonian order who staffed the kitchen of the college and preparatory school, had been lifted several feet from the ground in the tornado's lethal embrace. The structure was turned about one-hundred-eighty degrees and slammed back to earth.

Two nuns were killed instantly. Twenty-seven year old Jacqueline Martel, known in religion as Sister St. John of God, would shortly be found dead, lying beneath a heavy radiator. Marie Alice Simard (Sister Mary St. Helen), forty-eight, was also found in the wreckage of the convent.

The Mother Superior, Mother St. Helena, staggered from the wreckage, bleeding from a deep cut in her forehead. Sisters Matilda and Mary of the Holy Ghost lay gravely injured in the ruins of the demolished convent. Young Brother Boisvert ran out of the main building and hurried over to assist the dazed and bleeding nun. Another Assumptionist, Brother Armand, who had been in his first-floor room emerged only slightly bruised and ran toward the convent. Even in the face of such a calamity, Brother Armand found remnants of sheets and curtains to replace the veils which had been torn from the nuns' heads, thus preserving the degree of modesty required by their religious calling.

Professor Lucien Desjardins of the college's Physics Department had been in the gym a few minutes before, and tried to open the door to the outside in order to determine the cause of the roaring noise he could hear. No matter how hard he pushed against the door, it refused to budge; it was as though it was nailed shut.

After a couple of minutes, the roaring subsided. He tried to open the door again. This time it opened easily...into a scene of unbelievable devastation.

A quarter-mile southwest, in her home on Assumption Avenue, Professor Desjardin's wife heard the rising howl of the wind and felt the house shudder. Almost without conscious thought, she ran upstairs to get her diamond engagement ring. She searched feverishly but unsuccessfully for a few frantic moments. Then she ran downstairs for the first floor once again, reaching the kitchen just as the tornado's force blew away part of the room's walls. The refrigerator toppled over onto her legs, pinning her against the chimney. After a few minutes of struggle she managed to squirm free and struggle from the wreckage of her home.

Lucky, Assumption's mascot, was cowering in his doghouse, quivering with fright, when the roaring funnel hit. The doghouse was whirled aloft with its canine occupant still inside. It was carried nearly two hundred yards through the air and dropped onto the same baseball field hurriedly vacated moments before by the Greendale School's team.

When someone, later that evening, spotted the doghouse and recognized it for what it was, Lucky was still inside, fearful and reluctant to let himself be coaxed out. When the animal was removed, he was found to have sustained two broken legs, most likely when the doghouse was slammed back to earth. Lucky was rushed to a veterinarian, as the only member of the Assumption community qualifying for such treatment.

At about the moment when Lucky was being whirled aloft, the Greendale School baseball coach and a couple of boys jumped into his two-year-old Cadillac and began to pull out onto Burncoat Street. When the funnel hit, it toppled a tree, which fell across the car's trunk, its crushing weight immobilizing the vehicle. However, the driver and his young passengers escaped injury. Moreover, pinned as it was, the heavy Cadillac escaped being rolled over or bounced around by the wind, as was happening to scores of other vehicles, both parked and underway, which found themselves directly in the tornado's path.

In the main building at Assumption, particularly on the second and third floors, several of the priests and brothers who were in greatest danger managed, through luck, quick thinking, or a combination of the two, to escape serious injury. Eighty-six-year-old Father Francisco happened to have just stepped into an elevator as the tornado struck.

As the elevator doors closed in front of him, the power in the building died. After the elderly priest had spent several minutes in the inky blackness of the elevator, Father Garcia managed to pry the doors open. What greeted Father Francisco was a scene nearly as shocking as that which Professor Desjardins was contemplating at that very moment.

Father Odilon, who had an artificial leg, and who, like Fr. Francisco, was quite elderly, was in the large chapel when the tornado hit. He escaped with only slight cuts from flying debris.

Brother Jules Viau was in his second-story room when the two floors above collapsed and came through his ceiling. Incredibly, a cut on the head from a falling brick, together with a nasty raised lump, were his only injuries.

Father Clair, whose room was two doors away from that of Brother Boisvert's, found himself trapped in his room, since the sagging and buckling of the floor above had caused his door to jam in the closed position. The side walls of his room being only of wallboard, Fr. Clair chopped a hole in one of them, then crawled through it into the adjacent room. Finding the hallway door from that room also jammed shut, the determined priest broke through another wall, coming through to Bro. Boisvert's room, where he was able to make his way into the corridor.

Father Ulric Charpentier, a mathematics professor at the college, heard the roar of the approaching storm, which sounded to him like, "one rumble rolling into another". Moments later, he watched some of the roofs of the college's chicken coops sail past his window. A chest of drawers came hurtling by as well.

Then, the walls of the room trembling, the windows of Fr. Charpentier's room blew out. The suction pulled open the door of a storage chest, from which a stream of linen and graduation robes issued, fluttering across the room and disappearing out the window.

More solid objects, too, were flying across the frightened priest's room, so he crouched in a corner, covered his head and murmured a heartfelt Act of Contrition. Moments later, the winds quickly subsided and Fr. Charpentier found the profound silence which followed "unbearable".

Within minutes, Father Gerard Brossard came out to the ruins of the convent with holy oils, a stole, and the ritual for the anointing of the dead and dying. A Jesuit priest, Father Mueller, anointed and gave absolution to the dead and injured sisters.

Brother Boisvert started searching for stretchers; he located the janitor, who was pinioned by a leg in the ruins of a barn. Two brothers were already working to free him and he seemed, to Brother Boisvert, to be in relatively good condition, considering his predicament. The janitor, a Mr. Picket, handed over a large key ring.

After Brother Boisvert had tried a number of keys in the coach's door without success, he ran to the gym, grabbed a two-by-four and broke a window with it, gaining entrance to the coach's office in this manner. He grabbed a couple of stretchers and coming out of the door, met Brother Vianney, who also took two stretchers, then the pair headed back to the convent area.

Noting that a fire had broken out in the boiler room, the busy Brother Boisvert ran up the hill to Burncoat Street, where he spotted a parked police cruiser. Hurrying over to it, he told the officer to call for a fire engine to be sent to Assumption, and to make an appeal for a doctor to go to the college as quickly as possible.

Looking around, Brother Boisvert began to appreciate the magnitude of the disaster as evidenced by the battered homes that lined the street. Felled trees and utility poles, dangling wires and an occasional battered wreck of a car rendered the street virtually impassable to any vehicle larger then a bicycle.

The young cleric began going from house to house, offering words of encouragement and support to whomever he met. If a severely injured person was a Catholic, he or she was also offered absolution. One man, lying on a mattress on the corner of Assumption's grounds nearest Burncoat Street, appeared to have escaped serious injury, other than a possible broken arm. After conversing with the man for a few moments, Brother Boisvert passed on to another victim. He later learned that the man had suffered broken ribs, at least one of which punctured a lung. The man was dead the next day.

At one pile of rubble which had been someone's home, he came upon several men digging frantically to recover a woman believed to be trapped inside. Among the diggers were two of Boisvert's fellow Assumptionists. As he hurriedly doffed his cassock before pitching in, Brother Boisvert noticed that the right shoulder of his shirt was soaked with dried blood. Wondering how he could have sustained such an injury without being aware of it, he remembered than an hour earlier, in comforting Mother Superior, he had cradled her bleeding head upon his shoulder.

After about half an hour of feverishly lifting heavy pieces of rubble and shoving them aside, the woman was located. Her body, "cold and blue", in Brother Boisvert's words, was removed. This was the exhumation of Jane Montgomery, next door neighbor to the Walshes. Her nervous dog, for the benefit of which she had returned home early, was whining and wandering aimlessly around.

Mrs. Dion, with two sons on the Assumption campus, tried to telephone the college when she heard the initial radio reports. Unable to get through, she was about to hang up when someone came on the line with the terse comment that the college had been "blown away". The callous remark only increased the woman's apprehension.

When her younger son and his roommate were frustrated in their attempts at fighting the boiler room fire, they headed down the long front lawn toward West Boylston Street. Out of curiosity, the pair approached the vehicle which had contained the mangled remains of Ann Lovell and Joan Karras, and were warned to stay clear of the gruesome scene.

Running south along West Boylston Street, the two Richards intended to stop at the nearest pharmacy and ask for first aid supplies to carry back to the college. Others had the same idea and the pair found that the drugstore into which they ran had already donated its stocks of these items to needy neighbors. The boys jogged nearly a half mile further south to another pharmacy which still had a supply of first aid items. The druggist gave the boys all they could carry.

Before starting their run back to the college, someone commented on the fresh bloodstain reddening the back of Richard Harnois' tee shirt. Closer inspection revealed a sliver of glass embedded in the boy's back, where it had presumably lodged an hour earlier, despite his protected location in the closet. The pharmacist removed the sliver, stuck an adhesive bandage on the wound and the boys began the long run back to the college.

Those at Assumption College could see a wall of black smoke a half-mile to the southeast, generated by the fiercely burning three-deckers along the upper part of Francis Street. A member of the college faculty, Professor Valmore Gaucher, left the college at about 5:30 and threaded his way through the ravaged streets on the slope of Burncoat Hill en route to his home. He arrived to find that his house, situated just below the lowest three-decker, had caught fire and, like its larger neighbors, had been totally consumed in the flames.

On his way back to the grounds of the college, Brother Boisvert came upon Mrs. Desjardins, bruised, scratched, and seeming to the young cleric to be almost in a state of shock. She was sifting disconsolately through the shattered fragments of her home, still searching for her diamond ring.

A few minutes earlier, a neighbor of Mrs. Desjardins from around the corner on Burncoat Street, Mrs. Lillian Fortin, and her college-age son had come upon the woman standing dejectedly amid the ruins of her home. Shocked at the woman's condition, Mrs. Fortin anxiously inquired what she could do to help her devastated neighbor.

Mrs. Desjardins thought for a moment. "I must be a sight," she said. "My hair's a mess...Do you have a comb I could borrow?"

At about six o'clock, while Brother Boisvert and several other Assumptionists were offering whatever spiritual and physical assistance they could to persons in the devastated neighborhood, a flatbed trailer truck owned by an Oxford building materials company came grinding up the long, curving driveway to the front of the college buildings. Word had already spread of the condition of the area and the certainty of an enormous number of casualties.

Arriving at Hahnemann Hospital ten minutes later, the huge makeshift hearse - ambulance was waved off by someone at the small hospital, which was already enormously overcrowded. Down Lincoln Street the truck proceeded, then up Belmont to Memorial Hospital, where the dead were removed and taken to the hospital's morgue, and the injured began to receive professional medical attention.

6

The Two Mrs. Lelands

As the half-mile wall of wind crossed Burncoat Street it lifted the back of the two-story Waterfield home at 380 Burncoat, completely off its foundation. When the building was pushed forward, as with so many others that day, it collapsed internally. Seventy-year-old Bessie Newton, mother of owner Ethel Waterfield, occupied the first-floor apartment. As Mrs. Newton hurried from her kitchen into the bedroom to close an open window, the floor beneath her gave way, sending her sprawling into the basement, her brass bed sliding down with her and pinning her beneath its weight.

Three-quarters of a mile away, her frantic daughter, Ethel, had been en route home from her job in the downtown office of the city's public welfare department, when a tree crashed down beside her car on King Philip Road, one large limb immobilizing the vehicle. Not realizing that she was experiencing only the effect of winds on the fringe of an unbelievably powerful storm, the worried Ethel ran the rest of the way up King Philip to Burncoat, where she turned left and headed north into the broad swath of maximum devastation.

Ethel was stunned at the concentrated carnage with which she now found herself surrounded as she ran toward her home, still a half-mile away. The air, which moments before had been filled with wind-borne debris, now was thick with flying rumors, hearsay and half-truths. A neighbor whom Ethel encountered told her that her home was completely demolished, a pile of rubble, and that her mother must certainly be lying dead beneath the debris.

A few minutes after five, Joseph Sarli, 17, drove his sister's carefully restored 1933 Plymouth, which he had borrowed for the evening, into the parking lot of the Holmes 1941 House, an ice-cream parlor adjacent to the Waterfield home. Joe glanced up at the lowering darkness and assumed that a particularly vicious thunderstorm was about to break. He hurried into the building, where he had arranged to meet a friend, with whom he planned to go to the North High Picnic at the American Steel and Wire campground in Millbury.

When the building began to tremble, and the windows started blowing in, Joe and another young patron vaulted the counter and lay flat on the floor, the counterman flopping down on them. A heavy electric fan which stood in a corner near the telephone booths came arcing through the air and crashed into a wall near them.

As soon as the roaring blackness receded, Joe and his friend ran outside. A glance at his sister's battered car, now resting on four flat tires, showed that it was undriveable, but before the full extent of damage had fully registered on their senses, they ran next door and carefully entered the collapsed Waterfield home.

Crawling down into the rubble, the two boys carefully removed a radiator which was poised above the badly frightened Bessie Waterfield. The heavy radiator had been wedged in such a manner that a shift in the debris would have caused it to drop directly onto the bed. As it was, she was pinned beneath the heavy brass bed, which was carefully lifted aside.

Then the two men headed off in the opposite direction, crossing Fales Street and making their way along Paul Street. At one wrecked home, the two lent their strength to the delicate task of removing a wheelchair-bound woman from her wrecked home.

+++

When Ethel Waterfield arrived at her house lot a few minutes later, she saw that the destruction was as total as she had been told.

Her shock at the house's demolition was more than offset by her vast relief at learning that her mother had been extricated from beneath the heavy brass bedstead in the rubble-choked basement. Pinning her and causing permanent injury to Mrs. Newton's legs, the bed's bulk allowed a sort of crude airpocket to form around the woman, without which, rescuers believed, she may well have been fatally crushed or asphyxiated.

+++

Alexander Talbot, of Burncoat Street in Worcester, had taken a day off from managing his variety store and had gone fishing. He had been working a stretch of the Swift River in Barre, casting for trout, when an ominous storm not far away made him decide to wade ashore and call it a day.

He reached his car, parked a short distance away, at about 5:30. Getting in, he turned on his radio and heard a news bulletin saying that there had been a tornado in Worcester and that the first known fatality had been a Mrs. Leland, who had lived at 353

Burncoat Street. His home was directly across the street at 354. Mr. Talbot began driving homeward at the highest speed he could maintain.

Since the tornado's path had crossed his route several times in its progress to Worcester, the road was blocked at those points by fallen trees and fragments of homes. This required numerous detours and even some cross-country driving over small tree trunks and horizontal utility poles, a tactic of desperation which at some point caused Mr. Talbot's muffler to tear away. Throwing caution to the wind and ignoring the first roadblocks, which had already been established, the desperately worried Alexander Talbot made it home under his own power.

While the frantic Mr. Talbot had been occupied in trying to coax a trout to his lure, his wife, with son Walter, age seven, had been concerned by the sudden stiff breeze that sprang up, concerned enough to hurry into the back yard, and tie up her peonies as best she could.

The winds blew harder, no longer a breeze of any sort, so Mrs. Talbot raced inside and up the stairs to the second floor. She struggled vainly to close the windows; the tornado was upon her and in the face of the shrieking winds she could not budge them. She was halfway down the stairs when the window at the landing, in response to the plummeting atmospheric pressure on its outer surface, exploded.

A few more steps down and the worried housewife was peering through the small glass pane at the top of the front door, which was tightly closed. Staring in amazement across the street, she spoke aloud, half to herself, half to her son, who was staring, white-faced, up at her: "There goes Brennans'...there goes Lelands'...and there go my two rose arbors!"

Mrs. Talbot found she had trouble breathing. She shouted to her son, asking him if he was having the same difficulty. He wasn't. Lying prone as he was might have something to do with it she thought, so she lay down on top of him, partly to shield him as well as to protect herself from flying lumber and other objects which were crashing through the rear wall and sailing the length of the house.

As soon as the shrieking winds subsided and the inky blackness gave way to daylight once again, Mrs. Talbot walked north on Burncoat Street to check on the status of their store. "The biggest little department store in Worcester," as it was described in its ads, was in a shambles. Most of its inventory had been badly damaged, much of it was a total loss.

She walked back down Burncoat Street toward her home, on the opposite side of the street. A young man that she knew called a warning to be careful of the live electric wires which had been downed by the storm. She thanked him; until this moment she hadn't given a thought to that particular hazard.

Drawing opposite her own home, she saw elderly Fred Leland sitting in a chair in front of his ruined home, his wife lying on the ground nearby. "Agnes is dead," he said matter-of-factly, glancing up at his neighbor.

Mrs. Talbot protested that she couldn't be dead, she looked so peaceful...she was merely unconscious, surely. Margaret Talbot urged him to come across the street to her home. She knew he suffered from a serious heart problem.

"She's dead, I can't leave her," he repeated.

To reassure herself that the woman had merely been rendered unconscious during the demolition of her home, Mrs. Talbot walked over, leaned down and lightly touched her neighbor. The woman's body was already growing cold.

At their home on Ivernia Road, just off Burncoat Street, Ingvar Ahnrud and his wife were just sitting down to supper when the sunshine was replaced by darkness and the express-train roar could be distinctly heard. Ahnrud, an employee of Norton's Grinding Machine Division, ran outside in time to see the left side of the funnel passing Burncoat Street perhaps three hundred yards south of where he stood. The debris being whirled in the dark funnel and being spewed out in all directions, left little doubt in his mind as to what he was seeing.

Peter Matachinksas of Auburn was one of two pharmacists on duty at the corner of Burncoat and Fales that afternoon. The single-story building was not air-conditioned, and as usual the back door was standing open to admit the relatively cool breeze from the well-shaded parking lot behind the store.

At ten minutes past five, the two druggists felt the zephyrs of cool air suddenly freshen to a stiff breeze. At the same moment, they heard what they took to be the sound of a passing train. With the railroad a half-mile distant, why, they wondered, was the sound growing in volume.

Stepping to the door and looking out, they saw a large, dark cloud rolling toward them from the northwest, with what appeared to be birds wheeling and darting about it. Within seconds, these flying specks resolved themselves into pieces of airborne debris.

Not waiting to see more, the two alarmed men tried to close the back door. With the leading edge of the funnel nearly upon them, the gale-force winds made this impossible. Knowing that what was enveloping the store was no ordinary summer thunderstorm, the two men ran toward the front of the store, where they could crouch between the two heavy ice-cream freezers.

During the few seconds of this hurried passage, part of the building's roof tore away. The plate glass outer frames which formed the store's display windows exploded outward onto the sidewalk. The inner, sliding glass panels fragmented inward, but without real explosive force, and without causing injury to either man or to any of the customers.

By the time the two druggists reached the spot where they intended to take shelter, there was no longer much need to do so. Even though the center of the half-mile-wide funnel crossed Burncoat only a hundred yards south of the building, the relatively moderate damage and brief duration of the tornado's battering would seem to indicate that, in this particular spot at least, the tornado lifted from the ground, sparing this brick building and the frame houses directly across the street, anything like maximum impact.

Within a few minutes, neighborhood residents, dazed, cut and bleeding, wandered into the pharmacy, where they were given bandages, cotton swabs, gauze pads and adhesive tape, gratis. Some administered first aid to themselves; others took the items to their homes nearby. All were grateful for the consideration of the two pharmacists.

Glancing out back, Peter Matachinskas could see that the trees bordering the parking lot had been laid flat almost without exception. His 1950 Studebaker had been spared by the toppling trees; not so the large Packard of the meatcutter who worked in the adjacent grocery store. His automobile's roof had been flattened by the weight of a heavy tree trunk.

Later, when the large tree which had crushed the car's roof had been removed, the otherwise driveable car was given a unique open-air look by its owner. With the aid of a heavy-duty meatcutting saw, he proceeded to cut the now concave roof completely away, as though removing the lid of a gigantic tin can.

Alexander M. Naylor, Senior - "Sandy" to his friends and neighbors, sat in the small first-floor office of his home at 349 Burncoat Street, going over some accounts in connection with his plumbing business. A few minutes after five, the fifty-four year old master plumber saw through his office window enormous hailstones "as big as hen's eggs", he swears, bouncing off Burncoat Street, as the wind quickly rose and a roaring sound swelled in volume.

After a minute or two, Naylor got up from his desk and went through a small door into the hallway at the foot of the stairway to the second floor. He paused there, uncertain for a few moments, just inside the closed front door.

The Naylors' daughter, Lorraine, twenty-two, had gone to the attic as the wind rose, then hurried down to the second floor, intending to close the several open windows in the various bedrooms. Her mother was in the kitchen at the back of the house, peeling potatoes for supper.

When the cyclonic winds hit the home it tore roof and attic away and much of the second-floor walls. A downburst of air tumbled Lorraine down the stairs, where she landed almost at her father's feet.

Part of the north wall, an end wall of the living room, was torn away in the first seconds, which instantly created a tornado crossdraft. China, furniture and even the heavy piano, sailed, bounced or slid out through the gaping hole, lighter objects being whirled away to be instantly pulverized, the piano dropping three feet to the side lawn.

Lorraine, having just gotten shakily to her feet, was enveloped by the powerful crossdraft, So strong was the suction, it pulled her off her feet, body horizontal and several feet off the ground, fingers locked around the wooden molding on the side of the doorway.

Mr. Naylor reached out to help his daughter. As he did so, the heavy front door was blasted inward, tearing completely off its hinges, and smashing inward and downward, breaking Sandy's forearm in two places, rupturing two vertebrae in his spine and pinning him momentarily to the floor.

As Lorraine was summoning her last reserves of strength to maintain her grip in the doorjamb, more of the opposite wall carried away. The resulting dissipation of suction caused her to fall to the floor.

The Naylors' son Burt, 20, hurried down from the shower, clad only in a bathrobe. He and Mrs. Naylor headed for the cellar followed by Lorraine, who had won the desperate fight for her life, and the injured Mr. Naylor.

Sandy Naylor was convinced that the sudden, overwhelming destruction had to have been caused by an atomic or hydrogen bomb aimed by the Russians at the huge Norton Company abrasives company, but which had missed its intended target by about a mile. He was, at that moment, sure that the end had come and was thankful that the family would face it together. A married son, Alexander Junior, was at his own home in West Boylston, where he would be safe, his father believed.

When the roaring of the wind and the shaking of the ravaged home subsided, Naylor realized that his hearing had been impaired, a condition shortly to be confirmed as ruptured eardrums, possibly sustained when the front door slammed him to the floor.

Young Burt, still in his bathrobe, ran to the two-tenant home next door at 347 Burncoat Street. The home was demolished; it was nothing but a heap of twisted wreckage, yet the two second-floor tenants were alive and did not appear to be seriously injured when Burt climbed into the wrecked home, extricated the couple and led them to safety.

Mrs. Cleveland, the landlady and first-floor occupant had been speaking with Mr. Naylor two hours or so earlier, so he thought she must still be at home. Although there was no sound or sign of life from the ruined structure, Sandy Naylor was correct.

Not long afterwards, City Manager Francis McGrath, accompanied by Bishop John Wright of the Roman Catholic Diocese of Worcester, arrived in the neighborhood. Sandy Naylor rushed over to the pair, telling them of Mrs. Cleveland's presumed fate. The bishop, standing before what had been the Cleveland home, said a prayer that Mrs. Cleveland would be found alive, and followed that with a second prayer - a prayer for the deceased, that her soul be received into Heaven. Even before the bishop had finished saying these words, McGrath was heading for the nearest functioning telephone to place a call ordering the city-owned mobile crane to the scene with all possible speed.

It would be several hours, as darkness was falling, before the crane had moved enough of the collapsed structural timbers and wall sections to permit rescuers to extricate Mrs. Cleveland's body. It was discovered that she had died instantly, crushed by a collapsing chimney. A Mrs. Whitney, who resided with Mrs. Cleveland and was with her when the tornado struck, was helped to safety by Burton Naylor when he gave similar assistance to the second-floor tenants. Somehow, Mrs. Whitney escaped serious injury.

Lorraine Naylor had headed in the opposite direction, and two houses up the street, came upon the body of elderly Mrs. Leland, about the time Mrs. Talbot led the dead woman's husband away. Examining the woman's unmarked body for signs of the trauma that had killed her, the nurse came to the conclusion that the cause of death had been a massive heart attack.

Sandy Naylor had been driven to the Memorial Hospital emergency ward for whatever medical treatment was available for his injured arm. No sooner had he arrived, then he was overwhelmed by the number of people awaiting medical attention, including many who were gravely injured. Ambulatory, and with "only" a broken arm, as he then believed, he caught a ride back home without having received medical help, half-expecting the dropping of another "bomb", and wanting to be with his family when - or if - it happened. He pretended to his family that he had received medical attention. In the absence of any sort of cast, though, daughter Lorraine at least, was not deceived.

Five hours later, Sandy Naylor was sent back to the same hospital by his concerned family, with orders not to return again until his arm was properly set. The attending physician set the fractured radius and ulna, or so Sandy thought, applied a cast, then x-rayed the result. He saw that the jagged ends of bone had not been properly joined, so he removed the cast and repeated the process, with the same unsuccessful result. A third attempt at properly setting the fracture succeeded, and Mr. Naylor was returned home some time after midnight.

Just four houses north of Naylors' on the same side of Burncoat Street, stood a large frame dwelling, which, like the Vernon Drug diagonally opposite, was damaged only lightly, despite its location in the center of the seven hundred yard wide path of devastation. What is more surprising, however, is the fact that in this house at 363 Burncoat Street, the elderly owner, a Mr. Magnuson, sat absorbed in the reading of his Evening Gazette, which contained a prominent front-page story describing the damage and huge loss of life in the tornado that tore through Flint, Michigan, the previous day.

By all accounts, Mr. Magnuson remained for some minutes oblivious to the tornado which roared around his home, collapsing houses like matchboxes and killing three people in such homes within five hundred feet of where he sat contentedly reading. Unquestionably a man with exceptional powers of concentration. Possibly also, one might conclude, a man with a pronounced hearing loss.

A woman whose home was located on the east side of Burncoat Street near the corner of Inwood Road was sitting in her living room talking to one of her three sons. It grew suddenly dark and a howling wind come out of nowhere. The woman looked out of a window facing the side of a neighbor's home, as an enormous tree on the neighbor's property crashed to earth between the two houses.

Thoroughly alarmed now, and certain that whatever was engulfing them was no late-afternoon thunderstorm, she and her nineteen-year-old son ran from room to room slamming shut all the windows.

An older son, age twenty-two, had just finished showering and was dressing in his uniform prior to reporting for his annual Naval Reserve training period. The three of them rode out the remaining minute or so of the tornado's fury as every window, in quick succession, shattered inward. A loud ripping sound indicated that part of the house was tearing away.

The most frightening moment for the trio occurred as a heavy timber crashed through a window into the door, sailed across the room and into a closet, where it punched through the rear wall of the closet as though it had been a piece of paper, emerging in the bedroom, where it came to rest. Fortunately for the three frightened occupants, none of them was in the path of the hurtling timber, which may have been picked up by the tornado as it plowed through the Diamond Match lumber yard on West Boylston Street, less than a minute earlier.

The woman and her two sons, fortunately unscathed, emerged to a scene of utter devastation. A tangle of downed trees and utility poles made Burncoat and the side streets impassable; fallen electric wires lay everywhere, adding another deadly dimension to the horrified residents who picked their way along the littered sidewalks.

The first of the contiguous trio of three-deckers on Francis Street was already ablaze and the second was smoldering. Thick black smoke drifted to where the woman and her sons stood. In the opposite direction they could see smoke rising from what they later learned was a single-family home on Randall Street.

One of the two brothers ran across the street to check on the condition of an elderly woman who had been alone in her home when the tornado struck. Her house was a total wreck, roofless and without a single intact wall, yet the woman, still abed, was untouched.

Among the many articles of clothing and household articles scattered around their home the woman and her sons saw, draped on their hedge and still neatly suspended from coathangers, several priestly vestments blown there from the battered Assumption College, less than a half-mile away.

The older son headed diagonally across Burncoat and passed the small shopping center extending south on Burncoat from the corner of Fales Street, hoping to be of assistance to any of his neighbors who might be injured and perhaps trapped in the wreckage of their homes. He turned right, onto Lorion Avenue, and could see neighbors converging at the far end of the short street, in front of the Gurry home.

Coming closer, he could see that the tornado's winds had battered the house in upon itself. Word was growing around the gathering crowd that a girl was pinned beneath the wreckage. Willing hands working alongside him, huge sections of wall and roofing were lifted carefully away, or, if that was not possible, simply shoved aside. Finally, the rescuers uncovered the still form of a young girl, lying on a stairway landing.

The young man carefully lifted the girl in his arms, where she hung as limply as a rag doll. What the would-be rescuers feared was quickly confirmed by a physician, Dr. Victor DiDomenico, who had arrived on the scene. Susan Ann Gurry, age thirteen, was dead.

When he returned to his home, the young man took a closer look at his car, which had been parked in the driveway. Part of a large wooden utility pole was sticking into the vehicle through the driver's window.

Soon thereafter, the youngest of the three boys in the family, age thirteen, arrived home uninjured, to his mother's vast relief. He'd been caddying at Worcester Country Club, nearly a mile north of the tornado's path, when suddenly enormous round hailstones began to fall from the sky. These spherical ice chunks were of such a size and shape, he said, that it suddenly looked as though the fairways and greens were covered with practice balls.

The caddymaster may have realized what the huge hail presaged; in any case he immediately ordered all the boys into the clubhouse and told them to lie flat on the floor, which they did. They remained thus until the sky off to the southward brightened, and it became evident that the storm, of whatever kind, had passed them by.

Still later, the family circle became complete once again when the man of the house finally arrived; very late, very worried, and afoot. Like so many others heading home from the downtown area, he'd been unable to turn up any of the side streets from West Boylston Street that would take him home. Driving in a half-circle around the stricken Burncoat area, he finally parked nearly a mile away, not far from where his youngest son had earlier covered his head to protect it from the largest hailstones he had ever seen.

The man picked his way along Quinapoxet Lane, having heard from nearly everyone he encountered that a devastating tornado had plowed right across the upper section of Burncoat Street where his home was located. He'd had ample time to picture the devastation that undoubtedly awaited him, but tried not to dwell on the possibility of injuries to members of his family. His relief upon finding his wife and three sons without so much as a single cut, bruise or scratch among them is something that would probably have to be experienced to be fully appreciated.

In addition to residents of the densely-populated Burncoat neighborhood, who experienced the full brunt of the tornado but somehow escaped injury, there were a number of persons from outside the area making business deliveries or merely transiting the area when the funnel hit. One of the most fortunate of these was Maurice Leslie, an employee of Wentzell's Dairy, who was driving a milk delivery truck south on Burncoat Street at about twelve minutes after five.

Over his right shoulder, Leslie saw an amorphous black mass rushing towards him, just as he was passing St. Michael's Church. Assuming he was seeing an unusually concentrated and fast-moving thunderstorm, he continued across Fairhaven Road. Within an instant, he found himself within the funnel itself, in a state of zero visibility and with the truck rocking in the wind. Leslie instinctively pulled over to where he knew the curb must be and switched off the ignition.

The truck received the full brunt of the cyclonic winds, the same winds that collapsed Mrs. Cleveland's house only a hundred yards behind the rocking vehicle, and flattened St. Michael's across the street from where the woman lay dying, yet it remained upright, windshield intact. There is no way to explain Maurice Leslie's coming throughout his ordeal unscathed. What is virtually certain, however, is that if he had been ten seconds later as he drove along Burncoat, his truck would, at the very least, have been toppled, with serious injury very likely.

A woman who lived a few blocks farther north, just off Burncoat Street, remembers the fringe winds which did minor damage to her home, but has an even more vivid recollection of seeing their small family dog, Mike, "float" for a few seconds, across the yard.

The woman's husband and teenage daughter set off shortly thereafter to help in the digging out of their less fortunate neighbors a few homes to the southward. The young girl was equipped with a bottle of whiskey to be administered to any victim wishing to partake. Many traumatized persons availed themselves of a sip or two of whiskey that evening, hoping it might calm their shattered nerves.

Jim and Driane Leland were newlyweds, living with Francis and Helen Grenier, Driane's parents, at 227 Burncoat Street. Besides their recent wedding, each had graduated from college the preceding week, Driane only three days previously.

Now she had assumed, for the time being at least, the role of housewife. On this oppressive Tuesday she was doing some hand laundering in a metal basin in the kitchen, when her parents rushed through the door in a state of obvious agitation. To Driane's surprise, they yelled at her to get her hands out of the water, because there had been a terrible storm just behind them. They were sure it would strike at any moment. Jim appeared in the kitchen, curious as to the cause of the commotion.

The Greniers had just driven the half-mile south on Burncoat Street from the neighborhood grocery store, just as the tornado crested the hill and chewed its way across Burncoat, behind them. Intent on escaping its fury, at least for the moment, they did not spend time looking back at the looming black cloud or they would have been even more alarmed than at present.

The four watched as the large maples and other trees nearby swayed and groaned, and large limbs crashed to the ground, along with many smaller branches. As this was happening, the deadly funnel was passing them by, still headed east-southeast. The main funnel missed them by three-tenths of a mile, but strong fringe winds buffeted the home.

After about two minutes, the violent windstorm abruptly subsided. Jim and Driane immediately went outside to check for damage to the property. There was only a single cellar window broken, but such a large number of tree limbs had fallen or had been blown into Burncoat Street that it was nearly impassable. The young couple set immediately at work to clear away what they could of the fallen debris. Hardly had they begun this work, when the pair smelled acrid, pungent smoke, such as one would have smelled if located just downwind of the city incinerator.

Jackie Kelly, fourteen, was being helped on his Evening Gazette paper route that afternoon by a friend, Jackie Foley. Young Kelly had no fewer then one hundred thirty-eight Gazette customers on his paper route along Burncoat and side streets, and he was familiarizing Foley with the route so that he could turn it over to him when he departed shortly for a Boy Scout Jamboree in California. At about ten minutes after five, the two boys were delivering a paper to Arthur Bellerose at the corner of Rexhame Road and Greystone Circle. So quickly and forcefully did the wind arise that the Kelly boy was pushed off balance; he bounced off the house wall, unhurt, and managed to keep his feet.

Mr. Bellerose came to the door and practically pulled the two paperboys inside. Looking out to the north and northeast, the three watched as arborvitae and other supple evergreens bowed until they were almost touching the ground. Television antennas seemed to sprout from nearly every chimney or rooftop by mid-1953; now they were being bent like the trees, until they, too, were horizontal. And beyond, perhaps six hundred yards from where they stood, they saw the cause of the strange occurrences, a huge black funnel was sliding past, moving eastward.

The two Jackies did not know it, but the spot from which they watched the tornado's progress was beyond the range of the damaging fringe winds, and so the two hurried on their way, intent on finishing the route. This took them right across the neighborhood east of Burncoat, between Thorndyke and Brighton Roads, which constitute the broad area of "fringe" damage to the right of the funnel as it swept diagonally across Clark Street, heading for Great Brook Valley.

Despite the mounting damage as the boys went along, they completed deliveries as best they could. Not surprisingly, two or three customers were inadvertently overlooked, as refugees from the carnage further east staggered past them heading for Burncoat Street, while frantic husbands and fathers sprinted past them in the opposite direction, fearing the worst. One or two of these missed customers contacted the newspaper's circulation department complaining of the oversight and were appropriately compensated.

When Jackie Kelly finally arrived at his home on Thorndyke Road, opposite the elementary school, his mother pointed at the large tree lying on the school's front lawn and told him how she had stood in a living room window and watched it being wrenched from the ground by the tornado.

Twenty year-old Bruce Wells, a junior at Fitchburg State College, was driving north out of the downtown area toward his home in the upper Burncoat section of the city. Still a mile from his home, he was forced by the torrential rain and near-zero visibility, to pull over to the side of the road. His vacuum-powered windshield wipers were simply unable to keep up with the downpour.

After a few minutes, he was able to continue driving cautiously along West Boylston Street, entering an area strewn with debris which he assumed to be the result of a violent localized thunderstorm having crossed just ahead of him. Prevented by fallen tree limbs and other wreckage from turning up Whitmarsh Avenue, a side street which led toward his home, the puzzled Wells backtracked several blocks to a passable side street which led upslope toward Burncoat. Still unable to turn left toward Clark Street and home, Wells continued across Burncoat Street and drove another four or five blocks, until, on Ontario Street, he saw, ahead and below him, what remained of the duplex homes along St. Nicholas Avenue that had been directly in the tornado's path.

Nearly thirty-five years after the event, Wells described to the author a scene that reminded him of photographs he had seen of "ground zero" in Hiroshima, after it had received the explosive force of an atomic bomb. Many of the houses were nothing but piles of splintered wreckage. Others had walls and roofs sheared away, reminding Wells of gigantic, grotesque dollhouses.

Knowing now that what he saw was the result of no ordinary windstorm, and realizing the futility of trying to drive farther, Wells parked his car and headed on foot for his home at 59 Clark Street, less than half a mile to the northwest.

With devastation all around him, Wells feared the worst as he approached his home, but found the home basically intact, although shoved about eight inches off its foundation. The only occupant of the home, the family dog, was crouched in terror under the kitchen table. The cinderblock garage was almost totally destroyed - not merely collapsed, but virtually gone - except for a portion of one wall. Against that wall remnant rested his canoe, propped on its side, untouched.

Wells found himself assisting a stranger who was shuttling injured neighborhood residents to Hahnemann Hospital. He speaks wonderingly of the man who was impaled by a lathe which had punctured his abdomen below the rib cage, passing completely through his body to one side of the spine and projecting at least a foot behind his back. Wells recalls the man being conscious and lucid. He thought the lathe missed vital organs, and the man, he believes, survived.

All utilities, of course, were inoperative in the Burncoat area, so Bruce put his Coleman camp stove into use. Over its flame, he and his parents heated a very late and Spartan supper

Looking north up Burncoat Street, Jim and Driane Leland were able to see the flames shooting upward from a burning building half a mile away. The Lelands at that moment were unaware that they were looking into the zone of maximum devastation, where a fire from a gas stove was greedily devouring a multi-family home even as the flames were leaping to an adjacent, almost identical structure, dooming it as well. The pair began running up Burncoat in the direction of the fire.

Halfway to the burning buildings, the Lelands approached Clark Street and entered the swath of devastation - the so-called "area of total impact". Another few hundred yards, and it was, in Driane Leland's own words, "...as if we were in a foreign land. Nothing looked familiar." Now, as they reached the corner of Fairhaven Road, they saw diagonally across the street the source of the smoke and flame. Looming behind the flattened ruins of what had been St. Michael's Episcopal Church on the Heights, there was a hideous example of an unstoppable chain reaction, of what a later generation would come to call "the domino effect".

Again, Driane's own words: "We soon saw a three-decker, totally engulfed [in flames], topple onto an adjacent one. This second three-family home was devoured and fell onto a third. This house then collapsed and fell onto and burned a single-family home." People all around the stunned young couple were screaming for help, some in pain, all in fright.

These were the most terrible moments of all in every neighborhood through which the deadly funnel plowed, a period of minutes, often many minutes; the period of isolation, when virtually no one beyond the confines of the stricken area knew what had transpired. This was what now held the residents of peaceful upper Burncoat Street in its cruel grip, as the two able-bodied "outsiders" came suddenly upon the scene.

Members of a stricken family on Fairhaven Road whose property abutted the flaming homes on Francis Street called to the Lelands for help. One woman with a grotesquely broken arm was soon wearing a hastily-prepared makeshift sling; another adult woman was bleeding profusely from several deep cuts in her face, neck and scalp. She was laid prone. Then, closer examination showed that she had several knifelike shards deeply embedded. With no tweezers or other instruments with which to remove the glass, Driane worked carefully, and with her fingers removed the largest fragments.

Able to do nothing more for the bleeding woman, Jim and Driane, climbing over downed trees and picking their way through debris, headed across Burncoat Street toward the still-standing portion of the Naylor home, in search of Driane's girlhood friend, Lorraine, a registered nurse. They could see a portion of Lorraine's car, crushed beneath the wreckage of the Cleveland home next door. The portion of the Naylor second-story wall which still stood, looked like the false second-floor front above a saloon in a 19th-century cow-town. It seemed to be propped up from inside the room by a bureau which rested against it.

The house just beyond Naylors' had folded in upon itself. The occupants were a woman and her two young children, who had just been sitting down to supper. Large wall sections of the collapsing home had somehow settled into a tentlike buttress around them, from which they were able to crawl, unhurt.

Next to this was another blown-apart home, in the midst of which the Lelands and Lorraine saw elderly Fred Leland, unrelated to Jim, sitting placidly, while at his feet lay the body of his wife. The anguish of having seen his wife killed before his eyes had caused Mr. Leland to retreat into a semi-catatonic state, but he recounted to the three young people how his wife had met her end. When rushing downstairs from the second floor with the house collapsing around her, she was struck in the back of the head by the plummeting bathtub.

Knowing the elderly man's history of cardiac problems, Lorraine found his heart medication in his pocket and gave him a dose. She and the young Lelands could hear sirens wailing in the distance from several directions, but they knew that no ambulance or other rescue vehicle could get anywhere near them, so choked were the streets with whole roofs, sections of roofs and walls, and even entire buildings which had toppled into the street.

Fighting back the disquieting feelings of being the only persons in the area not being injured or in shock, Nurse Naylor and her two friends headed further up Burncoat Street and crossed over to the mouth of Lorion Avenue, a short street entering Burncoat at a right angle. Here was the house in which Driane had grown up, at least what remained of it. In the driveway beside the house lay the mud-covered body of a man. According to Driane's account, the "force of the wind had completely pushed in one side of his face while forcing out the other." A neighborhood resident said she thought the body might be that of Eben Rich, of Paul Street, just around the corner from the further end of the short street. The man's identity undetermined, he was covered with a rug and left where he lay.

The second home beyond had belonged to the Gurry family. Now it was a neat walk leading to concrete steps which led to a cellar hole filled with overflowing rubble. Entombed far down in the wreckage was Susan Gurry, youngest child in the family. At this moment, the hideous reality of the situation fully registered with Driane and she began to cry.

Jim walked part way home with her, then headed off to find their neighbor, Doctor Victor DiDomenico. With the doctor at his side, Jim headed back into the ravaged area, as a crude kind of order was beginning to take hold in the devastated neighborhood.

It was now a few minutes after 6 p.m., an hour since the tornado's lethal passage, Doors, ironing boards and other similar objects were being pressed into service as makeshift stretchers. The injured were being carried with as much care as circumstances permitted, toward waiting ambulances, station wagons and commandeered hearses that had approached as closely as they could.

Bishop Wright, spiritual leader of the Catholic diocese, had arrived, along with City Manager McGrath. An embryonic first aid station was taking shape near the corner of Fales Street, and rescue workers were silently grateful that two and a half hours of daylight remained before artificial light would be needed to further rescue operations.

Victor DiDomenico and Jim had soon gathered a small group of people for transportation to the hospital. They found a car parked nearby, unlocked and with the keys still in the ignition, probably left by someone intent on locating loved ones. The two men "borrowed" the vehicle, and drove several of the injured to Hahnemann Hospital. Dr. DiDomenico remained there, working continuously to treat a seemingly unending stream of patients, with almost every conceivable kind of injury.

Jim returned to the Burncoat area and parked the commandeered automobile as closely as possible to where he had found it. The next day, he would call a local radio station and give the license plate number, which was broadcast along with countless other items of emergency information. Presumably, the erstwhile ambulance and its rightful owner were reunited soon thereafter.

Because of the hour at which the tornado ground through northern Worcester, several newsboys besides Karl Walz and Jackie

Kelly were caught in the open by the onrushing funnel. One paperboy in the Osceola Avenue neighborhood, just off Clark Street, shouted a warning to one of his customers that a tornado was about to hit them, then joined them in the basement of their duplex. Another lad, who lived on Fales Street was delivering along Paul Street behind St. Michael's Episcopal Church when the tornado caught him. He had both the opportunity and presence of mind to wrap arms and legs around one of the strong new magnesium utility poles, and, despite the blasting winds, managed to retain his grip. It is tempting to rationalize the boy's survival by speculating that the funnel may have spared the frightened paperboy its full brunt by lifting or veering providentially, until it is realized that only fifty yards away, middle-aged Eben Rich, who may or may not have been outdoors, was battered into unrecognizibility.

A short distance to the northwest, and less than a hundred yards to the rear of the Vernon Drug building was the recently-built home of a Mr. and Mrs. Moriarty at 70 Fales Street. Unaware of approaching disaster, Mrs. Moriarty was amazed to see a large tree and an automobile go flying past a front window.

Sheltering in their basement, the couple could hear the demolition of their home in progress above them. With the attic and all that it contained went their daughter's carefully-stored wedding dress.

At 5:14 p.m., the enormous funnel slid across Burncoat Street, plowing southeastward, with three-quarters of a mile of closely-spaced residential streets in its path before it would reach the lightly-wooded eastern slope of Burncoat Hill, beyond which was a half-mile of undeveloped land, and then... more homes.

7

Children of Uncatena

At his home on 30 Rollinson Road, half a block west of Burncoat, Bertram Beyer was relaxing in a bathtub of warm water. After his bath, he would be heading off to a clambake. He sighed contentedly.

Just after five, his wife called to him, telling him that there was a strange sequence of weather happenings taking place outside. The flat calm and oppressive heat had given way to a sudden coolness and a fall of large hailstones. Hardly had these ice chunks begun to melt, than the sun was obscured and a wind had begun to rise. With a note of urgency in her voice, she advised her husband to get dressed before the storm broke upon them.

Quickly terminating his bath, Mr. Beyer hurriedly dressed. Just as he finished, the tornado hit. Although just inside the left side of the advancing funnel, the Beyer home and others on the street did not receive the full brunt of the tornado's impact. The storm, however, hit with sufficient force to tear away a dormer that had been installed nearly twenty years earlier, soon after Bertram and his wife bought the home. At that time, the builder had confidently assured the couple that the dormer had been built to stand up to any wind, however severe.

While still fairly new, the dormer had been carried away in the 1938 hurricane, and was rebuilt. Today, fifteen years later, it succumbed once more. The rest of the home remained intact, although flying debris, including many sharp-edged slates torn from the roof of Assumption College, shattered windows and thudded into the outside walls, with a sound like three or four lumberjacks wielding their axes against a stand of trees.

Venturing outside as soon as the roaring blackness slid away, Bert found his yard littered with a host of items; household contents and fragments of the buildings which had contained them. A six-foot high chain-link fence running along one side of the Beyer property, having offered minimal resistance to the wind, still stood. Plastered against its windward side were countless items, from pages of books and sheets of newspaper to clothing items of all kinds and torn and shredded sheets and towels. Nearby lay a yard-square section from the roof of the Norton machine tool plant a mile and a half to the west.

A teenage neighbor of the Beyers came hurrying up the street from the direction of Burncoat. She called over to him that rescue parties had already begun to form and were beginning the difficult work of lifting away heavy sections of blown-down houses, beneath which people were known or believed to be, entombed. The girl indicated that these rescuers were in need of all the manpower available, so Bert hurriedly grabbed an axe, a handsaw and a pry bar and ran off in the direction of Burncoat Street.

A few minutes later, Beyer was working elbow to elbow in the ruins of a home on Paul Street. The flattened house belonged to Eben Rich, like Beyer a veteran of the First World War, and at fifty-eight, just one year older. The men pushed, pried and lifted for some time, but without locating the body of Mr. Rich.

Word was received that a man's body had been found a short distance away, near the corner of Fales Street. The corpse was so extensively mutilated that positive identification was impossible for the moment, so the work went on. It ceased only when enough rubble had been removed from the site that it became certain that neither Eben Rich nor anyone else lay entombed.

At first it was believed that the unidentified body was that of a much younger man; after two days, positive identification would at last be made, and the remains of Eben Rich could be prepared for interment.

+++

Mary Bartlett, who lived at 16 Calumet Avenue, less than a quarter mile east of Burncoat, was taking a cooling shower when, over the hiss of the shower spray, she heard what she took to be a late afternoon freight train, passing about three-quarters of a mile away. As the sound continued to swell, and the wind rose in proportion, Mrs. Bartlett, a teacher and former geography major in college, guessed what was happening.

Jumping from the shower and hastily half-dressing, she ran from window to window of their Cape Cod style home, shoving each one up as high as possible.

Her husband Lee, a guidance counselor at Worcester's Commerce High School, and the couple's seven-year-old son, had gone to visit the senior Bartlett's parents who lived near Lincoln Street, a mile or so away. Expecting rain, and seeing dark clouds moving across Burncoat Street to the northward, Mr. Bartlett put the top of his convertible up, and with his young son, whose name was Lee also, headed for home.

Halfway there, small branches were flying past the car, some rasping across the canvas roof. Turning right into Rexhame Road, half a mile from home, they began to encounter broken tree limbs in the road. Driving carefully on, more and larger limbs were encountered and Lee edged past them.

Reaching the corner of Squantum and Longmeadow, still several blocks from their home, fallen tree limbs made any further progress in the car impossible. Mr. Bartlett told his son to run ahead as quickly as he could, to see if his mother was all right.

Just as young Lee began to scamper on ahead of his father, the two saw a straggling group of people approaching on foot from the east, from the direction of Sachem, Pocasset and Uncatena Avenues. Their faces were begrimed, their clothing torn, and a few were sobbing softly. Some were leading quiet children by the hand; one or two carried babies. Young Lee heard one woman wailing hysterically that she had lost her child.

Rushing as fast as he could, young Lee found to his delight that his mother was unharmed. Their home had been partially deroofed, and the chimney had been toppled. Gritty dirt that had underlain Chaffins Pond in Holden twenty minutes earlier, had not only been blasted into the the exterior of the house; it had filtered into every closet, every drawer, every cabinet in the kitchen and even into the stored utensils themselves.

Young Lee Bartlett's major concerns, after seeing that his mother was safe, were for the tree home in his back yard, and for the aloe vera plant given him by his second-grade teacher at Thorndyke Road School, Miss Salminen. The fragile plant, he found, had somehow survived; the tree house had not.

After finding his wife Mary unscathed, Mr. Bartlett was walking up nearby Beverly Road a few minutes later, when he saw his parents driving slowly toward him in their car. They had just heard a radio report of a terrible storm which had swept through the Greendale and Burncoat neighborhoods and they were anxious about their son and his family.

Lee assured them that all three were uninjured, then urged the well-intentioned couple to "clear the area", a theme that would be repeated again and again at every level of authority for more than a week, directed at those whose presence served only to retard the struggle to bring order out of chaos.

+++

Nancy Connor, a young mother of two children, was sitting in an upstairs bedroom at her 84 Clark Street home with her daughter Patricia, five, and son Jackie, three. With them was her sister, her mother, who was recuperating from recent hospitalization, and another older woman, a friend of her mother's. The corned beef which Nancy was planning to serve her family at suppertime was simmering on the kitchen stove.

Within a matter of a few seconds, at eleven minutes after five, it became as dark as night, or so it seemed to Nancy. She was sure that this signified that a bad thunderstorm was about to break over their heads, and the thought made her nervous. She had long disliked these violent, often destructive, outbursts of nature, and she admitted to herself that she was somewhat fearful of them. What puzzled the four adults in the room was the absence of the distant rumble of thunder and the flashes of lightning that usually heralded the approach of such a storm. Instead, they could hear a loud, deep-pitched roaring, which grew in volume. The wind rose steadily, and she began to hear the wooden structural timbers groaning under the strain.

"I think I'd better go downstairs," Nancy said, half to herself, as she rose, picked up young Jackie in her arms and headed quickly down the stairs to the first floor. She assumed the others would be following close on her heels. For some reason, however, they were not.

Just as Mrs. Connor and her son reached the first floor and walked into the kitchen, the entire east-facing end wall of the home tore away. Fighting both panic and the falling plaster dust which half blinded her and which she was inhaling with every breath, Nancy wedged herself into a corner of the kitchen. Clutching her terrified son to her, she murmured the most fervent Act of Contrition of her entire life.

Yet even then the worst was over. The roaring and shaking diminished, and a few minutes later she was looking out through the wide-open east side of her home at a tranquil blue sky. The three women and little Patricia picked their way down the littered stairway and rejoined Nancy and Jackie in the kitchen. Mrs. Connor had sustained some ugly bruises on her upper back and shoulders - how she came by them she had no idea - and the two Connor children had numerous fibers from rock-wool insulation stuck into their skin, material which was released when the roof and east wall tore away. Other than a few insignificant scrapes, there were no injuries, at least nothing requiring medical attention. All present were thankful for being spared. When they began to learn of the death and injury which the tornado left in its wake, they would feel even more fortunate.

Nancy's husband Tom was driving home from work and, like many Burncoat husbands and fathers, heard of the catastrophe in a news bulletin on his car radio. He was forced to park four or five blocks away and came running up Longmeadow Avenue toward Clark Street, just a block up the street from his home. At the corner of Clark, a Mrs. Jones, wife of a local physician, called to him to reassure him that his family was safe, despite the ravaged appearance of their home.

After a heartfelt reunion, Tom and Nancy began taking inventory of the battered home's interior. Nancy had a vague recollection of having glimpsed the sturdy wooden high chair sliding across the kitchen floor and being sucked out through the yawning opening on the eastern side of the house. They found, too, that many garments which had hung in a first-floor closet had ended up in the second-floor bathtub. Presumably a strong updraft had been created as the east wall began to tear away, which had simply sucked these relatively light articles of clothing upward.

The same scouring wind that emptied this large closet carried away Mrs. Connor's carefully folded and stored wedding gown. It was later found, in dirty shreds, hanging from a nearby utility pole. The car belonging to their next-door neighbor, Mrs. McAuliffe, which had been parked in the driveway between the two homes, now sat, still upright, a dozen yards away, in the middle of Clark Street.

+++

Diagonally across Clark Street from the Connors and two houses down from Bruce Wells, lived Charles and Helen Blodgett with their sons, Gary, sixteen, and Curtis, thirteen. That afternoon, Helen had spent hours on hands and knees planting flats of flowers in beds behind the house. Five p.m. found her trying to steady a trellis her husband had made and was now attempting to nail to the railing of the front porch. In the rapidly rising wind, the couple was increasingly frustrated. Charlie finally gave up in disgust and the two went inside.

Within a few minutes the wind had increased to a roar. First one kitchen window shattered, then another. From somewhere upstairs the family could hear another window blasting. At Mr. Blodgett's urging, the four hurried to the cellar where they waited out the remainder of the storm. With the return of quiet above, the Blogdetts emerged. Their house had sustained only broken windows and the loss of most of the roofing shingles.

Damage to adjacent homes on the same side of Clark Street was similarly light, but looking behind Phil Hall's home next door, the Blodgetts could see across Brandon Road to the homes which faced west. With the passage of the tornado, they could not be said to face anything. The single-story house of Clifford and Charlotte Stott and the larger one of the Chambers family next door to it looked like piles of debris after the wrecking ball had done its work, waiting to be loaded into dump trucks and hauled away.

Five or six minutes earlier, Clifford Stott had hurried down to his own basement, but not in an effort to seek shelter from the onrushing tornado, of which he was blissfully unaware. His furnace was equipped with an extremely sensitive General Electric control which had a habit of malfunctioning any time there was electricity in the air or whenever a lightning bolt contacted the earth, even a half-mile away.

Hoping to avoid another seven-dollar service call, Stott reached the basement, hurried over to the control and reached for the switch to flip it to the "OFF" position. Then the world fell in on him.

When he regained consciousness, he was lying on the driveway in front of where the garage had stood. At first, he could only crawl, shaking his head and trying to clear it. He looked at his home. It had been pushed rearward, completely off the foundation. The walls were no longer vertical, but were canted steeply, giving the building a half-collapsed appearance.

Across the street, the home of Merle Hebb and his wife stood empty; they were both at work, leaving the doors locked and the windows closed. The tornado, which had exploded scores of buildings up to this point in its passage, and would similarly demolish scores more in its erratic path, engulfed the story-and-a-half cape with its triple agents of destruction, a front wall of wind moving at better than 300 miles per hour, followed by plummeting barometric pressure pulling walls outward and roof upward, and another blast of incredibly powerful wind as the rear of the funnel passed over.

This particular structure, for whatever reason, perhaps exceptionally sturdy construction, stood up to the three-pronged attack better than most. The enormous outward pressure exerted by the relatively high-pressure air inside the closed up building bowed the walls outward. So pronounced was this bulging that a gap was created at each corner of the house, tapering from a maximum of about a foot at the midpoint of each corner of the house. Amazingly, although the walls pulled away from the floor at the base leaving a gap of several inches, upper walls and roof did not separate; perhaps the gaps created by the grotesque opening of structural seams sufficiently equalized interior and exterior pressures so that danger of actual bursting was reduced.

Whether or not this was so, the walls did not fully resume their normal shape with the passing of the tornado, and if Clifford Stott had had the interest or energy to look across the street as he picked himself up from his driveway, he would have seen something which resembled an enormous white pumpkin as much as a house.

+++

John Mulhern, who lived at the corner of Clark Street and Acushnet Avenue, had read about the tornado which had torn through Flint, Michigan, the previous day. When he and his wife saw the first pieces of lumber which came whirling out of the roiling clouds toward them, he recognized the storm for what it was.

Mr. Mulhern shouted to his wife Mary, their seventeen-year-old son Jack and daughter Mary, thirteen, to get down to the basement. As young Jack struggled to open the cellar door against the suction caused by the sudden drop in atmospheric pressure, the bathroom window shattered. As Jack succeeded in wrenching the door open and led the family down the stairs to the basement, Mr. Mulhern ran to the bathroom to investigate the shattering of the window before following his family to the relative safety of the basement.

At that moment, the full force of the tornado struck, collapsing the roof and second story, and trapping John Mulhern under tons of debris, even as the entire dwelling was shoved off its foundation and moved several feet to the southwest.

Minutes later, Mrs. Mulhern and her two children were able to climb out of the basement through the gaping aperture under the front of the house. The only injury to the three of them was a severe laceration to one of Jack's ears, which would require ten stitches to close. The three of them shouted for Mr. Mulhern, but there was no answer.

Young Jack, a makeshift compress held tightly to the side of his head over his nearly-severed ear, walked and climbed his way from Clark Street to the point where vehicular travel became possible. There he encountered a friend who agreed to drive the young man to a hospital.

Scarcely had they started off, than they encountered Father Edward Connors, a priest of Jack's acquaintance, heading into the damage zone and Jack told him about his father having been trapped in the wreckage of what had been their home. The priest hurried to the scene as fast as the rubble-choked streets permitted, and, squeezing into the wreckage, got as close as he was able to where John Mulhern had been located. The former army chaplain had been a part of the Ninth Infantry when it fought its way from the English Channel to the heart of Germany and had anointed many men who had been killed or were dying painfully. Now, as had so often been the case then, he said the words but there was no response or sign of life. He would perform several more such somber ministrations before the night was over.

When a crane eventually lifted enough debris from above Mr. Mulhern's body, it was determined that he had been electrocuted by a live, exposed wire, rather than being crushed by the collapsing building.

+++

Carl Carlson was hot, tired, and more than a little annoyed. It was five o'clock, and Sam Gow should have been home a half hour or more ago, so that the two of them could drive out to Chaffins Pond in Holden for a few evening hours of yellow perch fishing.

Carl, a painter by trade, who worked for the Norton Company in Worcester, had applied the first coats of paint to the exterior of the Gow home at 35 Brandon Road when it was built twenty years earlier, and had repainted it several times since. On this hot, muggy afternoon, he was wielding a paintbrush, high on a ladder propped against the side of the house.

A few minutes after five, Sam pulled into the driveway. Carl walked over to meet him. He'd been about to quit for the day anyway. Edith Gow had already called to Carl several times to come in before the storm broke, and he didn't like the look of the black clouds boiling in over Burncoat Street from the west.

As the two men were hurrying inside, Mr. Carlson glanced up at the black clouds whirling overhead and saw a mattress, perhaps sixty feet above the ground, spinning through the air. Now thoroughly alarmed, the pair ran inside, collected Mrs. Gow, and headed quickly for the basement. Like many Worcesterites, they had read and heard about the tornadoes which had plowed through Michigan and northern Ohio the day before. That morning, over breakfast, Mrs. Gow had wondered aloud to her husband what the essential difference might between a tornado and a violent thunderstorm, which made the former so much more destructive. Sam had told her laughingly that she need not be concerned, since she'd never experience a tornado. Now, as they clattered down the cellar stairs, that fearsome word was in each of their minds.

Carl Carlson had read or heard somewhere that it was best to try to ride out a tornado by keeping close to water pipes - or was that true in a thunderstorm so that the pipes would ground the electricity if the home was struck by lightning? He couldn't remember, but the three huddled close to the pipes as windblown debris slammed against, or crashed through, the shuddering building.

Within two minutes the roaring above had abated and was replaced by total stillness. The trio went upstairs, fearful of what awaited them. A huge "two-by-eight" plank, perhaps fifteen feet in length had come crashing through the window above the breakfast nook and now lay on the kitchen floor. Moving to the front of the house, they saw that a smaller plank had been thrust through a corner of the dining room wall, just above the floor level, missing every piece of furniture and coming to rest against an opposite wall.

The screened-in sunporch opening off the dining room was now minus its enclosing screens. Gone too was every piece of furniture, including the new leather lounge set.

Upstairs, on the second floor, as expected, the Gows found that every windowpane had been shattered, and glass littered the floors. A third airborne plank had plowed through a window of Mrs. Gow's west-facing sewing room, and was protruding, spearlike, from a closet opposite the point of entry.

Several large sections of hardwood flooring, probably blown from across Burncoat Street were found wedged against the Gows' foundation.

The apple tree in the backyard was still standing, but had been stripped of every leaf. Draped in its branches, in a sort of bizarre compensation, was a woman's fur coat. The family dog was found in a closet unharmed, but despite a thorough search, Mrs. Gow's cat, Marietta was nowhere to be found.

Behind the Gow home, across Eunice Avenue, stood what was left of the Perry home, minus its roof and most of its walls. In the middle of what, until a few minutes earlier had been the kitchen, stood a fully-set table upon which sat a ham and the rest of the family's supper, untouched by them or by the raging winds.

A few homes away, at the corner of Brandon Road and Quinapoxet Lane, a wooden utility pole, snapped off near its base by the violence of the wind, had crashed through the roof of the home of the Gilbert family, burying itself in the second story like an enormous axe in a gigantic chopping block.

+++

Mr. & Mrs. Karl Walz of 24 Purchase Street and their daughter Constance headed for the cellar as soon as it became evident that the roaring blast presaged no ordinary storm. Karl Junior was out on his paper route, delivering the Evening Gazette on Rowena Street, exactly in the center of the intended track of the tornado's half-mile-wide funnel. Clinging to a swaying tree, the boy was seen by his teacher, Mildred Nally, who called to him from the doorway of her home. Just as young Karl staggered through the front door, the trunk of the tree to which he had been desperately clinging, snapped in two and went whirling away.

+++

Mrs. Barbara Williams was with her five-year-old son David, in the kitchen of their Purchase Street home. She had just begun to cook supper when the tornado struck. The front porch and part of the living room, as well as the roof above the front of the house were ripped away.

Young David, terrified, jumped into his mother's arms and clung to her. Mrs. Williams watched her remaining first floor windows blow out and saw her curtains instantly shredded. She remembers having the presence of mind to turn off the burners of her electric stove. She recalls little else, beyond struggling with the blown-in back door, which was wedged across a small landing between the kitchen and the top of the cellar stairs.

She and David were somehow able to push past it and hurry down the stairs to the basement. She and David crouched against the southwest corner of the cellar wall, under the stairs. She later learned that she had inadvertently chosen what is generally acknowledged to be the corner of a basement offering the greatest degree of safety.

After the deafening roar of the tornado abated, not a sound could be heard, and Mrs. Williams and her son cautiously climbed the cellar stairs and went out the back door. They saw that the rear wall of their home, though still intact, had been bowed by the torsion of the powerful funnel.

Moments later, Mrs. Williams' husband Reg, who had parked at one end of the debris-choked street and hurried home on foot, appeared. Even as he thankfully hugged his wife and little boy, he noticed several welts and bruises on Barbara's face. How she received these bruises, she was never able to recall.

+++

Seven-year-old David Gilmore, his two brothers and a young friend were playing in the Gilmore home on Acushnet Avenue when the tornado ripped into the house. Mrs. Gilmore rushed into the living room where the four boys were and lay on the floor beside them, huddled together against the storm's fury. The end wall on the north side ripped free and was whirled away.

The story-and-a-half cape, set about twenty feet back from the sidewalk, was shoved off its foundation and pushed at least ten feet towards the street. None of the frightened occupants of the house were injured during the short but terrifying trip.

+++

Mrs. Mary Hehir spotted the whirling funnel through her kitchen window and recognized it for what it was. She began rounding-up her three young daughters and three-year-old nephew, just as her husband Eddie arrived. He told her she was overreacting to what was undoubtedly just a severe thunderstorm approaching.

Mary had never seen or heard a thunderstorm that looked or sounded like the thing bearing down on the back of their home, so she hustled the children down the cellar steps and quickly followed them. Seconds later, possibly before the first of the Hehirs' windows blew in, her husband somewhat sheepishly followed them down.

For what was probably only a couple of minutes the family listened to the windows imploding and household furnishings and lighter pieces of furniture crashing to the floor or scraping and bouncing around. When they ascended to the first floor again, they would find every window in the house shattered, with windowshades and drapes blown completely away.

The chimney had been toppled, but the roof remained more or less intact, despite the fact that the house was almost exactly in the center of the funnel's path. Every room in the house was a wind-scoured mess, including the living room. One article in the living room was undisturbed, however. From its frame on the wall, the face of Mrs. Hehir's brother, a Catholic priest, gazed calmly out on the wind-ravaged room.

Like Mary Hehir, a block to the west, Gladys Gray was standing in her kitchen at 42 Housatonic Avenue. However, her kitchen faced east, unlike Mrs. Hehir's. Mrs. Gray was listening to a train passing through "the cut", a mile to the northward, a spot where the roadbed had been blasted through a ledge of solid rock, and from which the roar of a locomotive passing through would reverberate, sometimes carrying for several miles.

+++

Down the street, Annie Balitis had just come home from work. Her brother Albert had been taking a nap but at the sound of the rising wind he awoke and came out to the kitchen, where Annie, who had just made herself a sandwich and poured herself a cup of coffee, was sitting at the table.

Apprehensive, she hadn't yet begun to eat. In the gathering darkness, she told Albert a particularly bad thunderstorm was about to hit. A strong gust of wind slammed the bathroom door shut as the alarmed pair stood in the kitchen. Through a window they saw the roof of the Maillett home next door begin to lift from the house.

Running into the living room, they looked across the street. The second story of the Johnson home had vanished. Realizing at last what was happening, Albert yelled to his sister over the wind's roaring and the two headed for the cellar. As they opened the door to the cellar stairway, the living room windows blew in and the wind lifted the heavy piece of plate glass which had covered the coffee table, carried it across the room, through the cellar doorway to whirl down the stairs ahead of the hurrying pair.

As hand tools whirled and clattered in the half of the basement that was partitioned as a workshop, Mary said a fervent Act of Contrition. Finally, the roaring and smashing sounds above them died away.

When brother and sister climbed the stairs, the door was not only closed, its frame was badly warped. Rushing to the foot of the staircase leading to the second floor, Mary looked upward - at the sky. The ceiling of the first floor was now the shattered home's roof. Looking into Albert's bedroom, they saw that a jagged two-by-four had plunged into the pillow where Albert's head had been resting earlier.

+++

The roar, oddly, continued to grow in volume. Mrs. Gray had been in the front of the house moments earlier, had seen the looming blackness in the west and had called to the Evening Gazette paperboy, Bobby Spano, to come inside since a thunderstorm was about to break. Bobby had declined, however, hurrying between the houses opposite Gray's toward Rowena Street and the general direction of home.

Mrs. Gray called to her daughter Martha, asking her to go out to the front steps for the newspaper which was lying there. Seconds later, her daughter's voice came from the front porch. In it, Mrs, Gray could hear both wonder and alarm. Martha wasn't making sense. She was saying that trees from the yard of a neighbor, Mrs.

Olson, were blowing up the street. Mrs. Gray, in consternation, ran out to her daughter, saw instantly that in fact this was happening, and in the same moment realized that the noise she'd been hearing was unrelated to a train.

What Mrs. Gray and her two children couldn't know at the moment the tornado struck, was that they were just inside the left, or northern wall of destruction as the storm angled through the neighborhood. This spared them the pulverizing blast which flattened and fragmented homes and took lives elsewhere in the neighborhood. Even so, the house was deroofed and nudged several inches off its foundation, the front porch was torn away, and the garage roof was caved-in on the top of the new Ford, driven home by Mr. Gray just a week earlier.

The windows on the north side of the house imploded, so violently that glass shards were embedded in the wall opposite. Fortunately, no one was in the path of the flying shards.

It was an immensely relieved and thankful John Gray, who, after several mandatory detours and a mile on foot through steadily worsening debris, finally arrived to find his wife and two children, sitting uninjured in front of their battered home.

+++

Just as Roy Erickson cautiously resumed his interrupted homeward drive along Brooks Street, his brother Andrew pulled up in front of his family's home on Uncatena Avenue. He had just come from a shopping trip to Spag's Supply in Shrewsbury with his wife and young son.

The screaming wind seemed to come from nowhere, shaking the car as the driver eased it up to the curb. Mr. Erickson opted for staying in the car for whatever protection it might afford from the mysterious windstorm. His wife firmly vetoed that idea, and the three ran for the house.

Mr. Erickson opened the cellar door, thinking that the three of them would be safest there. The cellar windows had already shattered, however, and a whirling cloud of windborne dirt was visible below, The three Ericksons crouched together just inside the cellar door, a location as protected as any in the house, above the level of the ground. The windows exploded and small items of debris flew about, but none of the three received the slightest injury.

The first thing Andrew Erickson saw through a shattered window was his overturned automobile, lying on the front lawn. The wind had rolled it over and pushed it up the sloping front lawn to where it now rested. Mr. Erickson was glad that they had followed his wife's advice against remaining in the vehicle.

Roofing shingles had been torn off and blown away, the cedar shingles with which the exterior of the house was covered were split and broken in many places. The back of the house, which faced west was thickly studded with pieces of slate roofing shingles from Assumption College, a mile to the northeast. So firmly and deeply embedded were many of these slate fragments that later, attempts to extract them even with the use of pliers, would, as often as not, cause the slate to snap in two, leaving the subsurface fragment as firmly embedded as ever.

Hardly had the tornado passed beyond the neighborhood, when Andrew Erickson ran across backyards to the home of his mother and brother two blocks west, on Rowena Street. He came upon his brother's car, or what was left of it, parked in front of the driveway.

Harold Erickson had apparently pulled into his driveway just as the full force of the tornado burst over him, at about 5:14 p.m. Before he could exit the automobile, the cupola on the Erickson garage was torn from the structure's roof and slammed by the wind down upon the vehicle, shattering the windshield, buckling the roof, and inflicting massive injuries upon the hapless driver.

Andrew Erickson, with the assistance of willing neighbors, managed to force open one of the car's doors, both of which had been badly sprung by the cupola's impact. It seemed to Andrew, from his brother's sprawled position on the front seat and bloodstains on the interior surfaces of both doors, that he had tried vainly to open the driver's door, then the one on the passenger side, before losing consciousness.

Harold Erickson was alive when pulled from the wrecked car and placed as carefully as possible in the back of a volunteered van for the trip to the hospital. His brother Andrew rode in the back with him. In his service as a Navy Pharmacist's Mate in the Pacific theater during the Second World War, Andrew had seen or treated many casualties. Andrew Erickson could see that his brother had suffered a badly-crushed chest and felt certain that massive internal injuries had resulted. Bleakly, he concluded that Harold's chances of survival were virtually nil. A few minutes later, while the van was still en route to the hospital, Harold Erickson died.

+++

Like numerous other youngsters in the Burncoat area, Billy Phillips and his sister Nancy busied themselves picking up king-sized hailstones which were falling around their home at 21 Sachem

Avenue, Eleven-year-old Billy brought some of the largest into the house to show them to his mother.

At about twelve minutes past five, Helen Phillips heard the roar of the approaching juggernaut. A minute later she heard one of her windows blow in. This barely registered in her consciousness, since she was completely absorbed in the astounding sight of an automobile which had been parked across the street, suddenly being lifted into the air, soaring upward and over the utility wires, like a pole-vaulter clearing the bar, then crashing back to earth a splintered wreck. At this, Mrs. Phillips and her two children ran for the basement.

Clattering down the stairs, she remembered a bit of World War II civil defense advice concerning precautionary measures to be taken in case of an air raid. She pulled Billy and Nancy into the space beneath the staircase. There, she knew, they would be afforded the greatest degree of protection and increase their chances of surviving the destruction raging just over their heads.

As the Phillipses crouched in their place of refuge, the tornado demolished a cinderblock home across the street, wrenching the roof from the crumbling structure as it did so, and sending it whirling across Sachem Avenue to land in the Phillips' yard.

From somewhere, a roofing shingle came whizzing across the street, probably at a speed approaching that of the rotating funnel itself. The Phillips' front door having been blown open, the shingle shot through the doorway and buried itself deeply, like an axe in a chopping block, in one of the risers of the staircase leading up to the second floor.

Helen Phillips could hear the wind howling and furniture and furnishings being thrown around and smashed, but she had no conception of the nature of the damage. With a stream of air swirling through the house, as powerful as the water from a high-pressure hose, the hinges on the top of the family's piano stood no chance, and it was torn completely off the instrument. Moments later, a large fragment of a shattered mirror which had hung on the dining room wall sailed from that room around and behind the second-floor staircase and on into the living room, describing an arc of one hundred eighty degrees in its passage and coming to rest on the piano's sounding-board.

The carpet in the living room was drawn upward and inward by the wind, with the center of the large rug standing, tentlike, several feet off the floor.

+++

Mary Gagnon was thoroughly miserable as she hurried down Clark Street just after five p.m. She had gotten off the Burncoat bus at Slattery's Spa and was walking as quickly as she could to cover the five hundred yard distance to her home at 3 Pocasset Avenue. Usually, she rather enjoyed the short, downhill walk, but just now she found herself in the midst of a fall of hailstones - bigger than she ever knew existed. The fact that she was pregnant merely added to her discomfort.

Having covered only a third of the distance, she considered running up to the door of George Wells, whose home she was opposite and seeking refuge from the pelting ice. The hailstorm ceased as quickly as it had begun, however, so she continued on her way, unlocked her front door at twelve minutes after five, and stepped into her front hall.

Looking to her left, she could see out a dining room window facing north, which overlooked Clark Street, It had been broad daylight when she had come through the door, yet as she stared in perplexity through the window, a dusky gloom became steadily darker until it seemed as black as night. As the daylight was extinguished, the wind rose abruptly to a screeching roar which made the house tremble.

Just as Mrs. Gagnon had hurried up to her front door, a man had emerged from the just-completed house next door, feeling a deep sense of self- satisfaction as he locked the door behind him. The man was a carpenter, and he had built the story-and-a-half cape himself. He had just finished work on the chimney that afternoon, and the house was at last ready for occupancy. Savoring his accomplishment, he hurried down the walk and got quickly into his car before the thunderstorm which was obviously imminent, could break over him.

As the self-satisfied carpenter was about to start his car, the thoroughly alarmed Mary Gagnon started upstairs. Before she reached the second floor, much of the roof tore away. In the first howling downdraft of wind, the sewing machine which was standing near the top of the stairs was toppled and came bumping and sliding its way down the stairway toward her. She quickly retreated to the first floor and , on impulse ran into the bathroom. With shuttered windows and the crossdrafts that were set up, Mary felt as though she was in a wind tunnel, and she clung to the frame of the bathroom doorway.

The doorbell chimes were torn from the wall and flew past her head. She could hear the kitchen cupboards being emptied, as the wind, like a giant, invisible hand, swept dishes, cups and bowls from the shelves to shatter on the kitchen floor. Suddenly, her dog appeared from somewhere and slunk past her into the bathroom, to cower, trembling, under the washstand.

Almost before Mary realized it, the winds abated and the sun shone brightly on the shattered dwelling. Shakily, she walked into her living room. As she expected, it was a shambles, and she winced inwardly at the sight. Then she looked downward at her coffee table, which had been covered by a sheet of plate glass. Beneath the table, debris had been wedged, packed tightly by the raging winds. The glass top was still in place, without a crack, chip or scratch, sparkling now in the late afternoon sunshine.

After the most terrifying two minutes of his life, the carpenter next door regained his senses. He was still behind the wheel of his car, but the vehicle was tilted halfway into the cellarhole, of the home he had so carefully constructed. It had been blown into fragments, one of which, a shattered two-by-four, was deeply and painfully imbedded in his thigh.

+++

One of the more unusual suppers being served on Burncoat Hill that evening had been prepared by Sadye Steiman, who lived with her husband and two children at 9 Pocasset Avenue. Her husband, Israel, was an avid and accomplished fisherman, and the supper was being served a little earlier than usual that evening, since he and a friend would be heading out to try their luck at a nearby fishing spot this June evening with its several hours of remaining daylight.

Mrs. Steiman had broiled some trout which her husband had caught earlier, and scarcely had the family begun to enjoy them when a roaring sound and what appeared to be the sudden arrival of night, caused Israel Steiman to turn in his chair to see out of the kitchen window toward the northwest. He saw full-grown trees bend nearly flat, while the wind - and there was plenty of it - seemed somehow to be blowing in the opposite direction. This he told his wife, half-disbelieving the evidence of his own eyes.

Mr. Steiman grabbed his young son Mark, and Mrs. Steiman put her arms around young Lynne. Almost without a word passing between the two adults, the four headed for the safety of the cellar, where they huddled close against one of the walls, taking care to keep well below and away from the small cellar window. For an interminable period which probably lasted less than two minutes they crouched there.

Cautiously returning again to the first floor, they found that their entire supper had been blown from the glass-topped kitchen table, save for a single, unspilled glass of milk. In the living room, a wooden utility pole had penetrated lancelike through the front wall of the duplex apartment, the top coming to rest nearly touching the television set.

Looking out one of the first-floor windows, most of which, surprisingly, were unbroken, the Steimans could see their automobile lying on its side, a considerable distance from where it had been parked. Stepping outside, Mrs, Steiman heard a low but sustained moaning, a sound which was the simultaneous product of several of the injured in the immediate vicinity and a sound which Sadye Steiman recalls clearly after thirty-five years.

Mr. Steiman crossed his backyard to Osceola Avenue, the next street over, to see if he could render assistance to any injured neighbor he might come upon. He returned to his wife a few minutes later, ashen-faced and on the verge of tears. He had seen the body of a young boy who had been killed.

In the doorway of another duplex on Osceola Avenue, Mr. Steiman had seen a woman who was holding a baby in her arms. She seemed to be on the verge of hysteria as she called to an older child on the second floor. The woman's husband had been in Flint, Michigan, the previous day and had called his wife to assure her of his safety.

Shortly thereafter, the Steimans came upon two girls who lived on Osceola and whose parents, for whatever reason, were not in evidence. Both the girls, like countless other victims, had been peppered with tiny slate particles with which tarpaper roofing shingles are coated. These tiny particles had been driven at high speed into and through the girls' skin, producing hundreds of tiny but painful, bleeding cuts.

Nine-year-old Lynne Steiman held one of the small girls in her lap, comforting her, while Mrs. Steiman picked what particles she could from the little girl, then wiped away a mixture of dirt and oozing blood. After the two little girls had been cleaned up, Mrs. Steiman put them to bed. Not long afterward, the girls' grandmother appeared. The girls were awakened and turned over to her, to be taken to her home a couple of miles away.

+++

Schuyler "Scotty" Benedict and his wife Louise, along with their teen-age son and younger daughter, headed for the basement as soon as Mr. Benedict spotted large fragments of airborne debris flying around like so many windblown autumn leaves. They clustered near the house chimney, close to which Mr. Benedict had installed a jackpost to support a weak area of the floor above. Young Dick was standing with his back to the chimney as the west-facing house was lifted from the front and moved backward almost completely off the foundation. In the same instant, the roof tore away and vanished into the maw of the funnel. The resulting compression caused the chimney to buckle. It snapped through in two places, jackknifing against Dick from behind, just as an I-beam came down in front of the boy. The pressure of the buckled chimney pinned him against the beam as tightly as though he was caught in a vise.

With strength born of desperation, Dick's parents acted to free their trapped son. Mr. Benedict quickly positioned himself so as to be able to exert maximum upward pressure on the six-foot length of chimney thrusting against his son, while Louise Benedict got a firm grip on the I-beam. Scotty heaved upward with a force he hadn't known he possessed and succeeded in momentarily lifting the chimney from Dick's back, while in the same instant his mother tugged the heavy I-beam aside, as Dick half-rolled, half-fell to one side.

His son now safe, Scotty Benedict became aware that he and the others with him were being bombarded by large-diameter pea-stone gravel from the driveway, blown in by the blasting wind. Protecting themselves as best they could, the Benedicts heard and felt the tornado's winds moving away. Mr. Benedict felt his side pockets sagging from weight. Shoving his hands into these pockets, he pulled out many pieces of the flying stone.

+++

Jack Hildreth had come home early from work that afternoon. He and his wife Jeanette were observing their fifth wedding anniversary that day. Coming west on Route 9 toward Worcester, Jack noticed that the leaves on the trees he was passing were hanging limply, as though longing for a breeze to stir them.

Just after five, Jeanette remarked to her husband that the birds "seem to be going crazy". Small birds in the back yard of their duplex home on Pocasset Avenue, probably either starlings or sparrows, seemed to be fluttering nervously, as caged birds are sometimes seen to do. Some flew quickly from ground to tree limb and back to the lawn again.

Their two small daughters in the kitchen with them, the Hildreths, like so many others that evening, became conscious of the sudden looming blackness, which was characteristic of a fast-moving, severe thunderstorm. However, they became increasingly aware of an odd roaring noise which was not typical of such a storm. More from curiosity than alarm, Jack Hildreth looked out the back door of the apartment, off toward the west and northwest, the quadrant from which such storms generally approached. Perhaps there might be lightning flashes or some other indication of the storm's proximity. What he saw, with initial disbelief, was the southern edge of the funnel, sharply delineated and heading right for him and his family.

He yelled to his wife to run for the cellar, and scooped up the older of the two girls. Jeanette, for some reason, demurred and reached for the handle of the back door. Before she could touch it, the door was blown completely off the back of the house and whirled away. A steel bulkhead cover crashed horizontally through the kitchen window, sailed across the living room, and sliced completely through the wall at the front of the house. This was the last they saw as they sprinted for the cellar door, their daughters in their arms.

Across the street at 37 Pocasset, Sylvia Davidson looked out a living room window. Like Jack Hildreth, Mrs. Davidson realized that she was looking at the edge of a broad tornado funnel. She gathered up her two small children and ran through the dining room into the apartment's kitchen, living room windows shattering behind her.

She tried to open the door at the head of the stairs leading down to the cellar, bur suction held it tightly closed. Pushing one side of the refrigerator away from the kitchen wall, Mrs. Davidson, her mother and the two children wedged themselves into the protective angle thus formed.

Crouched on their cellar stairs, the Hildreths watched sparks like fireflies dancing across the basement. Mrs. Hildreth told her husband that she was afraid these sparks indicated that a fire was about to break out.

What caused this sparking is uncertain. It may have been electrically charged particles of some sort, but a less exotic explanation is more plausible. Small stones or gravel whizzing through a basement window at several hundred miles per hour, and striking the stone or cinderblock cellar walls were seen by the other survivors to have struck sparks.

Within two minutes, the eerie performance in the Hildreth basement had concluded and the noise of the destruction above, as well as that of the wind causing it, had subsided, The ensuing silence was total - a stillness so profound that it reminded Jack Hildreth of another moment eight years earlier. He had been serving in the Pacific aboard an aircraft carrier, the Ticonderoga. A Japanese aircraft, forerunner to the dreaded kamikaze, had slammed into the carrier. The young sailor had been impressed by a sudden stillness after the moment of shattering impact. So it was again, nearly nine years later.

Like other occupants of duplex homes along both sides of Pocasset Avenue, the Hildreths emerged from a home that was badly battered, but still standing. There were surprisingly few injuries, it was discovered, as neighbors began counting heads and comparing experiences. Most residents had apparently succeeded in making it to the basement, where they had ridden out the worst of the tornado.

Scarcely had the debris stopped falling, or so it seemed to Jack Hildreth, than he saw Scotty Benedict walking down Pocasset Avenue toward him. The man was carrying a jug of water in one hand and grasping the handle of an axe with the other.

Someone, in a house diagonally across from the Hildreths', yelled that he'd found an injured girl. Jack, and his next-door neighbor in the duplex, Tom Sampson, ran across the street.

The girl was fifteen-year-old Dorothea Rice, who lived four blocks away on Longmeadow Avenue. Dorothea had been babysitting for a family named Kaufman at 39 Pocasset. Pushing little Barry Kaufman, who was about a year old, down on the floor, Dorothea was seated on the living room sofa, her back to the window and to the approaching funnel beyond. A wooden beam hurtled through the window, smashing into the girl with tremendous force, hurling her to the floor unconscious and causing massive internal hemorrhaging.

Willing hands carefully lifted the unconscious girl and placed her on a folded blanket on the bed of Tom Sampson's panel truck. With Jack Hildreth seated beside him, Tom drove the mile and a half to Hahnemann Hospital, were waved off, and continued to Memorial. Jack remembers that the horribly injured girl clung to life as the makeshift ambulance made its way to the more distant hospital.

Just as the truck pulled into Memorial's horseshoe drive, Jack heard a muted gurgling sound from deep within the girl's chest and saw blood gush from her mouth, He fought down his worst fears while a doctor hurried over to the truck as it came to a stop near the entrance to the emergency ward. The physician quickly checked Dorothea for vital signs. Finding none, he shook his head in resignation.

A few minutes later, the two men were back on Pocasset Avenue, taking aboard the truck a number of tornado casualties, among whom were Louise Benedict and her son Dick. None of these had sustained life-threatening injuries, but all required medical attention, including some with gashes which would require a large number of stitches to close.

While her husband was helping Tom Sampson transport injured neighbors to the hospital, Jeanette Hildreth turned the basement of their duplex apartment into a gathering place for the numerous neighborhood residents who had been dehoused, to use a term which utterly fails to indicate the shattering psychological trauma endured by the unfortunate. Soon she had a tiny Sterno heater employed in heating soup or hot water or in warming baby bottles.

With the heater in constant use, it did not take long to deplete the supply of this fuel, and when a Salvation Army automobile, its trunk loaded with sandwiches and other refreshments arrived in the neighborhood, it was gratefully received. Its foodstocks were quickly apportioned among those most in need. Other Salvation Army vehicles, and Red Cross vehicles, the latter mostly of the specially-constructed mobile canteen type, were soon to follow. They would maintain a welcome and reassuring presence in the neighborhood for days to come.

+++

Catherine Jackson, a forty-two-year-old housewife was living in a duplex home at 29 Osceola Avenue with her husband and two young sons, Jimmy, age ten and six-year-old Bobby. Her husband was at work and the two boys were seated on the living room floor, watching the Gabby Hayes show. The time was 5:14 p.m.

Mrs. Jackson, hot and tired, headed upstairs to take a shower, which she hoped would better enable her to face the job of preparing supper. She paused to close the front door before climbing the stairs, since it had suddenly become cooler, darker, and a breeze was blowing up.

No sooner had she reached the second floor than the wind rose alarmingly, and with it a roaring sound such as she had never before heard. The house began to shake as the outer winds preceding the tornado slammed into the front of the house.

The frightened woman rushed down the stairs and from this point, directly inside the front door, called the two boys to her, intending to shelter them in her arms from the fury of a storm that had already become like nothing she had ever before experienced. The two boys were at least as frightened as their mother, and scampered quickly to her.

The boys reached their mother's side just as the the front of the funnel plowed into the facade of the west-facing building, shattering every window in an instant, and blowing the front door inward with the force of a piledriver. The door missed Jimmy, but smashed little Bobby to the floor with such a crushing blow that he died instantly. His mother was struck down by the door also, with her left leg doubled under her and her right leg outstretched and vulnerable to window glass and other debris which crashed down on it.

More seriously injured than she could possibly have imagined, but still conscious, her maternal instincts prevented her from accepting, at least on one level, the reality of her son's sudden, violent death, although it had happened before her eyes. "Get Bobby a pillow of some kind - quickly, Jimmy!" she moaned. The sobbing ten-year-old grabbed a cushion from the living room sofa and tried to wedge it under his dead brother.

His mother gently but irrationally chided him. "Not this, Jimmy; a real pillow." Why she said this, Catherine Jackson has never been able to explain. Perhaps it was a manifestation of her desperate resolve to do something - anything - for Bobby, hoping thereby to postpone, even for a few moments, coming to grips with the terrible reality of his death. Nor has the passage of thirty-five years dimmed the image of Jimmy's tear- stained face, the very picture of agonized helplessness, as much a victim of nature's rage as his dead brother.

Finally, neighbors came and tenderly carried Bobby's body outside, laying him on the front lawn and carefully covering the small form. Shortly thereafter, Bobby's remains were removed to a hospital morgue.

Mrs. Jackson, still clinging to consciousness, was driven to Hahnemann Hospital, two and a half miles away, with the pain of her internal injuries exacerbated by every jolt and bump. Because of the seriousness of her injuries and the overcrowding at Hahnemann, Mrs. Jackson was sent on to Worcester City Hospital, where in the initial confusion of that tragic night, and with unintended irony, she was placed for a while in the morgue.

TORNADO!

Sedated and flitting in and out of lucidity, Mrs. Jackson today claims that she was moved later in the evening to a third hospital, St. Vincent's, where she was finally located about midnight by her frantic husband and her relatives from the city of Lynn. At last, more than seven hours after the tornado's fury had altered forever the life of her family, Catherine Jackson's day was at an end, as she finally fell asleep.

+++

Alice Mateiko was home with her ten-year-old son Teddy at 37 Osceola Avenue when the black cloud enveloped them. Her first thought was of a nuclear attack, a hydrogen bomb dropped by the Russians. She remembered having been in a downtown bank the previous day during a Civil Defense air raid simulation drill.

Two cardinal points had been stressed; in taking cover one should avoid being in line with windows, with their potential hazard of flying shards of glass. Also, if a basement is nearby, everyone above ground should seek shelter in it immediately. With son Teddy at her heels, Mrs. Mateiko put the advice to immediate use and raced down the cellar stairs.

In the adjacent unit of the duplex home, Mrs. Dolan had just attempted to acclimate her three sons, ranging in age from four to a year and a half, to the noisy thunder that had accompanied the rain shower moving through the area a little while earlier.

Showing by her own calm manner that the thunder was not to be feared, Kay Dolan read to the boys, absorbing them in the story until their concentration was broken by the clatter from a fall of huge hailstones. Not long afterward came the roaring noise, the darkness... and the wind.

Mrs. Dolan gathered the boys around her as the tornado began blowing in windows and battering the walls with airborne objects. Unable to decide whether to try to ride out the storm where they were, or go down to the basement, she temporized by taking her three frightened sons to the top of the cellar stairway and gathering the boys close around her on the first step down from the kitchen.

In a matter of seconds, one whole wall of the Dolans' apartment, the duplex's south wall, tore away and vanished, sucking many of the household furnishings, large and small, out of the yawning opening to immediate destruction.

Alice Mateiko huddled with her sons as the tornado raged above her, looked up at one point and believes she saw blue sky through a shattered cellar window, saw what she is convinced was the "eye" of the tornado passing above her.

Just across the firewall and up the basement stairs from Alice and her son, Mrs. Dolan and her own three boys were as close to the centerline of the building as they could get. The four Dolans weathered the remaining moments of the tornado without injury. When the noise and battering subsided, Kay Dolan descended the basement stairs. Calling through the wall to Mrs. Mateiko and being answered, Kay Dolan learned to her relief that her neighbor and son had ridden out the savage storm in safety also.

A few minutes later, both anxious husbands came running up. Like most of the other residents of the stricken neighborhood, they had been forced to park at least five blocks away. Ted Mateiko swears that his "feet never touched the ground" during his sprint through the deepening debris field, even when a neighbor who has seen Alice and Teddy emerge unscathed, called a reassurance to him as he churned past.

Paul Dolan had been driving north, up Burncoat Street. He was opposite the site on which a new junior high school was being built. He and a passenger friend, a Mr. McKeown, saw a young girl, head bent, trying to walk up the hill, but barely making headway against the strong winds. He stopped his car and told his passenger to offer the girl a ride.

Like most youngsters in such a situation, the suspicious girl refused, whereupon one of the men got out of the car, carried the girl to it, dumped her in and proceeded to drive the terrified youngster to her home. Stopping to pick up this unwilling young passenger who was walking well outside the tornado's fringe area, may not have saved her life; however, since the tornado at that moment was crossing Burncoat Street a half-mile ahead of them, it is possible - even probable - that this considerate act, albeit unappreciated, kept the two men from becoming casualties.

After his overland dash into the damage swath and reassuring himself that his wife and sons were unharmed, Paul Dolan walked two houses down Osceola to become one of a small knot of neighbors standing a sad vigil over the small blanket-covered body of Bobby Jackson.

As with the Hildreths a block away, the basement of the Mateiko apartment became a gathering point for several neighborhood families. Somehow, Alice's roast beef and lemon meringue pie survived the tornado's battering and were free of glass fragments. The pie was soon devoured by hungry neighborhood youngsters; carefully sliced for sandwiches, the roast lasted somewhat longer.

+++

TORNADO!

David Connors had been living in a duplex on Uncatena Avenue for only about two years but he had made many friends in the neighborhood and he was not happy with the thought that he would soon be leaving the neighborhood. David's family would be moving to Peabody in a few days so that his father could be closer to his job with the Federal Aviation Administration at Boston's Logan Airport.

David remembers that his family had hamburg, mashed potato and another vegetable that evening, sitting down to the meal shortly before five. As they were finishing supper, they could see through the open front door enormous raindrops splatting on the concrete walk. This was followed almost immediately by a fall of hailstones, which seemed, in the eyes of the nine-year-old to be "golf ball size or larger".

Suddenly the family saw the wire fence which enclosed the yard of the other half of their duplex "go right up in the air". It quickly grew pitch black, and David describes having heard a "whirling" or whirring sound, not the jet-engine or express-train roar described by so many of the survivors. Heavy metal rubbish barrels, which had stood behind nearly all of the housing units, began tumbling by.

"Mom," David said, "I think we should go down to the cellar." He repeated his plea, more insistently, so his mother agreed. With David leading the way, the family started down the basement stairs. In addition to David, his mother, and young Dennis, there were his two sisters, Judy, fourteen and Patricia, seven. Two or three steps down, David came to a stop. Small stones were flying through the broken cellar window, across the stairs and striking the opposite wall with such force that some of the stones caused sparks to fly. The scene reminded him of the World War II movies he'd seen, with the bright streaks of tracer bullets zipping past.

The five of them huddled on the top two steps for what seemed like an eternity, but was probably less than two minutes. Then, dust and plaster from above started sifting down on their heads. Mrs. Connors exclaimed aloud, "Oh, Dear God, help us!"

They looked out a window, then, in the sudden stillness, they cautiously went out through the front door. At that moment, David now recalls, he felt like Dorothy in the film "Wizard of Oz", after being caught up in a "cyclone" and whirled far away from her Kansas home. The dramatic difference, he says, is what greeted his eyes; not a scene of magical beauty, but one of devastation and disarray, with the street looking as if "rubbish trucks had just come up the street and dumped rubbish everywhere. Clothes, rubbish...houses were down...broken telephone poles, wires down...", David remembers the kitchen clock. It was stopped at 5:14.

A neighbor a few houses away was going around to those houses which had natural gas service and was shutting off the supply from the gas main - if he could reach the shutoff - in order to prevent explosions.

Mr. Preston, who lived four doors down the street form the Connors and whose daughter Maureen was a classmate of David's came walking up. "You didn't happen to see a 1948 Dodge come flying by, did you?" he asked. The Connors told him that they had taken shelter and not seen anything of that kind. The man noticed a mud-covered automobile lying on its roof, wheels in the air, in the Connors' driveway. Hesitantly, he walked over to the wreck and rubbed some mud away. It was the Dodge.

At about 7 p.m., the Red Cross was on the scene, helping to evacuate residents and find them temporary shelter. David has a recollection that there was talk among the adults of the possibility of another tornado - a rumor completely without foundation as it turned out, but a possibility which the survivors found too bitter to contemplate.

A Mrs. Lapinsky, next door neighbor of the Connors, was married to a Navy man who had told her exactly what to do in such an emergency. Laughingly, but with a trace of pride in her voice, Mrs. Lapinsky told how she had grabbed the family's cashbox, scooped up her children, and wedged herself with them in an interior closet.

David recalls that his family was initially given shelter by a young couple in their twenties, who lived only a block or two away. Some hours later, they were removed to the home of the parents of either the husband or the wife, who lived in another part of the city. His mother had hastily scrawled a note on their front door in lipstick, telling Mr. Connors where he could find them. Eventually, he and his brother did. At about two o'clock the following morning the family was reunited and set out for David's uncle's home in the Brighton section of Boston.

Judy Connors had been scheduled to baby-sit that evening at the home of the Wilson family, a few doors from her own home; a duplex apartment, like all such homes in that block of Uncatena. The apartment was destroyed, with only a staircase leading to a nonexistent second floor surviving, still somehow attached to the wall of the adjacent apartment. The Wilsons escaped serious injury, however, and Mr. Wilson would receive his military discharge in the mail a few days later. It had been found lying on a lawn by some-one in Jamaica Plain, a Boston borough forty miles to the east.

+++

The kitchen of the Preston apartment at 116 Uncatena was filled with the savory aroma of simmering spaghetti sauce. When the high winds tore into the building, Mrs. Preston quickly shepherded her daughter Maureen, seven, and the girl's three younger brothers down the cellar stairs. As the storm raged above them, Mrs. Preston talked soothingly to the frightened children clustered around her, keeping her voice just loud enough to be heard over the blast of the storm, and she sang familiar songs with them until the roaring died away.

When mother and children ascended the cellar stairs to the the kitchen, they found the room a shambles, with both windows broken and with spaghetti sauce splattered on all four walls as well as ceiling and floor. To their amazement, the adjacent apartment unit had virtually disappeared.

The curious Preston youngsters began to roam about the neighborhood, encountering death for the first time in their young lives when they came upon Bobby Jackson's covered form. As they stared uncomprehendingly at badly injured neighbors being helped from their shattered homes, Mrs. Preston called them to her and brought them inside. They had seen more than enough suffering for one day.

+++

Further up the street, Dorothy Glavin heard and saw her home coming apart around her. When a door fell from its demolished frame it landed near her, becoming wedged between the kitchen refrigerator and a remaining portion of the wall. Mrs. Glavin, a nurse by profession and not easily panicked, crawled into the triangle of space beneath the propped door. Emerging shortly from this comparatively protected spot, Mrs. Glavin would find ample opportunity to exercise her nursing skills for the benefit of her injured neighbors.

+++

At about five o'clock, Jacquelyn Smith, who had been playing with her friend Beverly Clement in front of the Clement home, heard her mother calling her to come home. Mrs. Smith felt that a bad storm could break at any moment and she wanted Jacquelyn at home when it happened.

Mrs. Smith's husband John would have been on his way home from work at that hour but instead he was resting in the bedroom, recuperating from a painful tooth extraction. When the roaring wind began in earnest, Mrs. Smith saw large objects rolling and bouncing like tumbleweeds between the houses and across the street. She called to her husband to come into the kitchen.

He joined them, just as windows began to pop. Then the roof tore off, walls started to buckle and household furnishings began streaming out of the openings. The three Smiths had no time to get to the basement and so they dropped to the floor in the middle of the kitchen. When the wind died a minute or so later, they were still lying where they had dropped, not a serious injury among the three, but with the house and all its familiar furnishings completely vanished. The floor itself had started to lift in one corner.

Mrs. Smith, a trained nurse, began giving what first aid she could to her injured neighbors. A Doctor Haig, who lived in the neighborhood, was doing the same, while a priest from devastated Assumption College, over a mile away, arrived shortly and anointed a number of the dead, dying and injured, sometimes lending his strength to help free someone pinned in the rubble.

+++

"Look, Mommy! What's that in the sky?"

Irene Howe ran to the window. Standing beside her five-year-old daughter Barbara, Mrs. Howe peered off to the northwest, across the back yard of the Smiths next door, saw a churning black cloud and heard a roaring noise, getting louder each second.

The home's windows had been closed because of the fall of large hailstones and in anticipation of the rain which Mrs. Howe felt sure would quickly follow. With a crash, a front window exploded and in an instant a mirror hanging on the wall a few feet away was plucked from that position as by invisible fingers and was whirled out through the shattered opening.

Mrs. Howe ran to the back bedroom where little Judy, who had just turned two, was asleep in her crib. She picked the toddler up and cradled her protectively in her arms, Barbara at her side. Around them, they could see, hear and feel their home being destroyed by the kind of storm Irene Howe had never imagined could exist.

The next thing Mrs. Howe remembers is regaining her senses on the sloping front lawn. She was lying close to the unpaved street, an immense diagonal wound in her upper left arm, where a piece of the toppling chimney had gouged flesh from her arm, like some enormous rough-toothed saw blade. A large splinter from a fence picket protruded like an arrow from her right leg and her right ear was bleeding profusely, although that cut would prove to be the least serious of her injuries.

Barbara was in tears at the sight of her mother. The girl did not seem to be badly injured, her mother noted, seeing her daughter through the veil of her own excruciating pain.

Mother and daughter heard from nearby the familiar loud wail of a frightened infant. Barbara walked toward the sound of the crying, carefully lifted aside a piece of their former home and found beneath it the hysterical Judy. The wall fragment had somehow landed leaning on another object, sheltering Judy from the fall of additional objects.

The toddler had survived the total demolition of her home without suffering any sort of injury.

Far less lucky than Judy Howe was the experience of William Heyde, thirty-two, whose family lived next door to the Howes. In the whirlwind demolition of his home, he was struck on the head by some airborne object. Neurological specialists would fight vainly to save him; he would succumb to his massive trauma within a few days.

+++

Clarence Clement had left work soon after 5:00 p.m., as he always did. Leaving the Paul Revere Life Insurance Company building in downtown Worcester, he headed up Lincoln Street toward home, where his wife and daughter awaited him. The sky in that direction was ominously black; doubtless the Greendale and Burncoat neighborhoods were catching the brunt of a fast-moving thunderstorm. At Brittan Square, where Lincoln Street bore to the right, traffic was being diverted into the left fork, Burncoat Street, which also led in the general direction of home.

Puzzled at this odd re-routing, Mr. Clement tried to suppress a deepening foreboding as he continued on. By the time he passed Rexhame Road into what was loosely termed "upper Burncoat", his misgivings began turning to genuine alarm. Steering around downed tree limbs past Thorndyke Road, the anxious driver covered two more blocks before he encountered more and larger limbs.

His car now slowed to a crawl, Clarence turned right and headed east, down Brighton Road toward his home, a half-mile away. At the far end of this short street, where it ended at Bay State Road, he could see signs of serious storm damage ahead. Correctly assuming that Ontario Street, his most direct route home, would be impassable, he got out of his car and ran toward Uncatena Avenue.

Struck by the sight of utility poles, broken off or leaning crazily, with wires trailing on the ground beneath, Mr. Clement hurried on. A block further and he was passing half-destroyed homes.

Running as hard as he could, he crossed the crest of the low hill between Pocasset and Osceola and saw what remained of the row of new, single-family homes on Uncatena Avenue, the neighborhood that Clarence Clement, his wife Jennie and their nine-year-old daughter, Beverly Rae, called home.

The five-room Cape Cod and ranch-style homes along the still-unpaved Uncatena Avenue had been built on concrete slabs, rather than on foundations with finished basements beneath. What met Clarence Clement's disbelieving eyes was a row of slabs, looking like gigantic grave markers, flush with the green grass around them. Some of the slabs bore the twisted wreckage of houses that had once rested upon them; others were nearly bare. In front of one of the latter, a woman, bleeding, her clothing in tatters, stood silently.

Mr. Clement ran toward his wife and started to embrace her, then stopped when her realized how badly she was injured. "Beverly's dead," the woman said. Clarence saw his daughter lying on the slab. As he moved toward her, he could see that she had suffered what a physician would call a "massive trauma to the head", which no one could have survived.

Numb with grief, the couple was half-aware of other people around them, limping past or trying to dig through the shattered fragments of what had been their homes. A friend, Doctor Haig, came by and offered Mrs. Clement a sedative, which she mutely accepted.

He briefly examined the woman and found that her back was peppered with embedded particles; wooden splinters and gravel, driven under the skin and into the flesh beneath, almost with the force of buckshot.

While the doctor was thus occupied, the distraught mother described to him and to her husband the manner of Beverly's death. In the maelstrom of wind as the pulverized home was being blown away piecemeal, Beverly had been flung to the slab upon which their home had stood. The heavy hot water tank had struck her in the head, fracturing her cranium and causing instantaneous death.

+++

Earlier that afternoon, fifteen-year-old George Steele, Jr., who lived next door to the Clements at number 145, had gone across the street to spend some time with his friend, Mike Sullivan. The two boys had been in the attic of the Sullivans' single-story home when the deadly funnel hit. Their bodies were found in the remains of the demolished attic and roof, several hundred feet down the tornado's track, as close in death as they had been in life.

+++

Malcolm Hannah and his wife Lillian turned from Burncoat onto Clark Street at eleven minutes after five. Their two children, Mary and David, would be waiting for them at home. Just over a minute later Mr. Hannah turned the couple's 1949 Chevrolet onto Uncatena Avenue. The wind was already blowing hard enough to rock the car as they continued heading up Uncatena toward their home, tree limbs breaking away and sliding across their path; trash cans whirling through the air and bouncing off the car and over it, to slam into the houses on the leeward side of the street.

As they approached their home at 151 Uncatena their car, already battered, began to come apart. As though in slow motion, the terrified couple saw their automobile disintegrate. The hood sprang up, tore free and spun away in a single convulsive wrenching. The windshield pulverized and vanished and the front fenders tore off. What remained of the battered vehicle, along with its two occupants, was flung past the Hannahs' crumbling home, coming to rest against a tree more then fifty yards away.

+++

Unaware of their parents' plight, when the tornado struck their home, fifteen-year-old Mary Hannah had grabbed her nine-year-old brother, locked her arms around him and planted herself firmly in the center hallway. The two youngsters stayed on their feet and conscious as they fought the powerful suction and watched what seemed to be most of the household's contents come flying past them and out the kitchen windows. When the end wall of the kitchen tore away with a roar, even heavy objects like the refrigerator slid out of the opening and into the tornado's maw.

When the roaring died away, Mary relaxed her hold on her brother and walked out of the ruined house. It was she who first saw her dazed father tottering toward her. He had apparently been thrown from the car as it had been flung down the slope and into the trees. Mr. Hannah mumbled to his daughter and gestured weakly back in the direction where his wife lay.

As her father continued dragging himself toward a neighbor's home which still stood, Mary ran down the hill and found her mother, face down, handless arms outflung, but still conscious. She asked to be turned over onto her back. As Mary tried to do as her mother asked, Lillian Hannah, her rib cage crushed and lungs collapsed, stopped breathing forever.

+++

When the tornado struck the home of the Dixon family at 152 Uncatena, Mary, age thirteen, and her eleven-year-old sister Katherine crouched in terror behind a large armchair in the living room. Like the majority of homes on Uncatena, theirs was built atop a concrete slab. Thus lacking a basement into which they could flee, the two frightened girls could only cling to each other as the roaring wind tore their home apart.

The girls either lost consciousness or briefly blanked out during the storm's demolition of the home; next thing they knew they were lying on the sloping front lawn in front of where their house had stood. They could see that the slab was bare, save for some bits of debris... and the family's bathtub.

The two girls began walking west, in the general direction of Burncoat Street. Halfway there, they stopped at the home of a woman they knew, whose home had been on the fringe of the tornado, and had escaped major damage. The woman was aghast at the two ragged, dirt-encrusted girls who stood before her.

She plopped the pair into her bathtub and they scrubbed themselves until their normal skin coloration re-emerged. The girls dressed in clothing belonging to the woman's own daughter. With her skin clean once again, it was discovered that Mary had somehow sustained a long gash on one side of her nose, which the thoughtful woman bandaged as best she could.

The girls then wandered back to their own neighborhood. The Montville home, a little farther up Uncatena from the Dixons' had been just outside the funnel, and was more or less intact. Mrs. Montville took the two girls in.

A few minutes later, the girls' frantic parents arrived, along with a third daughter, Phyllis. Beside themselves with worry, they had been forced to leave their car some distance away, and like Clarence Clement and numerous others, had picked their way over, around, or through debris which made passage as slow as it was difficult, injuring many who braved it.

At first the Dixons were unable to locate the site where their home had stood, since houses on both sides of Uncatena for a considerable distance had been totally destroyed and the debris blown off the hillside. As they were trying to orient themselves, the two girls came out of the Montville home and ran to their parents. In the joy of being reunited, other considerations were for the moment pushed aside.

+++

Five-year-old Brian Willett couldn't understand why his mother suddenly seemed so worried. He and his sisters had been sitting with her on the Montvilles' front porch, across the street from their home.

The two mothers had been talking; he and his sisters had been playing with the Montville children, when suddenly it began to hail; round pieces of ice the size of golf balls. They had been having a wonderful time throwing the ice lumps at each other. Even the hailstone that had hit Brian on the head before landing at his feet, had hurt for only a minute.

Now suddenly their mother was shoving the three reluctant children back across the street to their own home. There was a roaring noise, getting louder and louder. At the same time, it grew dark, almost like night, Brian thought, and the wind blew so hard it shook the house. A window burst from the force of the wind.

Their mother stood with them in the middle of the hall which ran the length of the house, as far from any outside wall as she could get. More windows blew in and the wind began blowing objects through the hall where they stood. It seemed to Brian that it was getting harder and harder to stand in one place.

Brian saw a heavy ceramic table lamp come flying into the hall and strike his mother on the head as it sailed past. She fell to the floor unconscious. The three frightened children could see the tops of the hall walls leaning inward toward each other. The effect reminded Brian of an Indian tepee.

Then the walls and ceiling came down on them and everything was dark and silent. The next thing Brian remembers was a ray of light appearing above him and a man's voice calling: "here's another one!"

Brian's little sister Mary Jo had been blown completely off the floor before the house had fully collapsed over Mrs. Willett and her two other children. Searchers spent several anxious minutes before one of them spotted part of the little girl's red and white polka-dot sunsuit. Mary Jo was almost completely buried in debris some forty or fifty feet down the sloping back yard from where the house had stood. She was badly cut, scraped and bruised.

Mrs. Willett regained consciousness and she and the three children were helped across the street to the home of the Brunell family. Brian's eyes were stinging and his vision was cloudy and blurred. Only later would hospital examination reveal numerous glass shards and bits of road tar in both eyes.

Since the tornado's destruction swath was so wide that rescue vehicles couldn't reach them, the Willetts joined the stream of homeless victims walking towards Burncoat Street. At Bay State Road, three-quarters of the way to Burncoat, the Willetts and many of the others were greeted by volunteer drivers who transported them to hospitals, the Willetts being taken to City Hospital.

+++

It had seemed to Yvonne Brunell that nearly every youngster under the age of twelve who lived on either side of that long block of single-family homes on Uncatena Avenue was playing in front of her house - and Mrs. Brunell didn't mind it a bit. Nearly all the couples from number 130 on up the street were in their late twenties or early thirties with one or more children. Most of the wives did not work outside the home.

One or another of the mothers was hostess to an informal kaffeklatch nearly every day and with their mothers came the energetic preschoolers, interacting loudly and vigorously with their neighborhood playmates. Yvonne Brunell enjoyed these gatherings, and she felt the same maternal pleasure now, as she sat with several other women watching the children play. There was a considerable number in sight; the school-aged youngsters having joined their younger siblings about an hour and a half before.

With the onset of an eerie darkness and a rising wind, the other women with Mrs. Brunell hurriedly gathered their youngsters and quickly departed for their homes. When Yvonne and her sister, Teresa Rivard, brought Yvonne's two children, Mary and Joseph, inside, Yvonne found to her annoyance that she was unable to close the door behind them, so fierce had the wind become. She gave up trying to accomplish this when she saw the family's heavy steel rubbish barrel go rolling and bouncing up the street. Throwing caution to the winds, literally, she darted out and gave chase. She recovered the errant barrel and dragged it back.

No sooner was Mrs. Brunell back inside than the funnel proper struck. The two Brunell children and a visiting youngster were pushed to the floor and a rug was hastily thrown over them. The two women attempted to give additional protection by lying atop the frightened and bewildered children. Mother and aunt offered up several fervent Hail Marys, in which the children joined without any prompting.

When the roaring and smashing sounds abated, the five disengaged themselves and stood up. They found that the low-lying ranch house which had been on the extreme right-hand edge of the funnel had stayed more or less intact. The long front and rear walls still stood as they had been built, but the two end walls were semi-detached, flaring upward and outward, away from the eaves. The roof showed signs of having been lifted from the walls.

Somehow - no one is sure just how - the Brunell home evolved very quickly into a meeting place for many homeless and disoriented neighborhood residents, and a collection point for people with a variety of injuries, some ambulatory, some not.

The Clements were there, having been led from the slab where their house had stood and where their daughter Christine had died. Mrs. Clement had been badly hurt also, but she was conscious and semi-lucid. Someone offered her a shot of brandy which she accepted and downed. Young Brian Willett was there, eyes burning and nearly swollen shut from being splashed with road or roofing tar when a large bucket of the stuff, plucked aloft from God-knows-where, had landed nearby like a liquid bomb, spraying the stuff in all directions.

When Mr. Brunell arrived home from work, on the dead run like most of the other worried men coming into the neighborhood, he carefully did what he could to flush the heaviest concentrations of the tar from the boy's reddened eyes. At about the same time, Malcolm Hannah, bloody, ragged, and hobbling on two fractured ankles, leaning on his daughter for support, shuffled into the house. A few minutes later he and several others of the most seriously injured neighborhood casualties were evacuated by truck to Memorial Hospital.

Soon afterward, word spread along Uncatena Avenue that a baby's arm and hand had been spotted projecting motionless from the rubble where a home had lately stood. Running to the site, rescuers carefully removed debris from around the arm and lifted forth - a doll.

+++

Bobby Jackson's back yard abutted that of the Williston family, who lived on the next street to the eastward, Uncatena Avenue. The Williston apartment, like that of the Jacksons, was a duplex building, with the O'Grady family occupying the other unit.

Steven Williston, four, and his twenty-two-month-old brother John had left their home with their parents a few minutes before five. Betty Williston was a waitress at Stuart's Diner on West Boylston Street, and just after 5 p.m., in the midst of a downpour, Harold Williston dropped his wife off in front of the diner and she hurried inside.

Mr. Williston and the boys started up King Philip Road, heading for their home a mile and a half away on the far side of Burncoat Street. The gusting wind rose quickly and the three could see branches falling into the street. Within seconds the car was rocking in the howling wind, and Mr. Williston told his sons to get down on the floor of the car, pushing them down with his hand as he spoke.

Although what the Willistons were experiencing were fringe winds on the southern side of the passing funnel, the storm was quartering across in front of them. A little further up the hill a huge tree limb was sheared off and thudded across the hood of their slowly-moving automobile. Mr. Williston got out and found that although the limb was far too heavy for one man to lift, he was able to slide it off the deeply-dented hood and push it out of the car's way.

The three turned left at the top of King Philip Road, drove north on Burncoat for about five hundred feet, then right onto Clark Street. Now, Harold Williston was entering the swath of destruction cut by the tornado only two minutes earlier, one of the very first motorists to find himself in this situation. Heading down Clark Street, he and the boys found themselves driving slowly around and through portions of roofs, walls and fragments of almost every conceivable article of household furnishing. Wherever they looked, the broken and twisted stubs of trees were festooned with shredded articles of clothing or bed linen.

Carefully turning off Clark onto Uncatena Avenue, Steven Williston can still remember arriving in front of where his two-family house had stood. Although built as a unit with a heavy firewall between the two-story apartments, the Williston half of the building had been fragmented and blown away, just as though the entire structure had been sawed in half.

Before Mr. Williston and the two boys could begin to wonder what had happened to the oldest Williston boy, Jimmy, who had been left with the O'Gradys, he came running toward them. The six-year-old had wanted to stay with his playmates, the O'Grady children, and when the rising wind began to give evidence that what was coming was no ordinary summer thunderstorm, Mrs. O'Grady had wanted to pull the refrigerator away from the wall and crouch behind it with the children.

Jim had protested, insisting that the best protection would be gained by going down to the basement, as he had been taught at Thorndyke Road School. Mrs. O'Grady had consented and they had run down the stairs, as quickly as they could, windows breaking behind them. Thus sheltered, they had ridden out the storm unharmed. When they returned to the first floor, the place was a shambles, including the kitchen, in which the refrigerator had been toppled and shoved across the room.

At this moment, the Willistons' only material possessions, literally, were the clothing in which they stood, their home having been fragmented and blown down into Great Brook Valley. Yet, as Mr. Williston said, embracing his boys, they were all safe, they had each other and they should all be thankful for that.

A little while later Steven would wonder about his friends in the neighborhood, especially Bobby Jackson. Steven had asked Bobby if he wanted to ride down to Stuart's with them, but Bobby's mother had thought that a storm might be brewing, so she had decided to keep her son at home.

+++

Edna Fitzmaurice lived with her husband and father-in-law in a large two-story frame house near the corner of Clark and St. Nicholas, overlooking Great Brook Valley. At around 1 p.m., she felt the temperature begin to drop from levels reached at mid-day. By mid-afternoon, her husband Henry, who was recuperating from recent surgery, came in from the yard for a light sweater, as did his father at about the same time.

Later in the afternoon, probably toward 5:00, Mrs. Fitzmaurice looked out to see a number of large hailstones concentrated in one corner of the yard, or so it seemed.

Edna had heard and read of the destructive tornado which had caused heavy loss of life in Flint the previous day, as well as the tornado in northern Ohio, which seemed to be moving eastward, toward western New York. When she and her husband were relaxing in their living room at about 5:15, they heard an express-train rumble and looking up Clark Street, could see the north side of the funnel bearing down on them.

Before either could formulate and utter the word "tornado", Henry yelled at his wife to lie down on the floor. Both fell flat on the floor, each holding a large sofa cushion as a body shield against flying glass or falling debris. Sharp-edged roofing slates came flying through blown-out windows to whiz across the room and shatter against the wall opposite, but none touched either of the prone figures.

Other than the broken windows, the house sustained no major structural damage, but when the screaming of the winds had subsided, the Fitzmaurices could see that what remained of most of the surrounding trees were grotesque stubs of trunk, snapped or twisted off in most cases many feet above the ground.

From the second floor, the senior Mr. Fitzmaurice saw the funnel approaching from the westward. He was certain that at least some of the whirling debris was aflame, an indication, if true, that at least one of the three-deckers that would shortly be engulfed in flames was already ablaze. The old man braced himself in a doorway as the tornado struck the home a glancing blow, the funnel proper sliding past to the south, still plowing ahead on an east-southeasterly course.

+++

Kathleen Loosemore was somewhat surprised when her husband pulled into the driveway of their duplex at 214 St. Nicholas Avenue. Her husband's arrival was considerably earlier than usual, and when he came in he told his wife he had a strong feeling that a bad storm was due and that he wanted to be home when it struck.

The young mother in the adjacent apartment was outside her back door, on the concrete patio shared by the two families. Her husband had just called from his downtown office at the telephone company to tell her that a "bad storm" was in the offing.

Very soon thereafter, Mrs. Loosemore noticed that the eldest of her three sons, who was all of three-and-a-half, had been staring intently out a window. Turning, the boy solemnly announced: "Daddy, the trees are lying down." Grabbing her four-month-old baby, and with her other two sons at her side, Mrs. Loosemore and her husband Bob ran for the basement as quickly as they could.

Once there, they crouched under the metal doors which covered the steps leading to the back yard. Bob hung onto the handles on the underside of the doors, feeling that he was thereby lessening the likelihood of their flying open and tearing off their hinges. Over the roaring of the wind, the Loosemores could faintly hear the young woman from the adjacent apartment calling to Mrs. Loosemore at the top of her lungs.

At the same time, they could hear sounds that were unfamiliar but which they were certain indicated that the house above them was being dismantled by the wind. As soon as the roaring of the wind and the tearing and crashing sounds died away, Bob Loosemore led his family back to the first floor, where they found their home a shambles.

Running next door to check on their neighbor, the Loosemores found nothing beyond the brick firewall separating the two apartments, except a small section of the front wall, including the door frame, with the door still tightly shut. Still crouched in its meagre protection was a very frightened but miraculously unhurt young woman, clutching her baby, which had also come through the nightmare unscathed.

Sucking aloft debris from the Loosemore home and scores of other smashed dwellings, and spewing fragments, large and small, in all directions, the funnel momentarily left a built-up neighborhood. It began churning down a lightly wooded grassy slope into Great Brook Valley, heading for the back end of the new housing project, visible across the shoulder of another hill. The nearest of these buildings was only about eight hundred yards ahead. The tornado would cover this distance in just under a minute.

Among the few photographs of the actual funnel in existence, this one is particularly riveting. It was taken by the late Henry Laprade from the rear of his Worcester home at 53 Wells Street, just off Plantation Street. Shot at 5:22 p.m., the distance to the tornado is three miles to the north-northeast, diagonally across Lake Quinsigamond, hidden among trees in middle distance. Funnel is moving across the Claflin property in Shrewsbury. Despite the eerie gloom and house lights in foreground, sunset is more than three hours away.   Photo courtesy William O'Connell

Two dozen people perished within the field of this photograph. Curtis apartments are to left; across Tacoma Street is residential neighborhood of single-family homes along Humes and Yukon Avenues, which run from Chino Avenue in foreground to Pasadena Parkway in middle distance. Thirteen died within this rectangular grid. Just above, beyond the gradual curve of Route 70, is a dark cluster of buildings, part of the city's home farm, where six men perished. Five others died at scattered locations shown in the photograph. To the right of the home farm, is the Lincolnwood project. The funnel moved from bottom to top in this photo.

Diane DeFosse and her sister Nancy, 6, at Holden District Hospital.

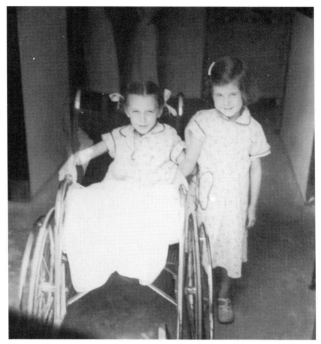

▼ *Front view of Worcester home of Carlson family at 55 Fales Street, Mrs. Carlson and sister blown from collapsing structure, landing unhurt on flattened front wall at left.*

▲ *Multi-family home with side wall sheared away. Burncoat Street near Fairhaven Road*

▼ *Debris littering the upper Burncoat area.*

▲ *This toppled three decker on Fales Street is where Tillie Pettigrew perished. Note the roof is only a few feet from the ground.*

Photos courtesy Davis Press/Lafayette Graphics

▼ *National Guard oversees issuing of resident passes at Vernon Drug, at Burncoat and Fales St.*

▲ Cover photo: Upper Burncoat Street. Lower left house belongs to "Sandy" Naylor.

Photo courtesy Mrs. Alexander Talbot and the Worcester Telegram & Gazette

▼ Winthrop Oaks in Holden where 60 out of 75 homes were demolished. X marks the spot where the 2 week old Oslund baby was found. Mother and son were swept up by the tornado and carried 500 yards through the air. Upon landing the baby was swept further away and not found until 2 1/2 days later.

Photo Courtesy Lafayette Graphics/Davis Press

Brothers Sam and Al Steinberg stand outside their shattered store, Greendale Salvage and Supply Co. a/k/a Jon's Railroad Salvage which was located at 651 West Boylston Street directly across from

Assumption College. It was reported the brothers slept out several nights protecting their devastated property from looters.

June 23, 1953

Lt. Col. John J. Pakula, Inf.
Commanding Officer
1st Battalion, 181st Infantry Regiment
Massachusetts National Guard
State Armory
Worcester, Massachusetts

Dear Colonel Pakula:

              The end of security duty by
1st Battalion, 181st Infantry at 9 p.m. Sunday
terminated a period of outstanding service by our
National Guard for this City and for its residents.

              You and your officers and men
down the line of command were called upon to help
in a situation such that more than ordinary duty
was necessary in many respects.

              Each and every one met the
challenge in a way that will be to the everlasting
credit of the Massachusetts National Guard and the
181st Infantry Regiment, with individual danger
and hardship ignored time and again.

              As Mayor and City Manager of
the City of Worcester, we extend this community's
heartfelt thanks.

              Sincerely yours,

              A. B. Holmstrom
              Mayor
              Francis J. McGrath
              City Manager

H/C

The city bus in which two died, seen here where it came to rest against one of the buildings in the new Curtis Apartments housing project. Of the nine surviving passengers, only Annette Bolduc emerged unassisted.

Photo courtesy Lt. Col. J. Bellino and CHMSGT M. Perna of the 212th, Engineering Installation Squadron; Air National Guard

▲ *The day after the tornado, freshman Senator John F. Kennedy surveys the devastation on Hapgood Way in Shrewsbury with Melissa Tyler, 14, and Richard Mayer, 15.*

▼ *National Guard Private William Ormond stands guard against looters on the grounds of Assumption College. At age 19, he had completed his Freshman year there, a few days before.*

▲ *Many hailstones were reported to fall throughout the area, some as big as "grapefruits."*

Photo courtesy Norton Company

▼ *Home of Hedlund family at 12 Hanson Avenue in Worcester's Greendale neighborhood with rear wall nearly sheared off.* Photo courtesy Richard Girard

At 5:22 pm funnel swept across Shrewsbury's Maple Avenue, missing the center of town by about 700 yards, moving from lower right to upper left in this aerial view.
The first three side streets off Maple Avenue from left to right are, Hapgood Way, St. James Ave., and

Crescent Ave. Second house in from Maple Ave on Hapgood Way is home of Steven Donohue. Unlike its battered neighbors, the home was utterly demolished.
Just to the right of center, in this view, is the large two-story home belonging to the Heitin family.

Drawing illustrates funnel's eastward march across Worcester County; a 42-mile, 80-minute course. Lower "fork" makes it appear that tornado split in two at Grafton; no such division occurred. Instead, a second funnel formed over Sutton at around 4:30 p.m. and plowed southeastward for nearly 30 miles, dissolving at Wrentham (off map) without loss of life. Born of the same turbulent supercell, this tornado was of a lower destructive order than the monster funnel.

Illustration reprinted with permission of the Worcester Telegram & Gazette

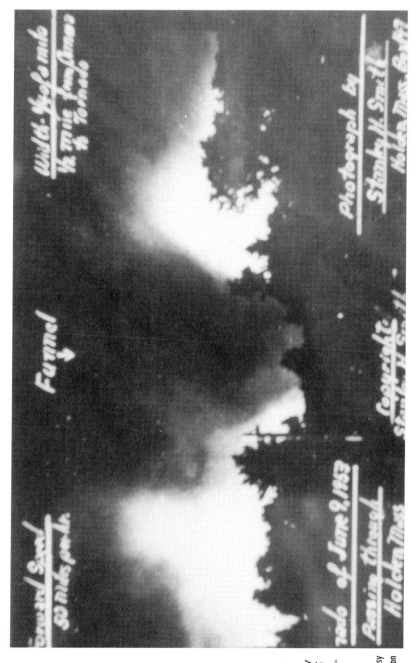

Photo of Funnel taken by Stanley K. Smith at 4:55 pm near the center of Holden.

Photo courtesy
Jim Duncanson

From 500 feet in the air, another view of the "Grid of Death," this one looking in the opposite direction, from which the funnel approached. Utter obliteration of these single-family frame homes is evident.

Photo courtesy Lt. Col. J. Bellino / CHMSGT M. Perna of the 212th Engineering Installation Squadron, Air National Guard

Despite the complexity of identifying and repairing telephone circuits as shown here, nearly all subscribers in the impact area across northern Worcester had service restored by Saturday, four days after the tornado. Power companies from across New England sent crews; one crew came from Indiana. A 17-day stretch of rainless weather assisted early efforts at recovery.   Photo courtesy Malcolm Arbour

▲ *Two nuns sift through the wreckage of their convent at Assumption College. Two other sisters perished.*

Photo courtesy Edward Kennedy

▼ *Before and After. 5:04pm Al Marcello's house in foreground.*

Photo courtesy Lafayette Graphics/Davis Press

From one of these west-facing windows on the third floor of the white painted house, thirteen year old Bobby Frankian watched the funnel's approach. His aunt, Anna Karagosian, and cousin, Nancy Aslanian died in the lower floors. The third floor landed on top of the masonry foundation.

Photo courtesy of Douglas F. Anderson, Jr.

▼ *Uncatena Avenue, where five died. Tornado moved from lower right to upper left, leaving debris-littered slabs. Squantum Street crosses at upper center; Clement home stood on second slab below Squantum, on left, Sullivan home opposite; Malcolm Hannah was first house beyond Squantum on same side. Willette's was four slabs beyond, just inside funnel*   Photo reprinted with permission of the Worcester Telegram & Gazette

▲ *Seemingly in shock, Ethel Waterfield, concert pianist, views the devastation at Burncoat and Fales Street.*
Reprinted with permission of the Worcester Telegram & Gazette

▼ *Damage on Rockdale Street, off Ararat in Worcester.*   Photo courtesy Lafayette Graphics/Davis Press

▲ Cottage belonging to Valmore Gaucher, Professor at Assumption College.

Photos courtesy of Lafayette Graphics/Davis Press

▼ One of three adjacent 3-deckers.

▲ *Jack Hildreth, front right stretcher bearer, helps the injured. He spent his 5th wedding anniversary aiding his neighbors*

▼ *Hot coffee and sandwiches served by the Red Cross Mobile Canteen. The served over 60,000 cups of coffee.*

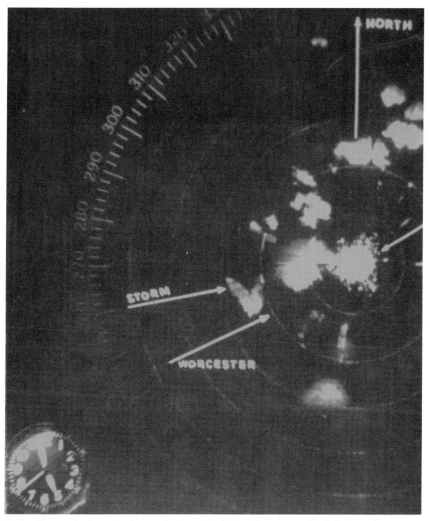

Radar photograph taken 40 miles away by MIT in Cambridge, shows storm. The clock shows the time to be 4:58 p.m. EDT, a few minutes before the tornado reached Worcester.

Photo courtesy Lafayette Graphics/Davis Press

Looking like a group of European refugees fleeing the ravages of World War II, Marian D'Agostino, her parents and her three daughters, walk from their demolished home on Worcester's Yukon Avenue. Marian's mother, Mrs. Riccardi, holds her aching head, injured by flying debris as she hurried downstairs from her second-floor apartment. Mr. Riccardi was not in the impact area when the tornado struck, and has just joined the rest of the family. The three girls had much of their clothing blown from their bodies and are clad in clothing and blankets given by neighbors.

Marian's hospital examination soon afterward determined that her injuries were inconsequential . . . and that she was one month pregnant.   Photo reprinted with permission of the Worcester Telegram & Gazette

Presentation of a check for $150,000 to Assumption College by Jean Kennedy on behalf of her father, Joseph P. Kennedy, Sr., in memory of his son, Navy Lt. Joseph P. Kennedy, Jr., who was killed in World War II. At center, accepting check, is Very Rev. Wilfred Dufault, Superior-General of the Assumptionist Order. At left is Bishop John Wright; at right, Jean's new sister-in-law, Jacqueline.

Photo courtesy
Assumption College

▼ Photo taken by National Guard Corporal Carmen Morabito. Exact location unknown - probably upper Burncoat area. Of those homes with walls still standing, most will have to be razed.

Photo courtesy Mrs. Carmen Morabito

Aerial view of Assumption College. The funnel approached from the lower right-hand corner of photo, exiting at top center. Note density of debris field in that area, including large light-colored fragments; all that remained of convent.

Photo Courtesy Edward Kennedy

Rear view of main building at Assumption College. Two National Guardsmen are standing atop wreckage

of wooden convent in which two nuns died.   Photo courtesy Edward Kennedy

Andrew Munter, Sergeant First Class, of Clinton Company M, stands guard.   Photo courtesy Andrew Munter

8

Diane

Francis "Bud" Senior had moved into the Great Brook Valley housing project with his wife and children only six months earlier, following the birth of their fourth child, Debbie. Now, all members of the growing family were about to sit down to supper, except the baby, who was not yet old enough to manage a high-chair. Bud, who had just been scanning the Evening Gazette account of the havoc wrought by the Flint tornado the previous day, put down his paper with a puzzled look on his face. "Since when," he asked his wife Chris, "can you hear a train in Great Brook Valley?"

Receiving the half-expected reply that this was unlikely, but that she could hear it too, Bud got up and looked out the large window in the rear of their apartment. From it, they could see Clark Street, curving down the northeast side of Burncoat Hill. Above the hill, black and menacing, and headed almost directly for them, was a massive funnel cloud, its accretion of whirling debris clearly visible. Feeling as though the newspaper story had just come to life before his eyes, Senior turned to his wife and said simply, "It's a tornado."

There was no cellar beneath the slab upon which the Seniors' two-story apartment building rested, nor did Bud or Rita think to secrete themselves and the children in a closet. Immobilized for the moment by indecision, they continued sitting in the living room at the front of the apartment. Bud's niece, Gail Braney, who was seven, the same age as Judy Senior, was visiting her cousin that afternoon, and both girls were wide- eyed with fear. The two younger children watched their parents' faces closely, but were not reassured by what they saw there.

The window through which Bud had watched the tornado's approach suddenly imploded, the shards of flying glass lancing across the apartment from back to front, accompanied by a banshee scream of scouring wind. Almost immediately, the front picture window, directly opposite the gaping frame, blew out, and the Seniors saw and felt household objects of all types go flying past them at blurring speed, many of them too fast-moving to be identified.

Mrs. Senior reacted first, Holding little Debbie tightly in her arms, she shepherded the other children into a semi-protected spot behind and beneath the heavy steel staircase leading to the second floor. Then, she took her husband by the arm and pulled him into this protected nook.

Finally the wind abated, leaving the gutted apartment a shambles. The irresistible crossdraft had sucked even such bulky objects as chairs out through the large hole where the front window had been. The heavy sofa, which doubled as a foldout bed, protruded several feet through the opening.

Rita and the baby were blood-soaked. When the family shuffled outside, Rita handed little Debbie to a neighbor, Marge McKern, who washed the baby clean. To the woman's relief, the baby proved to be free of cuts and gashes; the blood with which the infant and her clothing were covered was that of her mother.

Bud Senior had already carried Judy down the hill, at the foot of which was a large, open-sided truck. Bud saw a number of bleeding, dirt- encrusted casualties sitting or lying in the back of the truck. The driver told him he would evacuate the bleeding Judy with the others, so she was lifted into the back of the truck, which left shortly with a full load of casualties en route to the closest hospital, Hahnemann. At about the same time, Dickie, age four, was also taken by another volunteer driver to Hahnemann.

Bud and Rita, with little Diane and young Gail Braney, began the painful walk of more then a half-mile to the mouth of Tacoma Street, at the front, or eastern entrance to the housing projects. There, they found space in a large city ambulance which, like most other vehicles arriving after 5:45 that evening, received a brusque wave-off at nearby Hahnemann and was forced to continue to Memorial.

Although Bud and tiny Debbie had come through the tornado's fury practically uninjured, Bud's niece, Gail, would require thirty-five stitches to close the gashes on her face, arms and body. Gail's playmate Judy, who'd been among those turned away from crowded Hahnemann, was receiving a like number of sutures at City Hospital for similar lacerations.

Rita Senior was by far the most seriously cut. Her gaping wounds were deep and wide, and would require seventy-five stitches to close. She left the hospital with her husband and two children at eleven that night. The fact that this hideously lacerated woman was not admitted is indicative of Memorial's situation; with bed space obtained at the cost of wholesale early discharge of patients, the beds thus available were used for victims who were unconscious, or had suffered certain types of fractures or head injuries. An ambulatory victim like Rita Senior, although weakened by blood loss, after having her gashes cleaned was simply sewn up and sent on her way.

When Gail Braney's gashes were sutured, she was taken a quarter-mile down Belmont Street to the basement of Our Lady of Fatima Church, where cots had been set up. Later in the evening, Rita Senior's sister happened to be in the temporary shelter. She recognized the girl and was allowed to take her to the woman's home on Millbury Street.

At City Hospital, a similar chance recognition occurred when a friend of Bud Senior's recognized Bud's daughter, Judy. Her lacerations had been closed, so she was released in the friend's custody and was taken by him to her grandparents' home at 33 Fales Street. There, she joined her parents and two sisters, as well as her paternal grandparents, Aunts Kay and Patricia, and Uncle, Paul. Only little Dickie, safe in Hahnemann Hospital, was missing from the family circle.

The anxiety of individuals separated by medical evacuation, even though only temporarily, was felt to some degree by hundreds of families that day. Although few families were as large as the Senior clan, fewer still were so quickly reunited.

+++

At 5:16 p.m., the Lincoln Street-Great Brook Valley bus was nearing its last stop of the run, with only a handful of passengers still remaining aboard. The bus was nearly at the western end of the Curtis Apartments complex, about to swing left onto Tacoma Street, reverse direction and head back towards the Boylston Street entrance to the housing project.

What the driver, Ted Gaboury, saw looming just ahead caused him to brake to a stop, turn off the engine and turn around toward his passengers. In a clear, loud voice that easily carried to the back of the bus, Gaboury told them to quickly get out of their seats and lie flat on the floor.

Some of the passengers began to comply; others, including Mrs. Annette Bolduc, did not. Mrs. Bolduc had been released from the hospital only a week earlier, following surgery on a ruptured spinal vertebra. She therefore continued to sit upright - for about seven seconds.

TORNADO!

The tornado struck the bus, bouncing and rolling the heavy vehicle along the ground like an empty tin can being kicked along the sidewalk by a strolling youth. It rolled completely over several times, during which time some passengers recall that a young boy was sucked out through a shattered or open window. If these recollections are reliable, the lad survived, as no death which might be his, occurred at that spot.

The tumbling bus came to rest against the end wall of one of the apartment buildings. It was its final stop. Passengers had been flung about the vehicle's interior; a number of serious injuries resulted and several passengers lay unconscious. Among them was little Mera Pederson.

It had been sunny and warm at midmorning, when Mary Pederson, thirty- five, of 130 Tacoma Street, with her son, Paul, three-and-a-half, and daughter Mera climbed aboard the city bus near their apartment and headed downtown for a day of shopping. Tomorrow would be Mera's fifth birthday, and her mother wanted to do some last-minute gift shopping for the special day.

At a few minutes before five, after a long day of walking from store to store, Mrs. Pederson and her two children carefully carried their full shopping bags onto the Lincoln Street bus for the three-and-a-half mile ride home. As they approached Mera's stop, the girl wondered why it had grown so dark, and why the bus had begun to shake.

When the driver suddenly stopped the bus and told everyone to lie down, Mera and Paul flopped down onto the floor of the bus. Their mother lay on top of them, to protect their small bodies with her own.

The next thing Mera remembered was being taken out of the bus, dazed and with most of her clothing torn away. A blanket was put around her and she was bundled into the back of a station wagon and driven to a local hospital, suffering from a concussion. Her brother, who was not seriously injured, was taken to a different hospital. Mera's father and little sister had taken refuge in the apartment and were untouched by the tornado's fury.

Next day, Mera's aunt would tell the little girl as gently as she could that she would not be seeing her mother again. In the interior of the tumbling bus, passengers had been flung about, even as metal stanchions tore loose. One such stanchion caught Mrs. Pederson in the throat, nearly decapitating her. Although Mera would learn the details of her mother's death only later, her fifth birthday was one that she would never be able to forget.

+++

Roger LaPerle had been grocery shopping downtown and had two bags of canned goods and other items on the seat beside him as the bus rolled past the Curtis apartments. When Ted Gaboury yelled his warning, the thirty- two-year-old father of four fell to the floor of the bus and felt it being lifted into the air. Something - perhaps one of the cans of food he'd just bought - slammed into his head, giving him a mild concussion and causing him to lose consciousness for a few moments.

Coming to, he found that his shirt and trousers had somehow torn away, leaving him wearing only his underwear. Helped from the bus by one or another of the numerous volunteers who had run to the overturned bus, LaPerle was well enough to be embarrassed by his state of undress.

LaPerle was packed off to City Hospital, where he would spend about a week recovering. Had he not been an amateur boxer in superb physical condition at the time he was hurt, Roger's injuries quite possibly would have been more serious and his hospitalization longer.

+++

A Mrs. Gonyea, who lived at 45 Great Brook Valley, hurried along Main Street at about 4:35 p.m. to catch a Lincoln Street bus for the ride back to her apartment. She had originally planned to take the next bus, some fifteen minutes later. As it was, she arrived home a few minutes before the tornado struck at 5:16. The bus she would have otherwise taken, the one driven by Ted Gaboury, was caught in the grip of the tornado, coming to rest on its side against the apartment building, killing Mrs. Pederson and young Larry Demarco, who had taken the bus to visit his grandparents in Great Brook Valley.

Fortunate, too, was David Hayes, the manager of Great Brook Valley Gardens. He had just gotten into his car near the spot where the ill- starred city bus was about to make its final, unscheduled stop. Before he could start the car and drive away, the tornado flipped his car and rolled it over several times. When the tornado had passed by, Hayes crawled from the wreck, shaken but uninjured.

+++

Twenty minutes or so earlier, Donald Gannon, age five, had been driving through West Boylston with his parents, headed back to their apartment at 32 Great Brook Valley Avenue, after a day spent at Benson's Wild Animal Farm in southern New Hampshire. Suddenly hailstones bigger than any the Gannons had ever seen started bouncing off the car, denting the hood and thudding against the windshield, cracking it in several places. Donald could see that his father was upset and he heard him curse the cause of the sudden and unexpected damage.

At 5:15, the family arrived back home, and after playing outside for a couple of minutes, Donald was looking out a west-facing window of their second-floor apartment when he called his mother. When she came to his side, he pointed towards the huge black cloud which was looming above Burncoat Hill and heading toward them. Her hand tightened around Donald's arm like a vise as she yelled to his father.

Mr. Gannon quickly inverted a living-room sofa against a wall and pushed his wife and daughter into the protective wedge of space beneath it. Then he grabbed Donald's hand and ran down the two flights of stairs to the basement and safety. None of the four was injured, but the Gannon automobile, cracked windshield and all, was tossed in the air and smashed back to earth, a total wreck.

+++

Annette Bolduc had been seated about two-thirds of the way back on the bus. When it came to rest upside down she began crawling painfully forward. She could see that the front end of the bus had been partially torn away, but with the bus lying on its roof, it meant crawling over all the seats on that side. It was a tedious, painful process, and a gruesome one; at one point Mrs. Bolduc stepped over the still body of a pinioned woman, which she believes was that of Mary Pederson. Another woman, much older, was calling out in pain, asking would-be rescuers to give assistance to a much younger woman who lay nearby.

On her slow, painful way forward, Mrs. Bolduc picked up a small boy, possibly little Paul Pederson, who had been injured. She carried him to the front of the bus and passed him out to the waiting hands of the driver, Ted Gaboury. Then she was helped to the ground herself.

Of the passengers still aboard when the tornado struck, one person lay dead and all the rest had been injured. None were able to follow Mrs. Bolduc out of the wrecked bus under their own power. Annette Bolduc gave no thought to hospitalization for herself, but instead started walking toward her Chino Avenue apartment.

+++

Leo Boffoli, a World War II Navy veteran, lived in an apartment at 61 Great Brook Valley Avenue. A few minutes earlier, he had watched his four- year-old, Ann Marie, proudly push her tiny doll carriage along the sidewalk in front of their apartment building. When Mrs. Boffoli saw the black cloud rolling down the east slope of Burncoat Hill toward them, she called to Leo to get their daughter. He had scooped her up on the dead run, along with her carriage and raced back to the apartment.

Unable to close the door against the rising wind, Leo, his wife, the frightened Ann Marie and little two-year-old Salvatore had crowded into a closet, slammed the door and ridden out the storm untouched, while the wind roared through the apartment in a maelstrom of destruction.

With the funnel's departure, Leo saw the toppled bus and hurried to it. His brother Frank, who lived a hundred feet away, and who had been over on Constitution Avenue making a purchase from the Horton's Market "store bus", also hurried over. Seeing the pinioned woman, Leo raced to his car. He grabbed an auto jack from his trunk and hurried back.

Quickly placing a few bricks as a makeshift base, Boffoli tried to raise the section of the bus where Mary Pederson was pinned, in hopes of relieving the pressure of the metal on her body and permitting its removal. After a few strokes of the handle, the aluminum sheet metal against which the would-be rescuer was applying pressure, simply buckled, leaving the frustrated man boring a hole in the yielding metal.

This rescue attempt was soon given up. The last of the passengers, with one exception, had been carried from the overturned bus. Only one motionless figure remained on board, and it was now clear that there was no need for haste in removing her.

+++

Dora LaPerle, whose husband Roger survived the overturning of the bus in which he was riding, was in her apartment at 138 Tacoma Street with her four children when the tornado struck. Almost on impulse, the young mother yelled to the youngsters to crawl under the heavy double bed, which they hurriedly did. Then she quickly joined them.

In the ensuing noisy moments which followed, the apartment windows imploded and the howling winds reduced the interior to a shambles. Even many of the larger, heavier items of furniture were pushed this way and that by the blast of wind. The bed, however, did not move, and from beneath it emerged at length Mrs. LaPerle and her four children, unmarked. They got to their feet and stared in wonder at the transformation in their neatly-furnished apartment.

+++

TORNADO!

The James Keddy family was just sitting down to supper at their 135 Constitution Avenue apartment in the Great Brook Valley project. Mr. Keddy had not yet returned from work, and one of the daughters, Cecile, age thirteen, was at a Girls' Club swimming class. The others; Mrs. Keddy and five younger children ranging from twelve down to just over a year, heard the roaring wind and saw the approaching tornado through the apartment's picture window.

The door to the basement was at the far end of the apartment building and Jimmy, the twelve-year-old, knew they could never reach it in time, so he and his mother urged the smaller children to a spot on an inside wall where two bedroom doors opened and swung back, nearly meeting to form a wedge-shaped protected space. Jammed together in this protective "cubbyhole" as young Jimmy later referred to it, the family stole glimpses from between the doors. They saw front and rear picture windows shattered. A howling cross-draft was set up and the Keddys, jammed into their makeshift sanctuary and pulling the doors toward them as hard as they could, heard various possessions pulled across the kitchen and living room floors to vanish through the gaping rear window.

Mrs. Keddy saw her cedar chest and sewing machine whirl past; when little Priscilla saw her doll carriage sucked by she started for it but Jimmy held her back. The family began to say the Rosary; it seemed to have a calming effect, especially on the younger children, who were fidgety from being jammed into such a tiny space. Before they had said more than a few Hail Marys, the wind died away and the Keddys left their place of refuge.

Neighbors of the Keddys, the O'Connors, at 146 Chino Avenue, weathered the tornado in similar fashion. Mrs. O'Connor, her three children, a Mrs. Kennedy, and a total of six additional neighborhood children gained the safety of a walk-in closet with a sliding door. The door to the greatly- overcrowded closet would not slide shut, so the two women stood in front of the frightened children, holding onto each other and to the closet doorframe, interposing themselves between their young charges and the destructive forces of nature.

Those forces rapidly exploded a picture window, admitting a scouring, howling wind of unbelievable power, which whirled objects in the room to destruction, then sucked them away through the big picture window. Even the heavy divan was pulled through the gaping hole. Seconds later, the demonic wind seized a car which had been parked across the street, rolled and bounced it over to the building and upended it against the window opening.

Diane

Like many other residents in the housing projects, John and Catherine Monahan instinctively headed for a closet when the windows of their apartment began imploding. Mrs. Monahan held her twenty-two- month-old son Gary in her arms as her husband pushed her into a closet, then wedged himself in beside her. He could feel the door being buffeted from the outside, so he grabbed the doorknob and pulled on it, maintaining his grip until the roaring and shaking subsided.

In another apartment unit not far away, the Monahan's married daughter was home with her two small children when the blackness and roaring descended upon them. When a rolling, bouncing automobile crashed through their picture window and protruded into the living room, the young mother quickly pushed the children into a closet and rode out the tornado as her parents were doing.

+++

In addition to the woman who was killed in the battering of the bus, a second woman of the same name lived in Great Brook Valley. Mary A. Pederson was the mother of young children. She had been widowed a few months earlier, and lived with her son, age four, and five-year-old daughter in the Great Brook Valley Gardens complex on New Vista Lane.

Mrs. Pederson had been working as an unpaid volunteer at the Uncle Wiggly Nursery School that spring, while her two children attended that school. She did not own an automobile, so each morning she had taken the Lincoln Street bus downtown and boarded the Jefferson (Holden) bus for the nursery school. It seemed to her that she and her children spent as much time riding the buses as they did at the nursery school; the arrival of humid summerlike weather was the final straw. On Monday evening, June 8, Mrs. Pederson called the woman who operated the school and told her that she would not be coming to the school for the few remaining days of the session.

For this reason, Mary A. Pederson and her two children were not aboard the Lincoln Street bus which departed City Hall at 5 p.m. and which, seventeen minutes thereafter, was rolled over several times and slammed into an apartment building, resulting in the death of another Mary Pederson.

Instead, the woman and her two children had just sat down to their supper in the dinette area of their apartment's kitchen. Mrs. Pederson had just read the Evening Gazette's front page account of the Flint, Michigan tornado, and seen the photograph of a survivor being helped from the rubble-filled basement of his demolished home. Now, at quarter past five, she heard the deep-throated roar in the west and looked up to see the looming funnel cresting Burncoat Hill and heading straight for her home.

Her first thought was that this tornado was the same one which had devastated Flint twenty-four hours earlier. Just as the funnel reached her building, Mary pushed her two children to the floor and lay atop them.

Flying fragments of glass peppered her back as the apartment windows blew in, in rapid succession. The blast of wind coursing through the room lifted the carpet on one side of the room and folded it across the three of them, as though in an effort to protect them from further windborne missiles.

Forsaking this uncertain protection, and while the tornado was roaring around the sturdy brick walls that enclosed them, the anxious mother hurried her two children to the closet built beneath the stairway that led to the apartment's bedrooms on the floor above. There they rode out the remaining seconds of the storm's violence without further incident.

As soon as the roaring blast of wind subsided and the sky brightened once again, Mary ran to the telephone and lifted the receiver. Somewhat to her surprise, she got a dial tone immediately so she quickly called her parents' home on Belmont Street, having seen that the storm was coming from the northwest, and believing it might be headed in their direction. When her mother answered, Mary, fighting back hysteria told her what had just transpired and asked, somewhat shrilly, if they were all right.

First Mary's mother, then her father, assured her that they had experienced nothing like she had just survived, but agreed to come right down, and to bring her and the children back with them if the apartment was as badly blasted by the wind as Mary claimed.

+++

In the apartment at 135 Chino Avenue, toward which Annette Bolduc was walking as quickly as she could, her two children had been anticipating their mother's arrival at any moment. When the tornado enveloped the building, Marcia, who would be thirteen in two days, pushed her nine-year- old brother Alan into a two-foot-wide space between the end of the steel kitchen counter and the refrigerator.

Alan was hunkered down in a squatting position, his back to the wall. His sister leaned forward over him, facing the wall and the small window above. The window imploded; flying glass fortunately missed Marcia's face but deeply lacerated her left arm, both above and below the elbow.

As the two frightened children cowered in their semi-protected alcove, the punishing wind hammered the apartment. The wind blew out the picture window, twisted and mangled the venetian blinds, and tore from the walls the decorative objects which had been carefully handcrafted by Mrs. Bolduc.

Partitions between the bedrooms were punched apart by the wind as easily as if they were cardboard. A small wastebasket sucked out the window of Alan's second-floor bedroom was sucked into the first floor kitchen window and clattered to the floor.

When Mrs. Bolduc arrived fifteen minutes later, the relieved and overjoyed Alan ran to meet her. He described Marcia's injury to her mother and told her that a neighbor had driven her to Hahnemann Hospital.

Annette Bolduc set the loaf of bread she had carried throughout her ordeal on the kitchen counter, then with the uncertainty of her daughter's condition preying on her mind, she gazed around what had been her family's neat and attractive home and now looked as though a bomb had exploded there. Even the bruises, cuts and scratches suddenly seemed to hurt more, and she sank into a chair, overwhelmed.

She knew it had been a tornado. Her youngest brother lived in Curtis Apartments, and so he and his family would have been squarely in the tornado's path. She wearily picked up the telephone and called her father who lived in the southeast part of the city.

When her father answered, he started to tell Annette excitedly that there had been heavy wind gusts in their neighborhood. "Thought we'd lose our awnings, wind blew so hard," he said.

"Papa," she said, "There's been a tornado through here. Marcia's been taken to the hospital."

After a moment of stunned silence on his end of the line, her father told her he'd call another of her brothers, David, who lived on Idalla Avenue, in the Summit area of the city, which the tornado had missed by about half a mile. Her father said also he'd try to locate Marcia.

Minutes later a neighbor was driving Mrs. Bolduc and four or five other injured Valley residents toward Hahnemann Hospital. The small hospital, already overwhelmed, was, as noted earlier, forced to turn away any additional casualties not in critical condition. Arriving at Memorial Hospital, the other injured persons murmured their thanks and climbed painfully out.

Mrs. Bolduc did not budge, however. She had called her personal physician, Dr, Robert Lavoie, who was awaiting her arrival at St. Vincent's Hospital, several miles away. The driver suppressed a smile at the disheveled woman's determination and shrugged his shoulders. "OK, lady, St. V's it is!" he said.

When they pulled up in front of St, Vincent's, very few tornado casualties had as yet arrived, yet the hospital had been alerted to the catastrophe and staff physicians and nurses were waiting just outside the building's entrances. When Doctor Lavoie saw his bloody and bedraggled patient, who was also his medical secretary, his eyes filled with tears. She tried to tell him that she looked worse then she felt, but only half- believed it herself.

After Dr. Lavoie had examined her and determined that her contusions and abrasions were free of any visible foreign matter, her cousin, a member of the hospital's nursing order of nuns, scrubbed the dirt that had been blown deep into Annette's pores when the tornado's wind had blasted through the shattered windows of the battered bus. Then she was put to bed, across from a woman who was awaiting the surgical removal of a large wooden splinter which had been driven deep into her hip.

Meanwhile, Annette's brother Donald, finding that debris-blocked streets prevented his driving to his sister's apartment, ran the more than two miles, collected young Alan and continued on to his brother's home in the Curtis Apartments complex. His brother was away on a business trip, but fearful of a possible gas explosion, Donald gathered up his sister-in-law and her two children, then with his four charges in tow, he went out onto Boylston Street, where vehicular passage was impossible. Hailing a motorist who was on the point of turning his car around and heading back north, Donald virtually insisted that his group of refugees be driven to his home on Idalla Avenue.

At almost the same moment, Annette Bolduc's father was picking his way over, around and between injured tornado victims jamming Hahnemann Hospital's emergency ward. Peering intently into the face of any young girl who might possibly be his injured granddaughter, he had retraced his steps through the throng and just about decided that Marcia was not in the room.

About to leave, he heard a girl's voice. "Pepe, I'm here. It's me Pepe... Marcia."

His search over, he hugged his dirty and disheveled granddaughter.

+++

From Belmont Hill, two miles or so to the south of Great Brook Valley, there was an unobstructed view, off to the north and northeast. Many motorists on busy Route 9 saw the black mass moving to the eastward, but most assumed it was a highly localized thunderstorm which would soon be punishing the center of Shrewsbury. One such observer was Robert Achorn, a reporter for the Worcester Telegram. Driving east, down the long slope of Belmont Hill toward Lake Quinsigamond, he saw the storm off to his left and assumed that the northern part of the city was really catching it.

+++

The three young DeFosse children and their mother were at home in their third-floor apartment at 6 Great Brook Valley Avenue. The tornado smashed into the building, blowing out the DeFosses' windows and tearing off much of the roof over their heads. Diane, age seven, had fallen or been thrown to the kitchen floor, and was lying there as a steel structural beam exposed and loosened by the raging winds, plunged down. The heavy beam landed across Diane's legs, instantly severing her right leg above the knee and shearing almost completely through the left, which remained attached only by a shred of cartilage.

Thinking quickly, Diane's mother grabbed two shredded remnants of kitchen curtains and knotted them as tightly as she could around the pulsating stumps of her daughter's legs. The willing hands of neighbors quickly carried Diane downstairs, someone supporting her nearly-severed left leg. Despite the massive shock to her system, the little girl had not lost consciousness.

Someone near Diane yelled to a nearby motorist, asking him to drive the little girl to the nearest hospital. The man, seeing the blood-soaked curtains around the stumps of Diane's legs, declined. He had just bought a new car, he said, and did not want bloodstains on the upholstery.

Moments later, a volunteer driver was taking her up East Mountain Street toward Holden District Hospital, six miles away. Worcester's Hahnemann Hospital was only two miles distant, but the tornado's swath lay between; debris blocked every possible access route from the Valley.

Diane's mother, six-year-old sister Nancy, and two-year-old brother Albert were driven to the Worcester County Hospital, a former tuberculosis sanitarium in Boylston. None of the three appeared to have suffered serious injury.

Diane's driver kept up a continuous patter of encouragement, perhaps as much for his own morale as that of his hideously injured passenger. "We're almost there now," he assured Diane as they passed the Holden State Police Barracks. "Just a couple of minutes now."

Two minutes later, he pulled up to the ambulance entrance at the side of the hospital, and Diane saw nurses in white uniforms and men in white coats rushing towards her. She was lifted onto what seemed like a mattress on wheels and was quickly pushed into a brightly-lit room.

Now, someone was putting a piece of gauze over her nose. She knew what that meant. Sure enough, almost immediately Diane got her first whiff of ether. They had given her the same smelly stuff for her tonsillectomy and it had made her sick. Now she was struggling to tear the cloth away and breathe fresh air again, but she couldn't do it because someone or something was holding her arms. In a few moments she stopped struggling and lay still.

+++

Other children, many of them critically injured, were rushed to Holden District and to one of the several Worcester hospitals directly from the rubble of their demolished homes. In the haste of evacuation, they were often separated from their parents, who were in some cases evacuated to different hospitals.

If locating the children in the confusion and overcrowding so characteristic of that unforgettable evening was difficult for many distraught parents, making positive identification of a horribly battered or bandage- swathed child was even more traumatic, especially in cases where such identification was made in a hospital morgue.

Among a number of such tragedies, perhaps the saddest involved a family of three who were not Worcester residents, but who had just arrived from Pittsburgh, to visit friends in Great Brook Valley.

Dropping his wife off downtown with friends, Thomas Riley and daughter Sheila, age ten, continued on to the home of friends on Great Brook Valley Parkway. An uprooted tree crashed down on the Riley car, crushing and killing the two occupants.

When rescuers reached the flattened vehicle, the body of Mr. Riley was extracted with difficulty, but somehow, in the twisted wreckage, that of little Sheila was overlooked. Informed of the death of her husband, the grief-stricken Mrs. Riley began visiting the children's wards of Worcester hospitals in search of Sheila.

At City Hospital, she came to the bedside of badly-injured, bandage-swathed Martha St. Germain, who was the same age as her daughter, Sheila. Examining a ring on the girl's finger, Mrs. Riley said she was certain that she had found Sheila.

Not long afterward, Mrs. St. Germain, Martha's real mother, in search of her daughter, appeared at the little girl's bedside. As Mrs. Riley had earlier done, she checked the ring on Martha's finger and was convinced she had found her daughter. By way of additional confirmation, Mrs. St. Germain put her finger into the girl's mouth and probed for a space which had been left by the recent falling out of a filling. Her fingertip located the spot.

Also, as any mother would know, Mrs. St. Germain was aware that one of Martha's ears was slightly irregular in configuration. Examination of the injured girl disclosed just such an irregularity. Mrs. St. Germain had found her daughter.

Soon afterward, Sheila's body was discovered in the wreckage of the Riley car in Great Brook Valley. For Mrs. Riley, the search for her little girl had ended,

+++

As the tornado swept into Great Brook Valley, the fringe winds to the left, or north side of the huge funnel were strong enough to shatter windows of the new Clark Street elementary school, sucking out and scattering a small blizzard of torn books and paper, including many school records. Plowing the length of Great Brook Valley, west to east, the funnel was broad enough, six hundred yards or so at this point in its course, not only to punish the two new brick housing projects but also simultaneously rake across a residential neighborhood of single- family homes lying just to the south.

Parallel to Tacoma Street, along which much of the new Curtis Apartments had been built, were several unpaved residential streets. Humes Avenue lay closest to the project; then Yukon Avenue and finally Chino Avenue. The area had been gradually built up during the course of the preceding thirty years, the lots were large, with the land gently sloping and sunny. Numerous residents had beds of flowers; many had vegetable gardens as well.

The heat of the day seemed to emphasize the fact that all danger of frost was clearly past, so it was with confidence and anticipation that fifty-eight-year-old Joseph Falcone stopped at his neighbor's, Dino Riccardi's that afternoon after work. Mr. Riccardi had a greenhouse in which he grew flowers and flats of vegetables, many of which were sold to neighbors. One of his specialties was the cultivation of tomato plants.

Mr Falcone purchased some of the tall, sturdy plants from Mrs. Riccardi, since her husband had gone to a nearby store. Then

Joseph Falcone walked to his home next door. His wife Lillian, as she often did, came out to the front porch to greet her husband. If the couple paid any attention to the approaching blackness, they were not sufficiently alarmed to seek shelter inside the house. The tornado caught them in the open, seizing them and hurling them seventy-five yards through the air, even as it exploded their home into matchwood. They had been together for many years of their lives. When found a few minutes later they would have their arms around each other, in death as in life together still.

Seconds earlier, Oscar Skog, who lived up the street died in the rubble of his collapsing house. So youthful did he appear for a man of eighty-one, that his body would lie unidentified in a hospital for nearly three days. Diagonally across the street, Mrs. Anna Anderson was instantly killed in the same manner.

Almost across the street form the Falcones lived the Hutton family. At home that late afternoon was six-year-old Barbara Ann Hutton and her grandmother, Annie Hutton, seventy-three. In the suddenness of the tornado's onslaught, it is doubtful that either had time to realize what was happening to them. Several days later, two U.S. Savings Bonds belonging to Mrs. Hutton were picked up on lawns in widely- separated communities in southeastern Massachusetts. Both were mailed back to the Humes Avenue address. The owner would never cash either.

At the same instant the cutting edge of the tornado struck the Falcones, it sliced into the home of the Dagostinos on Yukon Avenue. For some inexplicable reason, Frank and Catherine Dagostino fled the home as the tornado hit, or, more likely, a few seconds before the funnel's impact. Perhaps fear had made them irrational; in any case they were running along the street when each was struck by flying debris. Mr. Dagostino was killed instantly. His wife lay in the street fatally injured, but still conscious and moaning for water. She would cling to life for thirty hours before succumbing Wednesday night at Memorial Hospital.

Seconds later, the funnel destroyed the Marcinkus home at 25 Yukon Avenue. Dying in the rubble were Victor Marcinkus and his wife Katherine. Nearby, Mrs. May Slack, at 3 Humes Avenue succumbed. In the next instant, Mrs. Slack's neighbor, a Mrs. Gleason, who lived around the corner at 71 Pasadena Parkway, perished in the sudden, hideous demolition of her home.

One woman who watched the black cloud churn toward her home was Marian Dagostino, daughter of the Riccardis and daughter-in-law of Frank and Catherine Dagostino, who lived a block away, on Yukon Avenue. She and her three daughters had finished an early supper, then retreated to the back porch, in hopes of catching some westerly breezes. Mr. Dagostino was working until 11 p.m. The wind had picked up considerably, and the sky to the westward, above Burncoat Hill, was dark, almost black. The boiling cloud drew nearer and seemed now to take on an odd, pinkish-brown hue. It seemed to Marian that she could see twigs and leaves whirling around in the cloud. Even if this were so, Marian wondered, why should she be able to see such tiny objects at so great a distance?

By the time the worried mother hurried her three daughters inside the house and tried to close the door to the porch, she could not do so. The wind was now such a roaring blast that the heavy wooden sliding door which gave access to the clothes reel was bowing inward from the tremendous pressure of the wind.

Marian abandoned her futile struggle with the door that would not close; it slammed open and in the same instant the tornado struck the house full force. Punctuating the express-train roar, the dazed woman could hear windows shattering and the louder sound of boards snapping and the groan of straining beams. Running into the kitchen, she saw curtains and shades streaming horizontally, wind roaring through empty windowpanes. In horrified fascination, she watched a huge hole appear above the windows, enlarging until it seemed the wall was dissolving before her disbelieving eyes.

She realized she was screaming for the children, but could not hear her own voice in the roaring vortex of sound. The children! She continued to scream for them as she staggered toward the bedroom. She was vaguely conscious of flying objects striking her with great force, but strangely she felt no pain. Calling on God to protect her children and to lead her to them, Marion Dagostino, her mouth full of dirt, staggered on. She bumped into something, climbed over it and - suddenly - she was outdoors.

The tornado had moved on. It had been replaced by a silence so intense that she thought her ears had become blocked. Standing in the rubble of her house she could see no life around her. She began to feel that perhaps she was the only one left alive. A flicker of movement in the cellar hole next door caught her eye. It was her aunt, uncle and cousin standing quietly, arms still folded across their heads in an effort to ward off debris that was no longer falling.

Suddenly Marian remembered her own children. Almost as soon as she began calling their names, something stirred and stood erect. It was Anita, so covered with wind-borne dirt that her mother had not seen her. Barbara was found lying in a lean-to which had been created by the bathtub propped against the fallen main beam of the house.

Something at Marian's feet stirred as she looked down. It was Margie. Her mother scooped her up and cradled her in her arms. The little girl was filthy, soaking wet and had not uttered a word.

Now Marian's uncle had climbed from the cellar hole of his home and was standing beside her. Then she saw her mother who had been on the second floor. The woman was rubbing the back of her head or her neck. She had been injured as she had somehow made her way downstairs while the home she shared with her daughter's family was disintegrating.

A neighbor rummaged in a storage chest and came up with a blanket for Margie, the oldest girl, a heavy, outside man's sweater for Barbara, and a sheet, which was wrapped around little, shivering Anita.

Marian's father, who had gone to the store just before the tornado struck, came climbing and running toward the ruins of his house. The frantic man somehow missed seeing his family who were huddled nearby, and he scrambled atop the pile of debris to gain a better view of the ravaged landscape. It was there, moments later, that they found him.

Dirty, disheveled and looking like refugees from a bombed-out World War II city, the five survivors and the stunned Mr. Riccardi began walking, past cellar holes rapidly filling with water from broken mains, past twisted tree trunks stripped of their bark, and men carrying still forms on improvised stretchers.

+++

Thomas "Franny" Forhan, his elderly father, and a friend from St. Nicholas Avenue, Lenny McGlynn, were hotter than most of the other residents of the neighborhood that afternoon. They had manhandled an electric water heater into position in the basement of Franny's home at 48 Yukon Avenue and had connected it to the water pipes.

With the first gust of wind before 5:15 p.m., Franny had gone out to move his car away from the apple trees which surrounded the house, in case a thunderstorm was brewing, as appeared likely. Ten minutes later, the winds immediately in front of the funnel hit. Franny started running around closing first-floor windows until his seventy-year-old father yelled that it was exactly the wrong thing to do.

There had been at least a partial vacuum created, however, and Franny Forhan remembers vividly the walls flexing and contracting, feeling as though he was inside an enormous diaphragm. Without further hesitation, the two Forhans, father and son, Lenny McGlynn and Franny's tiny daughter, helped along by her grandfather, headed for the protection of the basement. They had scarcely started down the stairs when, in Franny's words, " The whole structure was lifted from its foundation, walls exploding outward, as it toppled to one side."

It is nearly certain that all four persons blacked out momentarily, perhaps only for a few seconds, possibly for as long as a minute. Franny regained consciousness sprawled on the cellar floor, his head bleeding profusely from a gash in his scalp. He fought for breath; the air seemed thin and lacking in oxygen. This phenomenon, experienced and reported on by other victims was most likely the result of the drastic displacement of oxygen due to the enormous suction exerted at the center of the rotating funnel. The condition was transient, however, and quickly passed as the funnel moved away.

Franny had been sprawled atop his father and daughter, both of whom were uninjured, and he rolled off and got shakily to his feet. Then he and Lenny climbed from the basement. This was easily accomplished since there was nothing above the foundation now but blue sky.

An elderly couple, the Norths, were in their apartment above the Forhans when the tornado hit. Their apartment disintegrated around them, and the Norths were blown into the branches of the apple trees adjacent to the demolished structure. Landing in the yielding branches rather than on the hard earth beneath may well have saved them from serious injury.

Almost without being consciously aware of it, the two men began assisting - or attempting to assist - their injured neighbors. A neighborhood teenager, Eric Lund, appeared and joined the two men in trying to lift a large section of roof off Mrs. Skog, whose father-in-law lay dead in the ruins of her home across the street. The roof which had fallen atop Mrs. Skog, lay across a beam of some kind, which acted like the fulcrum of a see-saw.

When the trio tried, they succeed in lifting their end of the heavy roof, but this drew from the woman, who had at least one fractured limb, screams of agony, so they reluctantly ceased their efforts. Had their collective strength been sufficient, they would have tried to lift the enormous weight directly up and swing it away from her, but this was out of the question.

Nearby, a Mrs. McKiernan and her brood of seven children emerged from the basement of their now-vanished home. The woman had time to shepherd her children down to the cellar, before the tornado, roaring overhead, had blown their home apart. Had the building simply caved in upon itself, or been hammered downward, like Mrs. Skog's, the children and their mother would have fared far differently.

Mrs. Astrid Peterson, another neighbor, had been blown from her wind- blasted home into a nearby field. Her clothing in rags, she had suffered a gash on one leg which had laid open one thigh almost from groin to knee, right down to the bone. The femoral artery had not been severed, however, and there did not seem to be excessive bleeding.

+++

The broad funnel now pushed out across busy Route 70, enveloping more than a dozen passing automobiles. It overturned several, tossing them across the highway into the adjacent meadow and marshy area.

Charles Sokolowski, who lived just across the Shrewsbury town line on Holden Street, had driven a mile or so to the small convenience store where Lincoln Street and Route 70 diverge, a spot called Cozy Corner for some long- forgotten reason. Heading home with his eighteen-month-old daughter Charlene in the front seat beside him, he passed the front of the Curtis Apartments just as the tornado was ravaging the buildings. He saw the bus being overturned and slammed into the wall of one of the buildings; then the funnel enveloped the automobile.

The windshield and other car windows were shattered as Mr. Sokolowski tried simultaneously to pull over onto the shoulder, brake to a stop and lie across his daughter to protect her. The car was lifted and flung off the road, throwing the two Sokolowskis clear, as it rolled and bounced along.

Mr. Sokolowski's first conscious memory, after trying to shield little Charlene, was when he was walking along alone on Route 70, his clothing in shreds; hair, face and body coated with windborne mud. A neighbor, Joseph Bisceglia, stopped and helped Mr. Sokolowski into his car. So bloated was Mr. Sokolowski's head that his neighbor at first failed to recognize him, taking him for a resident of the Home Farm, instead.

Bisceglia drove north on Route 70 a dozen miles to the Clinton Hospital, since Lincoln Street was blocked by the debris field, preventing passage to Hahnemann Hospital only two and a half miles distant.

Charlene was found by a rescue worker later that evening. She was suffering from severe head injuries, and since the route to Hahnemann Hospital had become passable, she was rushed there and was later transferred to City Hospital for emergency brain surgery.

The Sokolowski vehicle, headlights on, was found on the bottom of a small pond on the property of the City's Home Farm. Mrs. Sokolowski's brother, recognizing the the two-week-old automobile resting just under the surface of the shallow pond, made repeated dives in an effort to locate his brother-in-law and niece, not knowing that both had been thrown clear before the car's immersion.

+++

A short distance behind Charles Sokolowski on the highway, Edgar Nichols was heading toward his home in the Morningdale section of Boylston. He had just left Worcester Envelope Company at 5:00 p.m., with a fellow employee and Boylston resident, Naomi Currier, whom he was driving home.

Nichols saw the tornado blast across the highway only a few hundred feet ahead of his vehicle. Moving from left to right across his front, it slewed some cars around as though they were resting on ice, shoved others off the highway, some to land upside down, resting on their roofs. A few cars were seen to lift completely off the ground and whirl some distance in the air before being dropped back to earth.

Nichols finally wrenched his horrified gaze from the scene before him and looked at his passenger. Mrs, Currier was nearly eight months pregnant and he was concerned for her. He could see, however, that she was as composed as anyone could possibly expect, given the suddenness of the catastrophe unfolding ahead. He relaxed a little; he would not be needed as a midwife today.

One of the airborne vehicles seen by Edgar Nichols to be whirled aloft was that of a couple from Sterling, a town fifteen miles to the north. As their car was tossed from the highway, Robert Burns, the driver, was thrown from the vehicle, as was his wife, Geraldine. Mr. Burns, badly injured, was found near the wrecked car and rushed two miles north to the Worcester County Hospital within a few minutes of the tornado's passage. His wife's lifeless body was found partially immersed in a swampy brook nearby.

+++

Seconds after Charles Sokolowski and his young daughter left the Cozy Corner store and headed down Route 70 into the path of the tornado, young Richard Higgins drove through the intersection. He was coming home from his job in Shrewsbury, at the Worcester Sand and Gravel pit and he continued west on Lincoln Street. At this point, he was a quarter mile from the Sokolowski vehicle and moving at a right angle to it.

Something prompted Higgins to look in the rear-view mirror of his Ford pickup. He saw the ugly black clouds angling across his field of view, and whirling in the funnel he glimpsed a black and white cow, one of the herd of Holsteins maintained by the Home Farm.

Across Route 70 from the front of the Curtis Apartments lay Brookside, more generally known as the Home Farm, where more than two hundred fifty indigent, elderly or physically infirm men from the city lived and worked. It had originally been built by the federal Works Progress Administration in the late 1930s. The farm centered around the care of a herd of dairy cows, some eighty Holsteins, and included a milk-bottling plant, a laundry and vegetable gardens.

Robert O'Brien drove his Cushman bakery truck onto the Brookside Farm property just after five o'clock to make one of his last deliveries of the day. He pulled up behind the building which housed the kitchen and parked his truck.

Within seconds, the dark funnel struck. When it passed, the truck was still upright and its badly frightened driver unhurt.

When Mr. O'Brien got out and walked around the truck to inspect it, it had come through the blow practically unscathed. Unscathed, that is, except for a jagged two-by-four, which had speared one of the truck's fenders and which protruded like an enormous arrow.

About twenty-eight men lived in three small, barracks-like buildings at the farm. On this early evening, most had just finished supper and were back in the Spartan barracks where they would spend the rest of the evening until bedtime. The tornado ripped into the flimsy structures, and within seconds four of the men lay dead in the ruins. Three others were missing and most of the rest lay injured in the splintered structures or were walking about in a daze. In the yard a short distance away lay the body of a fifth man, Frank Traupis, a tailor at the home. Fifteen residents would require hospitalization, with an equal number receiving first aid at the scene for minor cuts and bruises.

The roof of the main building's west wing was shorn off; the farm's power station was partially deroofed as well, and had been knocked out of commission. The hay barn was leveled; the cow barn also. Some of the animals were thrown hundreds of feet through the air, such as that glimpsed by Richard Higgins. Others died where they stood, necks broken by the stanchions in which they had been locked a little while earlier, when the blast of wind caused them to lose their footing.

Shortly after six p.m., Edward Kennedy, a local insurance agent and chairman of the city's Welfare Board, arrived on the scene. Kennedy had been enjoying the Holy Cross homecoming festivities a few minutes earlier when he received a phone call from his wife who relayed a cryptic message from someone at the Worcester Telegram alluding to some sort of disaster having taken place at the Home Farm. As the head of the board which administered the facility, Kennedy hurried to the scene.

The supervisor of the Home Farm had already begun directing rescue operations and was assigning volunteers to various tasks. Although Kennedy was in fact the supervisor's superior, under the circumstances he merely pulled off his suitcoat, rolled up the sleeves of his dress shirt and joined those who had already begun digging out, literally, debris-covered victims, dead and alive.

The grim work continued without a pause; by the time dusk had set in, about 8:30 p.m., high-intensity electric lights were in place and the initial cleanup efforts continued. A search for the three missing men continued, but without success.

Immediately behind and adjacent to the Home Farm and to the Shrewsbury town line was yet another housing project. Lincolnwood was a four-year-old conglomeration of barracks-like two-story structures, each housing six World War II veterans and their families. The development spread over a low hill, the crest of which overlooked Lake Quinsigamond.

Annie Holm sat with several neighbors in front of her apartment building while her five-year-old son Donnie played with his friends. A few minutes after five, her paperboy brought a copy of the Evening Gazette. Donnie paused beside his mother as she scanned the front page. She showed him a photograph of the damage from the Flint tornado the previous day, then hastened to reassure him. "You'll never see it here," she told her son.

Minutes later Annie had carried her two-year-old daughter Nancy up to the second-floor apartment and had begun peeling potatoes for supper. It had suddenly grown dark and she had switched on the kitchen light. A few drops of rain pattered down, it grew still darker and the kitchen light flickered.

Grabbing her daughter, Annie struggled to close one of the large, heavy windows, but a torrent of air seemed to be rushing out through the opening, making her loose-fitting dress stand out like a flag, and preventing her from closing the window. Running into her living room, she saw her draperies curling out through the window as though they were being pulled by someone or something on the roof.

A roaring sound was now clearly audible, and Mrs. Holm was becoming frightened. She ran to the adjacent apartment, pounded on the door, and heard the tenant, Mike Esposito yell, "Get the hell downstairs!" A foyer door slammed, separating Annie from her daughter, who had begun to cry.

Forcing her way through the door and grabbing Nancy, Annie ran down the stairs as the apartment walls above her buckled inward, touching at their apex and showering mother and child with plaster. The windowpane in the door at the foot of the stairs shattered, but the cloth with which Annie had covered the inner surface of the glass the previous week prevented the shards from flying inward.

Annie could feel the whole building swaying and when a hand and arm reached out of an apartment and a voice called to her, she reached out, took the hand, and still clutching Nancy, was pulled inside. Mr. Wise, to whom the hand and arm belonged, angrily demanded, "What are you doing up there? Did a water pipe burst, or what?"

As she was explaining to her puzzled and irate neighbor that she was in no way responsible for the water dripping from the ceiling onto the Wises' new refrigerator, the roaring and shaking subsided.

Annie went outside and looked up at the building. The roof had been torn completely away, the upper part of the chimney had been toppled, and large sections of the second-story walls were gone. Yelling for Donnie, the Espositos answered, assuring her that the boy was unharmed. She replied that she wanted to see him for herself, whereupon he dutifully stuck his head out of the apartment window and grinned at his mother.

Soon afterward, as Annie was poking through the debris which had filled her back yard, she spotted some fragments of her long-stemmed wine glasses. Her wedding and engagement rings had been earlier put into one of them and she began examining the shards more closely. Relief washed over her as she spotted her diamond solitaire and picked it up. She continued searching for her wedding ring, but it was never found.

While the Holms, Espositos and Wises had been fighting and winning their battle for survival, in another of the project's buildings a woman hastily scooped up her baby from its crib as their roof vanished and the rest of their dwelling seemed about to disintegrate. The building stayed more or less intact, however, and when the winds died away the young mother glanced into the crib again. A windborne brick had landed there.

+++

9

The Harveys

Fourteen-year-old Sally Belinskas stood transfixed on Regatta Point Beach, staring a mile down the lake at the moving blackness where moments before the lake's surface had reflected the blue sky. As the tornado roared across the northern end of Lake Quinsigamond and into Shrewsbury, it ran head-on into a westbound automobile driven by the editor of Norton Company's technical publication "Grits and Grinds", Enfrid T. Larsen - "Larry" to his friends and associates. He and the company's photographer, Norman Flink, had been in Boston all day. Larry had dropped Flink off near his home on Park Street near the center of Shrewsbury, just before 5:15. The blackness ahead he took for a thunderstorm, and he headed for his home on Brattle Street in Holden, seven or eight miles away.

With one eye on the turbulence ahead, Larsen had covered two of those eight miles when the blackness resolved itself into a whirling debris-laden funnel which engulfed his car. The vehicle was picked up and tossed over a guardrail. It rolled down the steep embankment and slid into a murky backwater of Lake Quinsigamond. Larsen had been thrown into the back seat and had just time enough to scramble out of the shattered rear windshield and across the trunk to safety, when the car, filling with water, slid completely under the surface with a gush of bubbles.

Almost fainting with the pain from an injured shoulder, Larsen half- climbed, half-crawled up the embankment to the road, where a passing motorist stopped. The man had already picked up three other injured victims, and took them, along with Larsen, to Hahnemann Hospital. Examination disclosed that his shoulder was broken, but as he later confided to Norton friends, he felt almost fortunate compared to some of the hideous injuries he saw at Hahnemann later that evening.

+++

When Louis Butts finished his day's work in Norton's shipping department at 3 p.m., he headed straight for Lake Quinsigamond for a few hours of relaxed fishing. He rented a boat at Carey's

Boathouse on the north end of the lake and was on the water by 3:30.

Just after 5:15 he saw a black cloud looming up in the northwest, but decided not to head for the boathouse on the eastern shore, at least not until it became certain that a storm was imminent. Two minutes later, the funnel swept across the end of the lake.

At the same moment Larry Larsen's car was tossed off the road which skirted the north end of Quinsigamond, the waterborne Butts, some three hundred yards to the southward, was caught in the fringe winds extending from the right side of the funnel. Shoved against the shore by the sudden tempest, Butts grabbed an overhanging branch to stabilize his rocking boat, while managing simultaneously to wriggle out of his shirt.

Reluctantly relinquishing his grip on the branch, Butts held his shirt aloft with both arms and hands, forming a crude tent; to fend off fragments of mysterious debris with which he was being pelted.

The wind and water subsided without the frightened fisherman suffering further harm, and Butts rowed directly back to the boathouse. There he apologized for the superficial damage to the rented boat. Mr. Carey, who had come through the sudden storm unhurt, told him not to give it a second thought, as he indicated with a sweep of his hands only the concrete foundation of his boathouse now remained.

Louis's car had been parked near the boathouse. Now it was badly damaged; dented, windshield and other windows broken; the luggage rack atop the car bent and twisted almost completely off. The car's headlamps had apparently been pulled from their sockets by the suction within the tornado's eye. They hung down grotesquely, like eyes popping from a human face. Fearing possible fire or explosion, Louis did not attempt to start the battered automobile.

As had just happened with the injured Larry Larsen, a passing motorist offered Butts a ride home, delivering him to his home on Belmont Hill. Finding his wife unhurt, as well as his mother, who lived nearby, Louis began to hear radio reports of a tornado across the northern part of the city. Trying to call Mrs. Butts' parents, who lived on Watts Road in the northwest part of the city, the couple found that her parents' telephone was out of order. Louis walked more than four miles across the city that night to check on his parents-in-law. He found them unharmed; their home had been on the fringe of the tornado and lost only a few roofing shingles.

+++

Between two and three that afternoon, Jack Monahan, a senior at Shrewsbury High School, had walked down the long hill from the center of town en route to his home on Constitution Avenue in the Great Brook Valley Gardens apartment complex. Two-thirds of the way along in his three-mile walk, Jack reached the home of his maternal grandparents, Lawrence and Nora Daly, at 71 West Main Street, almost on the edge of Lake Quinsigamond. The elderly couple doted on their grandson and enjoyed his visits, while young Jack fully returned their affection. When, at around 4 p.m., he said good-by, Jack did not go home, but went along instead to his job as a short-order cook at "Charlie's diner-on-wheels", a mobile canteen which operated in the northeast part of the city.

Just after 5:15, Jack felt the diner tremble in a way unconnected with the usual road motion. No one else on board could account for the severe buffeting, but the mobile canteen didn't topple, and presently the rocking subsided.

A minute later the swooping funnel churned across the northern end of Quinsigamond, simultaneously engulfing Carey's boathouse and the Daly home, two hundred feet to the north. Both structures were instantly fragmented.

The seventy-four-year-old retired building contractor and his wife were blown, along with much of their home, into the lake. If not actually unconscious when they struck the surface of the water, the Dalys were rendered thus by huge fragments of their home slamming down on top of them. When, at length, their bodies were recovered, both surprisingly still wore their glasses. Like the Falcones, who had died together ninety seconds earlier, the Dalys were found with their arms around each other in a last embrace.

+++

Joseph Krilovich, thirty-five, of 24 Old Mill Road in Shrewsbury had been home sick from his job with the Worcester Gas Light Company that day. Feeling a little better, he was in the kitchen at about 5:20 p.m., ready to sit down to supper, when he heard what sounded like the roar of an approaching freight train. Less alarmed than puzzled, since there was no railroad within three miles of his home, Mr. Krilovich got up and looked out his kitchen window westward toward Lake Quinsigamond and a wooded corner of Worcester beyond.

He saw the unmistakable funnel of a tornado blocking out the westering sun, apparently headed directly for his home. He knew exactly what it was that was bearing down on him and, with his wife, he headed quickly for the cellar.

Next door, eleven-year-old David Hight, his older sister Virginia and their mother were also about to have supper when they heard the roaring and saw the funnel cloud approaching. Mrs. Hight, however, feared being trapped in a rubble-filled cellar, so she called her children to her in the kitchen and prepared to face together, whatever came.

Less than a minute before the front wall of wind would have slammed into the back walls of these and neighboring homes, the tornado swung to its left, toward the northeast. The home of Edward Lundgren lay behind and at right angles to those of the Krilovich and Hight families, and while this home, too, was spared the full force of the twister, the winds were strong enough to completely scatter a flock of five hundred turkeys Mr. Lundgren had been raising for the fall market. The turkeys were never seen again.

The funnel continued across Main Street and struck the Lundgren and Jonaitis Dairy. Recently rebuilt after having sustained extensive damage in a fire, the dairy's main building, a milk-bottling plant, was struck full-force. The funnel ripped heavy planks loose, some of which became wind-driven spears, puncturing the walls, and in one instance the masonry foundation of homes on nearby Ireta Road.

As soon as the tornado had passed, Joe Krilovich ran cross-country through backyards, towards the spot on the Shrewsbury shore of Lake Quinsigamond where Carey's boathouse, now demolished, marked the funnel's arrival in the town. Nearby, he found a largely demolished home, and together with other volunteers, he pulled to safety the disoriented members of the family within. They were cut, scratched and bruised, but as far as Joe Krilovich could tell, none were seriously injured.

+++

Meanwhile, the adventurous David Hight, against his mother's strict orders, found a young friend and set off on a sightseeing tour of the neighborhood. They ventured as far as Holden Street, half a mile in the direction of the Home Farm, where David remembers seeing one or two homes that had been directly in the tornado's path utterly pulverized.

Upon returning home, David was scolded, as he had expected. Later that evening, the boy who had roamed with him throughout the neighborhood learned that one of his grandparents had been killed when the tornado demolished their home on Uncatena Avenue, only a few minutes before it roared past his own.

+++

Middle-aged Gosta Anderson, thoroughly alarmed by the roaring winds and rapidly approaching blackness, hurried out to the barn which stood near his home, to close the doors before the approaching storm struck. He reached the barn and was starting to swing the doors shut when the tornado hit.

The blast of wind hit him full force, sweeping him off his feet before he knew what was happening, then slamming him to the ground. He was bounced and rolled along for several yards.

Next door, and in the tornado's path, at 307 Main Street, stood the large eighteenth century farmhouse of the Claflin family. From the rear of their home one could see for several miles to the west and northwest where Mr. Claflin had spotted the darkness several minutes earlier.

A churning blackness could be seen several miles away to the northwest, in the approximate direction of the Shell Oil Company's gasoline tank farm. Apparently there had been an explosion or fire there, or so Mr. Claflin thought. Yet why was the smoke cloud so dense and approaching so rapidly, he wondered. He yelled to his fifteen-year-old son to pull one of the family's two cars into the large barn close behind their home, while he did the same with the other.

Young Bob dropped the Worcester Telegram, in which he'd just been reading about the killer tornado striking Flint, Michigan, the previous day, and ran to help his father. By the time he emerged from the barn, Bob could hear what sounded like an approaching train, over which he could hear the voice of his father, who was looking out a rear window of the house, urging other members of the family to "Come and look at this!"

Bob's mother and two sisters were reluctant to do so, but the boy himself was curious about the source of his father's excitement and why he was now hearing what sounded like the roar of a jet plane, low and closing rapidly.

Before he could satisfy his curiosity, Bob heard his father, in a voice filled with awe and disbelief, yell to the family that a tornado was bearing down on them and that they were to run for the cellar. With the funnel nearly on top of them, the five Claflins clattered down the cellar stairs just a few seconds before impact.

Bob heard the old house above their heads groaning and quaking from the tornado's right wall slamming into it. The Claflins half-expected the home to be either flattened by the tornado or lifted right off its foundation. They could hear, against the tornado's roar, the sound of shattering windows being blown in.

Less than two minutes after they had bolted to the safety of the cellar, the roaring sound was fading into the distance and their house still stood above them. They cautiously filed upstairs, then went outside. The damage to the south-facing front of the home was superficial - broken windows, and some roofing shingles torn away.

The rear half of the dwelling was in far worse condition and the rear half of the roof, from ridgepole to eave, had carried away. Of the barn, nothing but some flooring, partly of heavy plank and partly of poured concrete, now remained. The two family cars had been reduced to junk.

The Claflins, father and son, had a third automobile in the barn as well. This was a 1916 Peerless, a seven-passenger touring car they had almost finished restoring, which they'd planned to take to an antique car rally in Detroit in the near future. It was similarly demolished, virtually torn apart, when the barn walls abruptly vanished.

The extensive Claflin property included a number of acres on which the family's livestock was grazed. Mr. Claflin also owned and operated a factory in Worcester which produced wooden crates, for apples and citrus fruits. A large meadow to the east of the farmhouse contained a supply of the lumber needed in the manufacture of these boxes; one million board feet of rough-sawn planks.

As had happened ten minutes earlier when the black funnel had ripped across Diamond Match's lumberyard, the funnel scattered the carefully stacked planks, hurling many from its path; sucking up hundreds of others into its spinning vortex and carrying them forward. "Forward" in this case meant across the stretch of former pasture which had been converted some years before into a golf driving range operated by Worcester restauranteur Walter Cosgrove and his partner John Flaherty, a science teacher at Worcester's Classical High School.

Shortly before 3:00 that afternoon, Flaherty had arrived at the range with three or four students from Classical who'd come to the range each afternoon to locate and collect the hundreds of balls which had been hit during the day. Besides some exercise and a little spending money, these students would receive a few golfing pointers and a chance to hit a few balls downrange themselves.

On this hot Tuesday afternoon, Flaherty, Cosgrove and their young assistants had gathered the golf balls into piles at random points on the field, then the balls were put into burlap bags and tied. Finally, an old pickup truck drove around the range and the bags, like sacks of potatoes, were loaded in the back and driven back to the "clubhouse", a one-room shanty which sufficed as a storage place for the balls, a supply of clubs in racks, and on such days as this, a place of shelter from the hot sun.

Shortly before five, Cosgrove left his partner and the high-schoolers and drove about a mile to the refreshment stand at Carey's boathouse. Cosgrove quenched his thirst and cooled off a little by downing a milkshake, then he drove back to the range and joined the others.

By this time their work was finished and they were relaxing together in the clubhouse when Cosgrove returned. They had seen blackness looming in the west, no doubt presaging a thunderstorm, which hopefully would be over before suppertime and would cool things off.

While the group waited for the first drops of rain to fall, the "thunderstorm" approached; now less than two miles distant, its whirling funnel became clearly recognizable. Cosgrove stared fixedly at the advancing tornado, then gaped in astonishment, unable or unwilling to believe his eyes. "What's that?" Cosgrove finally asked, already knowing what the reply would be.

"That's a tornado," Flaherty replied, speaking in a somewhat detached tone, "...very rare in this area, so what you're seeing is a once-in-a- lifetime experience."

Asked if he were certain, Flaherty, somewhat annoyed that his identification should be called into question, replied that weather phenomena were included in the realm of science, his teaching field, so he was positive.

"Looks like Clinton's going to get it," he added, almost as an afterthought. Almost before the words were out of his mouth, he and the others realized that since this tornado wasn't heading north, but was moving instead almost due east, Clinton wasn't going to "get it", but they probably were.

What followed in the next couple of frantic minutes seems, at the remove of thirty-five years in time, to have been almost a comedic sequence of events fraught with potentially disastrous consequences. Alerted at last to the danger, the group ran across West Main Street to be further from the apparent path of the tor-nado. Finding themselves in the midst of a growth of poison ivy, to which Cosgrove was violently allergic, they ran back to Flaherty's car, jumped in and headed west towards Worcester - and the onrush-ing storm.

Realizing their mistake, they reversed course, sped past the dri-ving range and up the hill towards Shrewsbury center with the tornado close behind them. Cosgrove's apprehension increased sharply at the sound of a clearly audible Act of Contrition issuing from his normally taciturn partner.

Speeding into the center of town, Flaherty pulled the car into an alleyway between two buildings. Cosgrove for some reason chose to stay with the car; the others hurried into a hardware store, hastily blurted out their story that a tornado was about to hit, and in the same breath asked the proprietor if they could take refuge in his cellar.

The surprised man agreed; down they went, mentally preparing to ride out the tornado as best they might. After several minutes of uneventful quiet, the group, led by Flaherty, climbed the stairs. They were feeling somewhat foolish at their apparent overreaction. Then they heard the rising wail of the first siren.

+++

Three miles to the westward, from her vantage point on the porch of the main building of the country club atop Worcester's Green Hill, Walter Cosgrove's wife had watched the tornado rip through Great Brook Valley and the Home Farm, then chew its way into Shrewsbury. She could clearly see that its course and size were such that it passed directly over her husband's driving range. She was filled with concern for her husband and the others she knew would also be there.

In Shrewsbury, police cruisers with sirens wailing converged on the Maple Street area where the funnel, having unaccountably swung southeast to its right, had crossed West Main Street near the top of the hill and plunged into a residential neighborhood. Some fire engines and an ambulance were racing to the scene. West Main Street having been blocked by debris where the tornado veered across at a point midway between the driving range and the center of town, Flaherty and the others made their way on foot down the long hill, up which they had so recently sped.

As they had expected, the driving range's single building was completely gone, even to the heavy zinc-lined Coca Cola cooler. Gone as well were most of the estimated ten thousand golf balls that had been stored there. Gone too were the brand new pair of Florsheim shoes, still in the box, which John Flaherty had bought earlier that afternoon before coming down to the range. The battered pickup truck lay some hundreds of feet from where it had been parked.

This demonstration of the tornado's power was impressive indication, to each one of the group, of what would have happened to them if they had misjudged the tornado's path as it approached, or if they had simply tried to ride it out where they were.

After scattering the piles of boards and whirling across the driving range, the tornado continued uphill in the general direction of the center of town, a scant mile distant. It engulfed and demolished the large home of the caretaker of the town's rifle range. The house was lifted completely off its foundation, upended, and came to rest on its roof. Mrs. Murphy, the caretaker's wife, and her three children had seen the funnel approaching and were able to make it down to their basement before the tornado hit. All escaped serious injury, including the youngest child, a newborn baby.

+++

A hundred yards or so uphill from the Murphy home, a short dead-end street projects northward from West Main Street. The street had been named Monadnock Road, after a mountain in southern New Hampshire about sixty miles away, which was visible on the horizon on exceptionally clear days.

Four or five single-story homes had been built on this dead-end street when it had been cut through the previous year. One of these, number 7, belonged to an older couple, the Cushmans. On this late afternoon they were about to have a light supper on the patio behind the house. Ordinarily, the view across the valley to Worcester, with rolling hills and Mount Wachusett to the northwest, was a lovely one. At twenty minutes past five this oppressive late afternoon, there was nothing picturesque about the roiling black cloud noisily rolling toward the couple.

Mr. Cushman had lived in the Midwest and recognized the approaching tornado for what it was. He hurried his wife indoors and told her to run down to the basement, where he would join her as soon as he had called out a warning to Ruth Schervee. Mrs. Schervee lived with her husband Curtis at number 3, but was home alone on this afternoon. A backward glance at the onrushing tornado and Mr. Cushman knew he hadn't time to warn his neighbor and still make it to shelter himself, so he quickly followed his wife down the stairs to their basement.

The tornado slammed into these homes, ripping off roofs and tearing whole walls away, walls which were instantly reduced to splintered lumber, plaster dust and flying particles of insulation. Within two minutes the area was totally devastated.

Forty-five minutes later, one of the Monadnock Road residents was hurrying up the hill from the direction of Worcester. Marjorie Anderson, a Red Cross worker, who had had a late-afternoon dentist appointment after work, picked her way over or around fallen trees and wires. Two young men, who Mrs. Anderson did not know, approached from the opposite direction. As they passed they told her that every house on Monadnock Road now lay in ruins - or maybe one had been spared - they weren't sure. The two hurried on, leaving the heartsick woman to continue on her anxious way.

One home among the half dozen had indeed been spared serious damage and Marjorie Anderson saw in happy disbelief that it was hers. Her joy at this discovery was tempered by the sight of her neighbors' homes. Mrs. Schervee, who Mr. Cushman had not had time to warn, had escaped injury, but her home now resembled a crude cardboard shoebox house fashioned by a clumsy child, and then carelessly tossed aside. It had no roof or attic and was missing one entire end wall and most of the other.

The Cushman home was equally devastated, with furniture or pieces of furniture scattered about the yard, although the elderly couple had escaped physical injury. While the magnitude of this disaster was still registering with Marjorie Anderson, she saw Mrs. Cushman, a cloth in one hand, emerge from her ruined home. The woman walked slowly to where several chairs lay in various positions on the grass, carefully set them upright and slowly begin to dust them with her cloth.

The other homes farther up the street lay similarly devastated, yet the Anderson home had merely lost shingles from the northwest corner of the roof and a hefty tree limb smashed a window, sash and all, on the east side, when the tree of which it was a part proved unable to resist the cyclonic winds. The relatively moderate damage sustained by the Anderson home may be due at least in part to the fact that the couple had constructed the house themselves the previous year, making it far sturdier than Shrewsbury building codes required. Also, at least two of the windows had been left open an inch or two that day which may have alleviated somewhat the enormous atmospheric pressure differential accompanying the eye of the tornado.

+++

Still surging uphill, the tornado swept diagonally across West Main Street and into an area of fields and scattered hardwood trees. It came upon the rear of the sprawling Brewer Estate, which faced on Maple Avenue. Somehow, the large, elegant mansion, built in the style of an Italian villa, escaped with only the loss of a few roofing tiles. On the expansive grounds of the estate, however, were several smaller homes, one of which was occupied by two middle-aged women, Catherine O'Hearn and Ethel McDonald. Their cottage was demolished, with both women left dead in the rubble.

+++

Just after 5:20 p.m., two Shrewsbury construction workers, James Abdella and Melvin Johnson, were heading home from their Worcester job site. They drove along Maple Avenue in a flatbed trailer truck, upon which rested a tractor. Abdella saw a brick chimney attached to the side of one home, sway and topple to earth. As he pointed toward it and began to tell Mel, an entire roof sailed through the air, past the truck cab.

They stopped the truck as the spinning black cloud churned across Maple Avenue just ahead of them and watched in horrified amazement as several rows of houses were flattened, building after building, like toppling dominoes. Not far away, a sedan was spun through the air, dropping into the top of a large tree and coming to rest in an inverted position. Wedged between supporting tree limbs, it resembled the nest of some enormous primeval bird.

Moments later the blackness and roaring wind were gone. Within a few minutes, Abdella and Johnson, their rig still parked at the curb, had driven their tractor down off the flatbed and began clearing the scattered limbs and large trunks of the trees which had given the street its name.

A quarter-mile away, near the center of town, fourteen-year-old Donald Thompson was sitting with his mother in the office which his father, a home-builder, maintained in their home at 40 Westwood Drive. Hearing the roar of the passing funnel, young Donald dropped to his hands and knees and crawled beneath one of the two steel desks in the room, while his mother sought refuge beneath the other.

Seconds later, the wail of the air-raid siren atop the Town Hall assaulted the ears of the pair.

+++

Mrs. Gail Bailey and her three children were in their second-floor apartment of the two-family home on 101 Maple Avenue, when the left wall of the tornado crashed into their dwelling. She had seen the leaves standing "straight out" on the shade trees just outside her window and could sense the approach of a serious storm. The three children were hurriedly dispatched to close windows.

The four had started down the stairway, intending to seek shelter in the basement, when the funnel hit. Much of three walls were torn away and the chimney blown apart in the same instant, with huge fragments of chimney liner coming to rest on each of the two landings between the first and second floors. Fortunately, neither landing was occupied by either of the two boys, who had nearly reached the first floor, or their mother and sister Gail, who had just begun the descent.

Mrs. Bailey sustained a badly fractured arm in the process of the tornado dismantling their home, and her daughter was injured also, although less seriously. In the initial confusion, with neighbors wandering up and down the street to the accompaniment of wailing sirens, Mrs. Bailey held her painfully throbbing arm with her good hand, patiently awaiting evacuation.

At length, a member of the town's fire department, driving the chief's car, took the injured woman and her daughter to Holden District Hospital, a drive which involved numerous detours and delays en route. Once there, Mrs. Bailey would sit for a considerable time on an inverted wastebasket in the hospital's overcrowded emergency room, her daughter Gail beside her, while overworked doctors and nurses attended to the most seriously injured.

+++

Stephen Donahue, of 8 Hapgood Way, rarely took Tuesday off from his job on the editorial staff of the Telegram. Today, however, his wife had a mid-day medical appointment and Donahue had volunteered to look after their two sons, ages six and eleven.

After bringing the older boy to a midafternoon music lesson at the St. Gabriel studio in downtown Worcester, he and his younger son went to the campus of the Worcester Polytechnic Institute where he maintained a small office in Boynton Hall, from which he did part-time public relations work for the college.

Finishing his work at WPI, Mr. Donahue and his son returned to the studio for his older boy, then the three of them picked up his wife on Lancaster Street and drove to his mother's home on Longfellow Road, on the west side of the city. There, his sister told him there had been a severe storm which had affected Shrewsbury. Not wishing to frighten her mother by revealing the devastation which by 6 p.m. had already begun to be described on local radio stations, she merely told her brother that he ought to get home as soon as possible.

As the Donahues drove through Lincoln Square, they saw a police officer who was a close friend of Mr. Donahue, holding up normal traffic to allow a steady stream of emergency vehicles to pass through this traffic chokepoint en route to Memorial Hospital, one-third of a mile up Belmont Street. Officer Boyle confirmed that it had been a tornado, and that injury and loss of life had been heavy.

A few minutes later, pulling up in front of what had been their family home, they found nothing standing. All doors and windows had been left tightly closed in the family's absence, despite the oppressive heat, and someone later told them that the house had been seen to bulge outward, then burst apart as the huge funnel caused the atmospheric pressure to plummet, while the pressure inside the tightly closed house remained high, until the exploding building brought spectacular and instant equalization.

+++

As the whirling black funnel crossed Maple Avenue, it was perhaps five hundred yards wide at its base, with a course which took it directly down three closely-spaced residential streets that ran southwest off the avenue at right angles to it; Hapgood Way, St. James Road and Crescent Street. As the home of Steve Donahue was exploding into fragments, the tornado's front wall of wind reached 113 Maple Avenue, the home of the Aaron Heitin family.

Mrs. Heiten and her two younger daughters, Barbara, age fourteen, and Nancy, six, had run upstairs to close their windows, believing that the sudden darkness and rising wind signified that a particularly violent thunderstorm was about to break over them. Instead of a clap of thunder, lightning flashes and a downpour materializing, the home began to shake convulsively and most of the roof tore away with a rending sound.

Before Mrs. Heitin could shepherd her children downstairs to the comparative safety of the basement, a large portion of the heavy brick chimney toppled into the room where the three stood. It knocked Barbara to the floor, inflicting a massive head injury.

The nearby home of the Howard Bell family was so thoroughly pulverized that the storm-battered fragments collapsed into the basement, nearly burying Mrs. Bell, who had sensibly taken refuge there at the onset of the killer winds.

Providentially, Mrs. Bell was pulled to safety by willing neighbors, many of whom were homeless as well, just as the unconscious Barbara Heitin was being carried to a nearby vehicle for transportation to the nearest hospital. Because of the nature and severity of Barbara's head injury, after brief stops at two other Worcester Hospitals, she was finally brought to Worcester's City Hospital, to which all patients suffering severe cranial trauma were being brought.

A few houses up the street from the Heitins, at 125 Maple Avenue, no fewer than six members of the Breslin family required medical attention for their injuries. All were comparatively minor however, and after outpatient treatment at the Memorial Hospital they were able to return to their battered home, to sift through the rubble in search of their belongings.

+++

For Shirley Allison, thirty, of 56 Edgewood Road, the recollection of two especially violent thunderstorms the previous summer was still vivid, so when she saw and heard the enormous hailstones falling around her home at around 5:10 p.m. that afternoon, she had a sinking feeling in the pit of her stomach.

The wind rose steadily to a crescendo a few minutes later, and just after 5:20 windows began blowing in. She sent her two young sons, ages three and five, to the basement, but did not follow them immediately. Instead, she ran upstairs to the second floor to get her baby daughter, intending to take her to the basement as quickly as possible. Running now, daughter in her arms, she had gained the first floor and had reached the doorway at the top of the cellar stairs.

At that moment, the bulkhead covering the stairs up to the backyard from the basement, blew off. The roaring blast of air rushing up the stairwell prevented her from joining her sons. As she felt herself losing consciousness, she could hear the house around her coming apart. When she regained her senses, she was lying beside the wreckage-covered cellar hole that had been her home. Almost miraculously, the daughter she still held tightly was unhurt, as were the two boys.

+++

The Allisons' next-door neighbor, Barbara Ek, of 58 Edgewood Road, was alone with her twelve-year-old son Roger and daughter Suzanne, eight, that afternoon. Her husband, Edward, had taken the afternoon off from work to go fishing in the western part of the county.

At about five o'clock, Barbara saw hail falling; so large that she thought of it as "ice chunks". She used the freak of nature to create a game with her two children. She gave each child a bucket and told them that the first one to fill his pail with ice chunks would be the winner. The prize, if any, to be given to the winner, has been long forgotten. By about 5:15 p.m., one or the other of the Ek children had won and now were playing next door with two young cousins, the children of Mrs. Ek's brother.

With the approach of a sudden darkness and a sharply rising wind, the two young cousins ran into their home, Suzanne and Roger Ek with them. The apprehensive Roger urged his sister and cousins to run down to the basement with him, and the four youngsters ran down the cellar stairs just before the tornado struck.

Next door, Mrs. Ek was caught on the first floor, unable to gain the comparative safety of the basement, so she lay prone on the floor, covering her face with her hands. Although the house around her was half-destroyed by the tornado, Mrs. Ek suffered only relatively minor cuts and scratches, despite the blowing out of most of the windows, and the tearing away of huge sections of the home's outer walls. Some of her wallpaper tore away, and was later founds on the grounds of the Weagle Dairy, several hundred yards to the east.

Since Edward Ek's normal route home would have coincided almost exactly with the path of the tornado through Holden and Worcester, a series of extended but necessary detours delayed his arrival, frantic with worry, until about 11 p.m. To his immense relief, he found his wife waiting to reassure him that she and the two children had come safely through the sudden catastrophe, as had their young cousins.

+++

At the home of Herbert Olson, at 24 Lake Street, Herbert and four other men were relaxing over a beer in the kitchen, when it suddenly grew dark and the wind rose. Olson and one of his guests, William O'Neil, ran out to the backyard to close an beach umbrella that was blowing across the yard like a sail before the wind. Carl Whitman, of Waban, a western suburb of Boston, was another of the men who had been sitting in the kitchen and he knew what the "jet plane" noise signified. He yelled, "Its a tornado!" and headed for the basement with Norman Norton right behind him.

The pair flattened themselves on the cellar floor, as close to the west wall as they could get. Whitman heard a sound which sounded like "the sound you hear when you stick a can opener into a vacuum-packed can of coffee". In this case, the "swish" was the sound of the house above them blowing completely off its foundation.

When the wind abated a minute or so later, the two looked upward from their position on the cellar floor - and saw blue sky. Climbing up the cellar wall and over the foundation, they saw "Mr. Olson, covered with mud... [and] Mr. O'Neil covered with blood", walking around in a daze.

Stanley Manning, a Worcester labor union official and the fifth member of the group, was not located for forty-five minutes. After an intense search, a neighbor saw Manning's shoes protruding from beneath the wreckage of the Olson house. His body was uncovered a few minutes thereafter.

+++

Shortly after five o'clock, Emily Weagle, like so many others, stared in amazement at the fall of golf ball-size hailstones. Her father-in-law, Steven Weagle, had rounded up his dairy herd and led them into the barn for milking. One of his sons, Emily's husband Harold, was haying in a nearby field.

A second son, Donald, lived with his wife and two children in a home on the farm property as well. The Weagles had heard news broadcasts about the devastating tornados in Flint and northern Ohio the previous day, and had read accounts that morning in the Telegram, in which survivors spoke of a roaring akin to the sound of an approaching freight train as the tornado bore down upon them.

Donald's wife Doris, upon hearing such a sound, accompanied by a sudden blackness, quickly grabbed a couple of blankets, threw one around each of her children, then pulled them with her to the floor. The funnel struck the house full force, instantly demolishing the wall behind which Doris and her two young children lay huddled. On shelves against the wall had been Doris's collection of glass curios. Surprisingly, none of the three was cut or hurt in any way, possibly because of the hasty precautions taken by Doris, more likely because the wall was sucked outward by the tornado's partial vacuum.

Another indication that the windows and doors were probably closed at the moment of the tornado's impact is suggested by the fact that the roof over the kitchen portion of the house was lifted from the structure, the ends of the curtains wafting up and outward over the top of the wall, and the roof settled back into place once more. This bizarre phenomenon was identical to that observed by Philip White, near the Norton Company.

The tornado blasted the roof from the Weagle barn and demolished most of its walls. After the funnel passed on, Steven Weagle, dazed and with numerous scratches, a few of them bleeding, staggered from the ruins of the barn, having suffered no worse injury than a deep cut on his head. A young hired man was less fortunate. The French-speaking youth who was from Canada, was crushed to death in the collapse of the barn.

Emily Weagle saw pieces of straw which had been driven deep into the trunks of some of the trees which still stood on their property in the wake of the storm.

+++

Clarence "Skip" Quillia of Worcester had finished his day's work at Bay State Abrasives in Westboro and had started for home shortly thereafter. At 5:25 Quillia was heading west on Route 9 and was just opposite the Shrewsbury drive-in theater. Down the hill, a couple of hundred yards ahead, he could see a car stopped in one of the two westbound lanes.

The vehicle did not appear to be disabled in any way, nor was there any evidence of an accident. Just beyond the stopped car, Skip saw a looming black "something" cross the highway from right to left. It did not appear to be a thunderstorm, since these storms didn't usually extend to the ground, as this roiling mass was doing. Quillia noted too, the absence of lightning, though there was a clearly audible growling noise.

Within the space of a minute or so, whatever it was had passed, and the sky ahead quickly brightened. Skip drove the rest of the way down the hill and as he did so it became chillingly apparent why the vehicle ahead had stopped.

The road ahead was blocked with fallen trees, downed utility poles and hanging wires. Other debris was clearly recognizable as having been parts of buildings, including a roof and wall fragments.

As Quillia's mind groped with the problem of getting through or around the rubble-strewn road ahead, a teen-age girl came running down South Street hill, from the left, yelling that there had been a tornado and that people had been killed. Since the tornado had followed the route taken by South Street after crossing Route 9, it was impossible for Quillia or anyone else to turn up the hill and attempt to verify this near-hysterical report of casualties.

Anxious to get to a phone where he could call in a report of the disaster to the police, Skip carefully edged his car up onto the grassy center strip which divided the eastbound and westbound lanes of Route 9. The debris there, farthest from the sides of the road, consisted mostly of treetops and smaller branches. Quillia found that by keeping his forward speed to five miles an hour or so, he was able to brush past the tops of fallen trees, or drive carefully over small branches.

The swath of destruction was several hundred yards wide where the tornado crossed Route 9. Once past the worst of the debris, Quillia eased back onto the highway proper and drove another two miles to a bakery in the Fairlawn section of Shrewsbury, whose telephone he intended to use to call the police.

By the time he pulled up beside Sam's Bakery, radio news bulletins had already begun to hint at the magnitude of the disaster. Making a call to the Shrewsbury police, Skip Quillia got back into his car and continued on into Worcester. He did not go home, however; as a National Guard captain functioning as the 181st Infantry

Regiment's communications officer, he knew he would be needed in the disaster and expected to be busy establishing a radio communications network linking whatever units were called to emergency duty.

As he took his uniform from his locker in the Wheaton Square Armory and began changing, he wondered what would be involved in this emergency. He did not know, nor could anyone have guessed that he would not be seeing his home or family members for eleven days.

+++

The distraught young woman who Skip Quillia had seen and heard come running down South Street hill, shouting hysterically, was scarcely exaggerating the carnage on the crest of the hill behind her. Her identity will never positively be known, but it is likely she was the eldest of the four children of the Sanborn family, three of whom were at home in the two-family house they shared with the Fisher family.

The funnel tore the house apart, injuring Mrs. Goldie Sanborn, her father, Arthur Wilson, and her two children, Bradley and Marian. In the other housing unit, three-month-old Marlene Fisher's young life was instantly snuffed out; both parents were injured, her mother seriously.

Next, the tornado utterly flattened the buildings on the Fuller farm; farmhouse, dairy barn, outbuildings - everything. Miraculously, at least in the case of the Fuller family, it took no lives, nor were any family members seriously injured. Just beyond the Fuller place, South Street, along which the tornado was churning, passed through the middle of the Stuart Allen dairy farm.

+++

Dorothy Allen had collected the last of her three older children from their various activities in or near the center of town, shortly before five. Her youngest daughter, Elaine, four, was along for the drive.

Mrs. Allen had started supper before picking up her brood, so when they arrived back at their eight-room farmhouse at about 5:15, the two older girls went into the house with their mother and little Elaine. Son Dick, fifteen, headed for the large pasture where the Allens' dairy herd grazed. It was his job in the late afternoon to round up the animals and lead them into a smaller, enclosed "night pasture". Often his father would help him.

As Stuart Allen stood in the doorway of his barn, the car of a man who worked just up the road at the Fuller farm came into sight.

The man braked to a halt opposite Mr. Allen and yelled, "There's a tornado coming!"

Seeing the funnel cloud approaching from the west, Stuart Allen ran for the house as fast as he could, yelling to his family, telling them to get down to the cellar as quickly as they could.

At the same moment young Dick, beginning to herd the cows toward the night pasture, saw a churning blackness looming toward him from over the hill to the westward, accompanied by a swelling roar. Dick's first thought was that there had been an explosion of some sort at the Moors, a small nightclub about a mile toward the northwest of where he stood. Within seconds, however, the roiling cloud's cylindrical shape became evident and Dick knew what he was facing.

Reflexively, he fell flat where he stood and locked an arm around a hickory fencepost just before the tornado rolled over him. When it had passed, Dick found that his glasses had been knocked off and that his back had somehow been deeply and painfully scratched, but despite his exposed position, he had escaped more serious injury. Dick Allen did not know, nor would he, in all likelihood, have cared, but he had just joined a most exclusive club of survivors, composed of persons caught in the open, entirely unprotected, who were engulfed by the funnel and survived their ordeal.

Back in the house, the three Allen daughters, little Elaine, twelve- year-old Connie and Audrey, seventeen, ran for the cellar at their parents' urging. Somehow, Connie managed to grab a loaf of bread, and a jar of peanut butter and a knife while running for the safety of the basement. It was "in case Elaine got hungry", the practical Connie would later explain to her parents.

After a couple of minutes, the roaring above their heads diminished, and then stopped entirely, so the Allens cautiously made their way up the stairs to the first floor. They found that the big eight-room colonial home had been shoved four feet off its foundation. Many panes of window glass had been broken; when they went outside they could see that the roof of the house had been torn away.

Stuart Allen represented the ninth generation of his family to live on this farm since it had been established in 1725. Looking across the meadow, he and his family could see the twenty-two room structure aptly named the "big house", which had been built on the foundations of an earlier structure that had been destroyed by fire in 1912. This home had replaced a much older farmhouse, the original, which family tradition and town records both spoke of as having been destroyed in the "big wind" of 1815. Now the

Allens could see that the "big house" had collapsed inward upon itself to the extent that it was apparent to Mr. Allen, even from a distance, that demolition of the remainder would be the only practical step. Once again, nearly a century and a half later; a "big wind" had destroyed the venerable homestead.

Turning their attention to their own home once again, Mrs. Allen saw a bible lying on the floor of the porch. She stooped down, picked it up, and opened it at random. Her eyes fell upon the words: "In my Father's house there are many mansions..."

At about this time, Dick rejoined the rest of the family. His mother wanted to minister to her son's painful back, but Dick wouldn't even let his mother examine, much less treat, the deep scratches.

Meanwhile, Mr. Allen headed across to the battered "big house" to see whether the tenants who had been living in the now nonexistent second floor rooms, had been able to gain the safety of the basement before the house collapsed around them. The man who lived there, like Mr. Allen, had seen the black cone-shaped cloud approaching and had warned his family to get down to the cellar. He and they ran down to the first floor together. They continued on down to the basement, while he raced back upstairs to get a sweater.

Regaining the first floor once again, John was a few seconds from comparative safety when the tornado hit. It pinned him in the rubble of collapsing walls and it was in this condition that Stuart Allen found him. Mr. Allen managed to summon up the strength to lift the debris sufficiently for John to extricate himself. Fortunately, the man had escaped serious injury.

In the cellar beneath, mother and three children had used large boards propped against the chimney to create a sort of protective lean-to. However, they still received a coating of plaster dust which, as they climbed out of the cellar, made them look as though they had been dusted with flour.

The attic of the "big house" had been filled with an irreplaceable collection of antiques, the accumulation of two centuries. Now they were gone; the attic had been sheared off and its contents scattered, even as the floors beneath had buckled and the walls had cracked.

Soon after dark, the Allens heard looters picking through the ruins of the "big house" and saw the beams from their flashlights. These almost certainly were local people who knew what had been stored in the attic, but were unaware that these unique family treasures had either been blown miles away or pulverized beyond recognition - or both.

Mr. Allen and son Dick, armed with two-by-four cudgels chased them away. The looters did not return.

+++

A minute or so after it had so thoroughly scattered the Allen family's collection of irreplaceable heirlooms, the tornado churned its way across busy Route 20. This particular stretch of Route 20, about five miles in length and known locally as the Southwest Cutoff, has long had one of the highest motor fatality rates per mile of any highway in the state. What happened to one vehicle on the cutoff that afternoon, however, had nothing to do with poor highway design or driver carelessness.

Thomas W. Howe, eighty, of Eureka Terrace in Worcester, and his wife, Cecilia, seventy, and two married daughters, Ruth Carlson, thirty-eight, of Northboro and Harriet Loving, forty-five, of Worcester, were driving west toward the southern end of the city after a day of visiting with relatives in a Boston suburb. Before any of the four had time to realize what was happening, the car was engulfed by the onrushing tornado and sent spinning and bouncing nearly two hundred feet. The car was hurled across the eastbound lanes and the shoulder of the highway before tumbling off the road embankment and landing on its roof in a shallow gully beside the road.

The elderly couple and their daughter Ruth were killed instantly or succumbed moments later. Harriet, badly injured, was en route to Marlboro Hospital within minutes, where she would spend several painful weeks as she began her recuperation from a multitude of painful injuries.

The son of Ray Fuller, whose farm had been flattened scant minutes earlier, was driving his father's pickup truck along Route 20 when he spotted the convergence of people around the battered Howe automobile. He couldn't imagine what had caused the accident, but soon would be made aware.

The tornado demolished every building on the John Belinauskas dairy farm, its next target after rolling across the Southwest Cutoff. Then the funnel lifted from the ground.

+++

The same huge cell of instability that had spawned the deadly funnel an hour earlier now gave birth to a smaller tornado over Sutton, ten miles to the southwest. This newborn funnel caused damage on Leland Hill Road in the eastern part of the town of Sutton, near the Northbridge town line. It completely flattened the home of the Brigham family, which was accomplished without injury to any of the family members.

Then it raked across Frank Dakin's poultry farm. The tornado spared the eighteenth century farmhouse where Mr. Dakin lived with his wife Mildred and their son Robert. Yet the storm exacted a heavy price, destroying a large barn, a poultry house and ten range houses, home to a total of 1,500 Rhode Island Reds, the base of the Dakins' livelihood.

Almost as soon as the screaming winds subsided, the Dakins and their neighbors began combing the area, especially downwind, along the tornado's track, turning up one hundred birds in the process, some of them injured. The remainder, more than a thousand chickens were presumably spun off into eternity in the same manner as Oscar Nygard's Holden flock, and the turkeys that Shrewsbury dairyman Eddie Lundgren had been raising as a sideline.

Continuing to move almost due south, the newly-spawned funnel next touched down in Northbridge, damaging roofs and felling dozens of trees. It smashed squarely into a large, brick factory building, that of the Kupfer Brothers, which manufactured coated papers and employed about two hundred.

The roof and wall of the factory were torn away, inflicting minor cuts upon a few workmen, but no serious injuries. The wall of a bonding shed was collapsed by the tornado, allowing an enormous quantity of finished papers to be tumbled into the Blackstone River. Total damage to the factory and ruined paper was approximately $300,000.

Large hail like that observed in advance of the main funnel also fell in Upton. Although not in the size range of the ice chunks that fell in Worcester and further west, these hailstones were of sufficient size to break many of the glass panes at the Glen View greenhouses and to ruin hundreds of heads of maturing lettuce in a nearby field.

Wind-borne hailstones broke windows in homes throughout Upton, many of which had television antennas blown down as well. Nearing Milford, the funnel began to lose much of its punch. By the time it reached Wrentham a few minutes later and a few miles further south, this low-order tornado had dissipated entirely.

+++

The monster funnel which had obliterated the Howe automobile on Route 20, bounced into the air, still moving toward the southeast. About a mile west of the center of Westboro the tornado angled across West Main Street as the base of the funnel swooped toward ground, like a hawk onto its prey, virtually engulfing the farm of cattle dealer, Charles Aronson. A large, early Victorian mansion on the farm, complete with rooftop widow's walk, had stood on the spot since 1860. Unoccupied in 1953, it was instantly flattened.

The Aronson farmhouse, diagonally opposite the mansion, was lifted completely off its foundation and smashed to pieces as it slammed back to earth, debris scattering for hundreds of yards downwind. In the house at the moment of destruction were Charles Aronson, his sister-in-law Sadie, and her fourteen year old daughter Sheila. All were instantly killed.

Forty yards to the southwest stood two barns, one behind the other. In front of the open door to the barn nearer the farmhouse were two heavy wagons loaded with baled hay collected from the fields that afternoon. Hearing the roar of the approaching tornado, a farmhand who lived nearby came running out of the barn to see what strange sort of storm was producing such an unearthly roar.

Henry Bailey may have actually seen the tornado blast the Aronson farmhouse in the two or three seconds before it reached him. As it did so, it toppled one of the heavy, hay-laden wagons over onto him, crushing him to death.

+++

Angling south of the business district of Westboro, the funnel bounced into the air again, cruising along with its base twenty to thirty feet in the air, for more than half a mile. Crossing Charles Street, it clipped roof shingles from one house at the intersection of Baxter and Ruggles Streets. With its base still hovering above the ground, it grazed the roofs of homes at 6 and 4 Baxter Street heading closer to South street with every passing moment.

From the back porch of their apartment at 14 South Street in the center of town, several members of the Granger family watched the funnel slide past only a quarter-mile away. For a few terrifying moments it looked to young Jean Granger as if the "thing", whatever it was, had changed course and was now churning in their direction. Such was not the case however, and the Grangers continued watching with horrified fascination.

+++

At 5:35 p.m., Jane Harvey was in the kitchen of her home at 91 South Street, preparing supper for her family. Her four young children were with her, including a three-month-old daughter. Suddenly, a looming blackness overshadowed the house, and the wind rose so quickly that Mrs. Harvey saw most of a row of large, sturdy maple trees just across the driveway from the kitchen uprooted as effortlessly as she might have pulled an equal number of carrots from the family garden. She did not linger to see more. Scooping up the baby and telling the three frightened children to come with her to the cellar, she ran down the cellar stairs with the three older children scampering ahead of her. Just as she stepped down from the bottom step to the cellar floor, she felt the riser scrape the calf of her leg as the entire stairwell lifted up and away from her.

She and the children half-ran, half-dove a scant fifteen feet into the northwest corner of the fieldstone-walled cellar, feeling the wave of pressure change and hearing the roar just over their heads as the house lifted off the foundation and dashed to the ground to the southeast, the wreckage streaming out in that direction as though drawn along by the funnel.

In the basement, several factors combined in such a way that neither Mrs. Harvey nor any of the children received the slightest scratch or bruise. Whether by luck or instinct, they had flung themselves into the northwest corner of the cellar; as the windward side, it usually offers the best chance of survival. The floor of the Harveys' basement is a mere four-and-a-half below the level of the ground. The fieldstone wall was extended upward nearly two more feet, however, by a capstone of enormous horizontal granite blocks, butted end to end, each more than a foot thick, nine feet long and weighing several tons.

Several of these huge blocks along the south wall were dislodged and fell or were pushed by the whirling winds into the basement. Those two blocks which formed the west cap, and a third block on the north side which joined at right angles above the crouching woman and her children, held firm and contributed to their survival as certainly as their dislodging would have brought instant death.

Also, with the entire house torn away above them, like a lid being wrenched from the top of a can, the pressure differential which might have created a dangerous suction was suddenly equalized.

A hundred yards or so further southeast, Jane Harvey's husband Bob, had been in the large dairy barn behind his parents' home, loading hay. Now he was struggling against the rising wind in an attempt to close the barn's large sliding doors. After a few moments, he gave up the unequal struggle as a lost cause. He hurried through the barn and out, reaching a corner of the cinderblock milkhouse, where he and the tornado literally ran into each other.

As young Dick Allen had done ten minutes earlier, Bob Harvey fell flat to the ground and locked an arm around an iron post protruding from the concrete apron adjacent to the milkhouse. The funnel hit him full force; he was dimly aware of the cinderblock dairy barn being demolished. It seemed to Mr. Harvey that the tornado took only a few seconds to pass; when he got shakily to his feet, he discovered that his workshirt was a shredded rag, but his skin beneath was unmarked.

Looking around, Mr. Harvey saw that the barn was gone; the roof was lying on the ground at a crazy angle, but the walls had vanished. So, too, had most of the milkhouse, except for the corner nearest the spot where he had ridden out the tornado's fury.

He could see his parents' farmhouse still standing, but badly gutted and with every window gone. Walking closer to it, he discovered his mother lying on the ground, bleeding and moaning in pain. She had been blown from the house by the tornado and against the jagged point of a broken timber, sustaining a deep and painful flesh wound. Bob's father, Emory Harvey, made his way out of the house and hurried to his wife's side.

Bob crossed South Street, then picked his way through the wreckage of what had been his home and its furnishings. He passed the piano which had formerly occupied the family's "front room". It was sitting upright in the middle of the debris and appeared to be in playable condition.

Bob heard a hissing sound. Turning his head, he saw the natural gas meter lying near the foundation at the front of the house. Near it, the gas feeder line from the street had been ruptured, and the colorless gas was rushing from the broken line.

Fearfully, Mr. Harvey approached the cellar home and looked down. He saw his wife and children huddled there, and to his immense relief saw that they were unharmed.

After their joyful reunion, his wife described their near-miraculous brush with death. Somehow, having come through the tornado alive, the Harveys could view the desolation around them without being overwhelmed by it.

They recalled Bob's trip earlier in the day, when he took a load of calves to market. As was his usual custom, Bob had put the check he had received in payment on top of the refrigerator, until such time as his wife took it to the bank for deposit. Now, the refrigerator, weighty though it had been, was nowhere in sight; the fate of the check could only be imagined.

The couple's brand-new Buick had been garaged behind the house. The wind's force had blown the garage from around the car and the Buick itself had been shoved nearly a hundred feet across the yard, along with a steel plow weighing about three-quarters of a ton, which came to rest practically embedded in what had been the windward side of the car.

In contrast, across South Street, near the milkhouse where Bob had been caught by the tornado, a truck had been garaged. As with the Buick, its enclosure had been lifted off and had sailed away to destruction. Unlike the car, however, there had been not the slightest damage inflicted on the truck, not a scratch or dent, not even a rear-view mirror looked askew.

Four homes on the same side of South Street as Emory Harvey's and standing close to it were demolished. In two cases, the occupants were not at home.

Directly across the street from Bob and Jane Harvey's home and adjacent to that of his parents, lived the Quinn sisters. Both were seriously injured in the sudden demolition of their home. Behind the senior Harvey's just beyond, a Mrs. Cassinari was home alone. The home was caved in by the tornado's fury and Mrs. Cassinari badly hurt.

+++

After destroying the two Harvey homesteads and the other homes on the east side of South Street, the tornado apparently lifted from the ground again, passing over Cedar Swamp and continuing on a southeasterly heading. After a mile or so, the funnel swung sharply to the left onto a northeasterly course, angling back toward Route 9.

Reaching groundward once more, the funnel caught the edge of John Walkup's barn, solidly enough to tear its roof off, then it plowed squarely into a home on Flanders Road, that of Timothy Cahill and his wife. Even as the tornado, acting like a huge, horizontally-rotating buzz saw, demolished their home, it flung Mrs. Cahill from the structure, dashing her body to the ground.

+++

Whirling along toward the northwest, the funnel remained on the ground or close to it as it approached Southboro and bore down on busy Route 9, the Boston-Worcester highway.

+++

John Personis, who commuted daily from his Worcester home to Boston was returning homeward. He had just crossed the line from Southboro into Westboro and looking ahead saw what he took to be a severe and concentrated thunderstorm bearing down on him. Mr. Personis was not surprised; since the day had been steamy and airless, without a trace of a breeze, he almost welcomed it.

What struck his car, however, lifted the vehicle into the air and spun it around. Not a single revolution, but a dizzying whirl. At least twice during the spinning, his body hung partly out of the driver's door, which had been swung open. Only his tight grip on the steering wheel prevented his being tossed completely out of the gyrating automobile.

When the car settled back to earth, it slammed down on its four tires - and on the lower half of John Personis' body; the rocker panel across his pelvis, his legs angled under the car. The vehicle had spun across the highway's median strip and had come to rest squarely in the path of eastbound traffic. The possibility of being struck by an approaching motorist who might be unable to swerve in time competed in Personis' consciousness with an excruciating pain from his lacerated buttocks and with the possibility that gasoline leaking from the half-wrecked car's ruptured gas line might somehow ignite, causing a horribly painful death by burning.

A truck from the nearby power company pulled up; its crew hurried over and managed to lift one side of the car high enough that the trapped driver could squirm out. Moments later, an obliging New York motorist agreed to reverse direction and take Mr. Personis to a Worcester hospital, where he would begin a painful but steady recovery, despite being erroneously listed as dead in a Boston newspaper, next day.

+++

Bouncing into the air again at the Southboro town line, the funnel whirled along parallel to Route 9, in fact almost above it. At about 5:40 p.m., only a mile short of the Framingham line and seventeen miles due east of Worcester, the funnel dipped to earth one final time. Curving to its left as it dropped, it demolished a dozen homes.

Mrs. Jessie Cole, who lived nearby on Turnpike Road, as Route 9 was locally known, suffered head injuries, while forty-eight-year-old Gordon Johnson of Middle Road was the most seriously injured of those who had lost their homes. He was badly battered by the tornado, sustaining injuries of the head, back, and internal organs.

A woman and her son who had pulled their car over to the side of Route 9, were blown out of their vehicle onto the road. The dazed pair staggered into the home of Joseph Noberini, a patrolman on the local police force, and collapsed in the living room as the funnel hit full force. The windows blew out, household articles began whirling around shattering to pieces as they bounced off walls and ceiling. The house remained basically intact, however.

When things quieted down, Officer Noberini's sister went next door to the home of another brother, James, who lived there with his wife and year- old son, Robert. Others were already there, digging feverishly in the wreckage. The tornado's final earthward swoop left the structure looking as though it had been accurately dive-bombed.

James Noberini, only slightly injured, was soon freed from the rubble. His wife Irmgarde, twenty-six, was dead when she was located, as was her year-old infant son.

The Fayville post office was located in the same building, and the searchers lifted the dazed postmaster, James Trioli, from the debris. A dislocated elbow and several bruises were the extent of his injuries. His wife was removed to Framingham Union Hospital, where she succumbed a few hours later.

After demolishing the post office, the funnel had bounced back into the air one last time - and dissipated. Even more suddenly than it had begun, the funnel's eighty-four minute, forty-two mile march was at an end.

10

Helping Hands

At about 5:20 p.m. on June 9, 1953, a telephone call was received at the Red Cross Chapter House in Worcester. Mrs. Eleanor Connolly, a full-time Red Cross worker, took the call. Someone on the line was saying that "a house had gone down" in the area of the Home Farm. This report initiated Red Cross involvement in the disaster relief operations in the wake of the tornado which caused more deaths in central Massachusetts than any previous natural calamity. On-scene Red Cross assistance would take many forms, and would continue for a period of about one hundred days.

Mrs. Connolly immediately alerted the Worcester Chapter's Executive Director, Mrs. Astrid Johnson, as well as the Disaster Director, Richard Tait. Her third phone call was to Connie Kitchings, a Red Cross volunteer who was asked to hurry in to the Chapter House to staff the switchboard, in anticipation of the sudden, sharp increase in the number of calls, reports and inquiries that could be expected.

As the initial radio news bulletins indicated the scope and scale of the tornado damage, Red Cross volunteers and staff workers alike flocked to the Chapter House and Worcester's hospitals. So many blood donors responded that about two hundred sixty pints were drawn that first night, and by the afternoon, less than twenty-four hours after the tornado had struck, the local chapter would find itself in the unusual position of having to turn potential donors away, and even resorting to the shipment of surplus blood to Boston for storage.

Red Cross volunteer teams in each of the hospitals which received casualties assisted in the preparation, checking and cross-checking of casualty lists, which were as complete and accurate, just twelve hours after the disaster, as could reasonably be expected.

Emergency shelters were quickly opened for the newly-homeless at the National Guard armory, Worcester Polytechnic Institute and Holy Cross College. These were staffed with Red Cross volunteers.

Extra telephone lines were hurriedly installed in the Chapter House in an attempt to stay abreast of the developing blizzard of telephone inquiries from anxious friends and relatives. By 5:00 a.m.

Wednesday morning, a scant twelve hours after the tornado's passage, about a thousand such calls had been received from all over New England and from virtually every state in the Union.

The first of eight mobile canteens began operating almost immediately in the devastated neighborhoods in Holden, Great Brook Valley and upper Burncoat Street, with a stationary canteen soon functioning at the Chapter House and with others to be set up shortly at clothing and furniture distribution centers.

+++

Within two hours of the funnel's passage across West Boylston Street, the Salvation Army's Greendale Corps headquarters was operating as an around-the-clock disaster relief center. Located on the corner of West Boylston and Francis Streets, just south of Fortin's Market, the building had been on the edge of the funnel, and had sustained minor damage.

Commanded by Major Signe Turnquist, assisted by Major Alice Thileen, the Greendale Corp's location on the edge of the devastated neighborhood caused it to quickly draw Salvation Army personnel from the Citadel on Main Street and the Corps on Belmont Street and in Quinsigamond Village.

The Salvation Army's state headquarters in Boston broadcast an appeal for other Salvation Army workers in other communities to report to Worcester and offer assistance. Many did, including Captain William Hulteen and his wife from Quincy, along with a dozen other volunteers from the same community. From Somerville came Walter Nordstrom and his wife Elsie, bringing their young son with them.

The first urns of coffee were brewed and the first of several thousand sandwiches made before nightfall on that first day. Women worked preparing the food and men drove station wagons laden with the foodstuffs throughout the storm-devastated area - at first Greendale and Burncoat Hill, soon farther afield in Great Brook Valley to the east and in the opposite direction along Brattle Street and through Brentwood and Winthrop Oaks, with many civilian volunteers giving hours of service in the emergency, while continuing to work at regular full-time jobs.

Some of the hundreds of loaves of bread and hundreds of pounds of sandwich "fixings" were purchased by the Greendale Corps. Much more, however, was donated by local grocers like Simeon Fortin who cheerfully invited the workers to step into his wind-blasted market next door and help themselves to whatever they needed, or the local dairy which donated two hundred half-pint bottles of milk daily for a week.

Donated clothing was dispensed from the Greendale Corps building on an informal, walk-in basis, based solely on need. Later, vouchers to replace lost household articles were distributed by Salvation Army personnel going door-to-door, or more often, from one house lot to the next. Offered such assistance, one woman said she doubted she was eligible, since she was a Catholic. She was assured that this made no difference whatever. Another woman wondered if the voucher could be used in part to replace her lost clothesline. "Yes," responded Major Turnquist, "for whatever you need."

+++

Soon after 5:00 p.m. state Civil Defense officials were informed of the disaster by the State Police. The state's Civil Defense Control Center in Framingham and the nine regional control centers of the state were speedily activated, with some CD units immediately ordered into the disaster area, and the balance of the agency's resources across the state put on a standby basis.

Francis Logan was driving toward Worcester at about 5:30, travelling along Route 122 as he headed home from the Rutland Veteran's Administration Hospital, where he was registrar. He had made a stop or two since leaving the hospital about forty-five minutes earlier and was annoyed to find traffic at a standstill in Holden.

He was approached by a state police lieutenant whom he knew, William Mack, who told him about the tornado. Logan, an Army Reserve Lieutenant Colonel, was also the assistant to Worcester's Civil Defense Director, Robert Maloney, a full-time city police lieutenant. Lieutenant Mack told him to report immediately to the Worcester Memorial Auditorium, which had been earlier designated as the Worcester Emergency Control Center in the event of a natural disaster.

Making his way through and around the stalled traffic as best he could, Logan headed for the auditorium at the best speed the circumstances permitted. Arriving there, he assisted in getting the call-up network operational, which, at about 6:00 p.m., began its efforts to contact CD personnel and get them into a duty status without delay.

At the same time, calls for disaster assistance were streaming in. Logan recalls urgent pleas from the Upper Burncoat Street and Greendale neighborhoods, as well as from Assumption College. Initially, the control center had to make do with just two telephones, the city's civil defense line and that of Civil Defense Region III, which was under the operational control of Mr. Harold Rossi.

Francis Logan was to be on duty for forty-eight hours straight; others undoubtedly served similar marathon stints, kept going by the fact that this was no carefully rehearsed response to a simulated disaster, but reality.

The Framingham state Control Center coordinated the dispatch of materials, supplies, equipment and personnel into the disaster area, including a thousand blankets, a thousand units of blood plasma, and two hundred blood donor sets, which were sent to Worcester from the state warehouse in Natick.

Emergency lighting units began to arrive in the disaster area from the first of one-hundred-twenty-two towns and cities which sent this type of badly-needed equipment. Twenty-eight cities and towns within Civil Defense Region III responded by sending mechanics, nurses and policemen, as well as ambulances, trucks, street sweepers, bulldozers, fire engines, mobile radio transmitters and the trained personnel to operate them. Additionally, emergency power units, chain saws and engineering equipment arrived and were immediately put to use.

+++

Francis Moy, a Worcester ham radio operator, was on his way home from his job with an electronics firm in Southbridge, and had been listening to his car radio that afternoon, or at least trying to listen. There was static all across the AM band as he kept tuning the selector knob, trying to bring in an intelligible station. By the time he crossed the Worcester line, he was able to pull in WTAG with minimal distortion.

It was probably shortly after 5:30 p.m. when Moy picked up one of the early disaster emergency reports which would shortly become continuous. All doctors and nurses were being urged to report to their affiliating hospitals without delay. He switched on his car's ham radio and tried to raise CQ Worcester, the local controller on the ten-meter band.

Moving around the band, Mr. Moy picked up the voice of Zelda Edinburg, his employer's wife, testing from her home on Coolidge Road. Moy then moved back to CQ Worcester, the emergency frequency, and began to organize other operators for whatever lay ahead - this while still driving toward his home.

Once at home, Moy, whose call sign, W1SPG was well-known to other area ham operators, immediately got on the air and served as director/controller for the net from 6 to 11 p.m. An important part of the message traffic involved receiving messages from Red Cross chapters in Greater Boston. When Moy noted the kinds and quantity of relief equipment to be sent to Worcester from these points in eastern Massachusetts he would inform the local Red Cross chapter, coordinating delivery instructions so that plasma, blankets, folding cots, rations and sundry other items could be sent where maximum and immediate utilization could be realized. Even after he relinquished his network control function, Moy stayed on the air throughout that hectic night, continuing to expedite message traffic.

+++

Howie Fuller of Worcester, call sign W1JWM, was with his family in Shrewsbury working on their new home when the tornado passed through the town. The site was not directly in the path of tornado, so the Fullers, who sought shelter in their car, thought they were merely waiting out the passage of a summer storm. This they continued to believe, even though the fringe winds felled a large tree limb which dented a fender, and a huge hailstone struck the windshield, cracking it. Only upon emerging from the car and hearing the wail of several sirens around them did it dawn on them that something was seriously amiss. They turned on their car radio and found that the northern part of Worcester, where they lived, had been heavily damaged by a tornado.

Soon, a Shrewsbury police cruiser appeared. The officer, who knew about the Fullers' ten-meter, two-way radio, asked them to try to raise Worcester, since the tornado's swath through the town had knocked out all power and severed communications. Mr. Fuller agreed, and they drove to the Shrewsbury police station.

At 6:10 p.m., when he began to transmit, Fuller found that two operators in the Great Brook Valley housing development were already on the air. Through one of them, he relayed an urgent request from Shrewsbury police to the Worcester Gas Company to shut off the gas mains in the ravaged Maple Avenue and South Street neighborhoods. Already, ruptured gas lines in those hard-hit neighborhoods were proving to be a hindrance to rescue operations as well as a potential explosion and fire hazard.

From the police station, Fuller continued sending messages to Worcester for police, civil defense, Red Cross and utility companies, with an occasional personal message of an especially critical nature sandwiched into the traffic. When a telephone company car equipped with a two-way radio appeared, Mr. Fuller turned message traffic responsibility over to its operator, then drove to Worcester with his family to check on the condition of their home.

Finding their dwelling still standing but windowless, badly battered and in general uninhabitable, the Fullers decided to return to Shrewsbury. First, however, they headed in the opposite direction - west, since Mr. Fuller wanted to check on radio station WTAG's Holden transmitter. The tornado had passed by, more than a mile to the south, the transmitter was undamaged and the station's signal strength was unaffected.

Telephone communication with the city had been knocked out, however, so Fuller found himself functioning as he had in Shrewsbury. He sent several messages for the Holden police, who were particularly anxious to learn the whereabouts or condition of the Oslund baby, who had been snatched from his mother's arms two hours earlier. They were also trying to locate another missing child, probably Larry Faucher, who along with Liisa Hakala, were the only other two youngsters killed in Holden. Confirmed word that the missing children had been located would mean releasing two hundred fifty searchers - volunteers for other disaster recovery work.

Returning to Shrewsbury later that evening, the Fullers dropped their children at their grandmother's, then headed back to the police station where they resumed their handling of message traffic and continued for about eight hours, shutting down at 5:00 a.m. on Wednesday morning.

+++

Father Timothy Harrington, curate at St. Bernard's Church in Worcester and part-time assistant to Father David Sullivan, director of the new Diocese of Worcester's modest Catholic Charities organization, left his tiny office at 11 Ward Street at about 4:40 p.m. He drove a few blocks to the St. Agnes Guild in a heavy downpour, and ran into the chapel there for a few quiet moments of prayer and meditation. By five o'clock, he was back behind the wheel of his car, headed for the Nazareth Orphanage in Leicester, a few miles to the southwest.

Father Harrington was planning to take some of the Sisters of Mercy who served at the orphanage, to Our Lady of the Rosary Church in the Burncoat area of Worcester to hear a talk by a psychologist. He tried to call the pastor there to confirm this, but was not able to get through, and assumed that the Rosary's telephone was temporarily out of order.

Going ahead with his plans, the cleric and his passengers drove back to Worcester, stopping first at the sisters' mother house on High Street, opposite St. Paul's cathedral. They arrived at around 7:00, and were met by a visibly distraught sister. Assuming that the arrivals had heard of the unfolding disaster, she remarked: "Isn't it terrible about the tornado in Greendale" or something like it. This was the manner in which Fr. Harrington first heard of the calamity which would tax the resources, both human and material, of the fledgling Catholic Charities to the limit.

Fr. Sullivan had already been broadcasting on a local radio station that sleeping accommodations for children without shelter would be provided at the Nazareth Home, as well as at St. John's orphanage and at St. Gabriel's Home in the city. Hearing as well an urgent appeal for blood donors, Fr. Harrington drove immediately to St. Vincent Hospital. Here, at the Worcester hospital furthest from the affected area, he found himself at the end of a long line of prospective donors, so he reluctantly left.

Catholic Charities had also been leased space in the corner of one floor of the old Glenwood Building. originally a mill and in 1953, used for the offices of the Worcester Housing Authority. Wondering what would be happening there, Fr. Harrington called and got Barbara Kessler, a social worker. Asked what the situation was, she replied simply: "We're overwhelmed."

People were arriving by the busload and truckload from Great Brook Valley, some seemingly in a state of shock, others on the edge of hysteria, having been separated from family members and not knowing, in some cases, whether these were alive or dead. It occurred to the Father that the presence of the Sisters of Mercy would have a calming effect on the hapless victims, and so he drove a number of the nuns the short distance from the mother house. The sisters immediately set about giving what comfort they could to the victims, especially to the children, some of whom had been separated from their parents.

+++

The first tornado victims arrived at Hahnemann Hospital, the closest hospital to the devastated area in northern Worcester, at about 5:30. Hospital personnel had no inkling of the disaster's magnitude "when a man, blood streaming down his face, staggered across the lawn and into the door". According to an account in the Worcester Telegram, the man was initially assumed to be the victim of a nearby auto accident.

Within minutes of his arrival, however, the hospital driveways were rapidly filling with cars, trucks and station wagons, and victims were being carried into the building on "doors, boards, mattresses and sleeping bags". The notes of the hospital's superintendent indicate that more than eighty persons in need of medical attention arrived within ten minutes.

Three doctors had been on duty when the influx of injured began; within an hour there were more than forty physicians present, all working at top speed. Every available square foot of surgical and delivery room units were hastily preempted as makeshift operating rooms.

Minor wounds, according to the hospital superintendent, were treated wherever room could be found - in the library, the dining room, the accident ward and in corridors. The result of a hastily-organized system of triage, was to send all patients identified as having serious head injuries to City Hospital. By 8:00 p.m., the overwhelming pressure of numbers began to lessen as these and other serious cases were sent to one or another of the three larger hospitals in the city.

In all, more than three hundred were treated at Hahnemann, according to the estimates of hospital officials. The total number will never be known with any certainty, since it includes many slightly injured who walked into the hospital, received what little treatment was required, then simply left, without any patient record having been made.

+++

Albert Riopel and his wife Ellen lived at 4 Shattuck Street, just across Brittan Lane, which ran beside the hospital. Mr. Riopel - "Hop" to everyone who knew him - and a neighbor, Fred Salmon, hurriedly removed the hinges from a door and began using it as a litter to carry injured individuals into their home from the overflow of persons sitting or lying on the lawns adjacent to Hahnemann.

+++

At one point during the hectic evening, the hospital suddenly lost all power, but in just over a minute's time an emergency generator kicked in and continued running, to the immense relief of all in the building.

+++

No fewer then ten women from Worcester and nearby towns gave birth to babies at Hahnemann that day. One, Mrs. Emily Novakoski, was delivered of a daughter at 5:25 p.m., ten minutes after the funnel chewed across Burncoat Street, only a mile and a half to the north.

Another new mother, Irene Amsden of Rutland, had been delivered of a daughter earlier that day. She looked out a window of the maternity ward and saw below her on the lawn a number of people, all injured in one way or another. The westering sun gave a reddish tinge to the victims, a morbid visual effect in the eyes of the woman watching from above.

+++

Dr. S. Alden Guild had delivered one of the babies at Hahnemann that day, and at 5:30 was en route home to Grafton. He stopped at Fred Walton's electronics shop to pick up a portable radio for the family's imminent vacation.

While he was in the shop, a call was received by the owner telling him of storm-wrought devastation in Great Brook Valley and asking him to bring some needed electrical equipment there as quickly as possible. Not realizing the call's implications, the doctor arrived home a few minutes later.

Mrs. Guild told him that the telephone had rung, but because of all the electricity in the air she had not lifted the receiver. They would later learn that the call had been from Hahnemann. In the meantime, they heard of the disaster on the radio and Dr. Guild soon headed for Westboro where he would spend hours treating victims.

Another staff member, Dr. Fred Dupree, received a phone call at his summer cottage at Lake Waushacum in Sterling, twelve miles north of Worcester. Notified of the emergency shortly after 6:00 p.m., it took him two hours to reach Hahnemann because of traffic restrictions into the city on Route 12 from the north, and a consequent detour through Holden.

Dr. I. Gerald Shelby, another Hahnemann affiliate, was at his office near the center of Shrewsbury. He was close enough to the funnel to see debris flying through the air. When he began to appreciate just how widespread was the devastation, Dr. Shelby began making the rounds of some of his patients. When he saw the Weagle barn in ruins, he was surprised that Steven Weagle, who had been inside the structure, had survived the demolition of the building.

His youngest patient was Marlene Fisher, whom he had delivered in March. After struggling up ravaged South Street hill, he found that she had been killed.

Dr. Harold Constantian, a Hahnemann internist, had been in the house where he lived with two other interns which was owned by the hospital. Hurrying across the few hundred feet of open space to the hospital, Dr. Constantian was nearly swept off his feet by strong winds, although the funnel was a good distance to the northward. He made it to the hospital without losing his footing, however, and was there when the first victims began to arrive.

Dr. Constantian helped in the hurried discharge procedure under which many post-operative patients were sent home, including several who had undergone relatively serious surgery only a day or two before. Then he was given surgical responsibilities by Dr. Ljungberg, the hospital's chief surgeon. Those duties involved assisting during surgery on some of the more serious cases, and working independently in the treatment and suturing of numerous lacerations. Dr. Constantian recalls that during these same busy hours, two orthopedic specialists, Dr. Perkins and Dr. Matern, were busily engaged in examining and treating fractures.

+++

Still another Hahnemann affiliate, Dr. Robert Cox, had seen the last of the afternoon's patients at his home at 48 Kenwood Avenue, off Burncoat Street. His home was located midway between Hahnemann and the southern side of the funnel as it crossed Burncoat; about three-quarters of a mile from each.

Despite the distance from the tornado, Mrs. Cox saw the trees in front of their home bent double by the force of the wind, moments after the Cox children had run inside from their neighborhood play. Then a neighbor, Mrs. Reitzell, who lived a block away, called them with the initial report that a tornado had passed not far away. The Coxes went outside and looking down the street to their left, could see a looming blackness receding.

Since Dr. Cox was an affiliate at City Hospital as well as at Hahnemann, he drove as quickly as he could to the former, where he was soon in the children's ward, doing triage on the youngsters with dirt-and-debris-laden lacerations, some with glass fragments still embedded. Assisted by nurses, the two physicians examined the children, pinned a tag to each briskly describing the injury and directing measures to be taken. Then the children were passed along to other medical personnel for treatment.

+++

One of the physicians hurrying to Hahnemann Hospital in the wake of the initial report of a heavy influx of injured persons was Dr. Robert Johnson, one of only two neurosurgeons in central Massachusetts in 1953. Having moved to the city only a few weeks earlier, Dr. Johnson was able to make progress toward the hospital along traffic-choked Lincoln Street by driving against the traffic in the wrong lane.

At Hahnemann, Dr. Johnson moved through the mass of patients seeking out those who had appeared to suffer head traumas. He identified several cases of depressed skull fractures, others with compound fractures of the skull. One or two victims of severe head injuries had either just died or were about to succumb.

Particularly frustrating for him as a physician trying to employ his time as effectively as possible, were the cases of several women with long hair, matted with freshly-drying blood. Having no more efficient way to remove the hair to permit assessment and treatment of the wound, the doctor was compelled to wield a pair of scissors. More often than not, snipping the hair down to the bloody scalp, would disclose a laceration on the scalp; a laceration perhaps an inch in length, bloody and painful, but hardly classifying as a serious wound.

Some of the really severe neurological cases, however, were forwarded by Dr. Johnson to City Hospital to be treated there by the area's other neurosurgeon, Dr. John Carmody. Other patients needing the same type of treatment were stabilized to the degree possible, then sent to Memorial Hospital, whence Dr. Johnson soon went himself later in the evening. He began operating on the first of these patients at about midnight, continuing in surgery through the night.

+++

Staff at large St. Vincent's Hospital in the southeastern part of the city were alerted to the disaster and mobilized their considerable medical resources for the expected surge of casualties - a surge which never materialized. During the early and middle hours of the evening a total of twenty-seven tornado victims were brought to St. Vincent's. One reason for the lack of victim influx to the degree experienced by Hahnemann and Memorial was in the extra distance to St. Vincent's from the impacted area; about six miles from the damage zone. Additionally, as already noted, head trauma cases were vectored to City Hospital in many cases.

It should be noted, however, that among the twenty-seven victims arriving at St. Vincent's were a number of serious surgical cases being forwarded from the smaller, less well-equipped Hahnemann and bypassing the already overcrowded Memorial.

Dr. Raymond Gadbois, on the staff of St. Vincent's upon hearing of the tornado hastened to Assumption College, his alma mater, where he was attending physician for members of the college's religious community. He busied himself dressing the injuries of the priests, nuns and brothers, evaluating the more serious injuries, and helping prepare the injured for transport to Memorial Hospital.

Arriving at St. Vincent's in the early evening, Dr. Gadbois noted the spillover effect from the two overcrowded hospitals. Receiving a number of critically-injured victims from Hahnemann because of a higher level of care accessible at St. Vincent's, Dr. Gadbois and other staff members found themselves fully occupied.

+++

Doctor George Dunlop, a physician on the staff of Worcester's Memorial Hospital, had spent a pleasant late-afternoon couple of hours chatting with Clarence Brigham, the director of the American Antiquarian Society, a library for scholarly research in early American history located in the city. When he arrived home, at around 5:30, his wife told him that there had been an urgent call from the hospital asking that the doctor report there as quickly as possible.

Doctor Ivan Spear, a physician on the staffs of both Memorial and Hahnemann hospitals, had been en route to Memorial from his Elm Street office at about 5:15 p.m. when high winds forced him to pull over to the side of the road. At about this time, the tornado funnel was passing some three miles to the north.

Arriving at Memorial shortly before Dr. Dunlop, Dr. Spear was in advance of the onslaught of casualties as well. He began making his patient rounds, but before he finished, a telephone call was received at the hospital in which the caller said: "A house had blown down and they're coming in for treatment." The "they" turned out to be a small part of what soon became an avalanche of humanity.

The Memorial Hospital is located just east of the city's center on Belmont Street, a heavily-travelled east-west artery. Driving up to the hospital, Dr. Dunlop was passed through a cordon of Worcester police and civilian volunteers struggling to expedite the busy, rush-hour traffic past the hospital, diverting it away from the front of the building to the greatest extent possible, while making every effort to keep the horseshoe drive in front of the hospital as accessible as possible to the numerous ambulances and other casualty-laden vehicles which were arriving at Memorial in ever-increasing numbers.

Many of the near-ambulatory cases were being deposited on the hospital's front lawn, a few on ambulance litters or stretchers, some on blankets or having been laid directly on the grass itself. The congestion and confusion would increase steadily throughout the course of the next hour.

Probably no more graphic yet accurate description of this chaotic scene could be given than Dr. Dunlop's own words. The physician, a veteran of two years of post-combat surgery in the Pacific had seen or had been personally involved in treating, nearly every conceivable type of wound, Still, the enormity of this sudden tragedy comes through:

"As we approached the door, the street, walks and grounds were swarming with crowds of people, many attracted by the sirens, who came to watch the injured [being] unloaded. Others came to volunteer their services, and still others desperately attempted to locate members of their family.

Inside, one was met with a wave of humid heat, noise and confusion. Casualties were lying on the floor, desks and stretchers. Whole swarms of people were moving about, some working, some with looks of desperation stepping over bodies, peering under blankets, looking for loved ones. In one room, used as an office and workroom for hospital volunteers, were a variety of casualties. One woman with a broken arm and dislocated hip, appeared to stare through one open eyeball, glazed as if hit by a sandblast. One woman was dead. Several had minor lacerations. In a corner an obese male lay on his back with a head and chest injury, vomiting and aspirating gastric contents. Many had needles in their arms attached to intravenous solutions, with large swellings of fluids in subcutaneous tissue. I describe these details simply to give a picture of the confusion that existed as physicians began to arrive on the scene. Although I had seen hundreds of war casualties, I had never seen more dirt, gravel and grass than had been ground into the clothes, skin and wounds of these poor individuals."

Dr. Spear remembers a boy being brought in with a daggerlike shard of glass through his arm and penetrating his chest. Before treatment was commenced, the boy moved his arm, snapping the shard in two and leaving the tip embedded in his chest. The embedded portion was not at first detected by medical personnel, but when spotted later was carefully and successfully removed.

Doctor Foster Vibber, a neurologist, arrived and took in the Outpatient Department at a glance. He then seated himself calmly behind the front desk, smoking a pipe and surveying the crowded emergency ward, into which more victims were walking, hobbling or being carried every minute. To one of the senior staff nurses who saw him sitting there, the very image of tranquility and composure, Dr. Vibber's demeanor as he surveyed the hectic scene before him was deliberately calculated to convey an image of unruffled professional competence which would prevail, even in the present crisis.

Slowly, as the evening progressed, nurses and doctors, aided by dozens of lay volunteers, many with Red Cross or other basic medical training, began winning their battle to bring order out of chaos. By 3 a.m. the most critical cases had been treated and were for the most part stabilized.

Bed space was obtained by summarily discharging, according to Dr, Dunlop, more than eighty percent of the patients who had been occupying beds at Memorial when the onslaught of disaster victims commenced. The author was initially incredulous at this high an "eviction rate", until reminded that patients in 1953 were not subject to the "up and out" demands of medical insurance providers in the early 1990s. Thus the effect on these patients was in most cases merely a sudden interruption of a leisurely period of convalescence, which could safely be completed in the patient's home. Dr. Dunlop recalls with grim amusement one particular woman whose indignation turned to real anger when faced with summary discharge. Over her heated protests, the discharge was effected.

Eva Jones, a registered nurse from Holden, had been doing special duty with a youngster in the pediatric ward. She had gone down to the cafeteria for supper with some other nurses at a quarter to six. Almost as soon as they arrived in the dining room, a hospital janitor told them that the housing projects in Great Brook Valley had been leveled.

They walked into the emergency ward and saw that the first disaster victims had already arrived. Those who were not unconscious were sitting silently, staring straight ahead, speaking only when spoken to, and then in as few words as possible. At a glance, Mrs. Jones could see that many of these, if not most, were in shock.

Back on the third floor once again, Mrs. Jones supervised the consolidation of some of the older children in the wards of the pediatric section, thereby freeing up ten beds for the use of the newly-arrived children. Solemn-faced children, each carefully tagged, were brought to the third floor, where they were carefully examined for subcutaneous shards of glass or other foreign matter. If none were found, the child was scrubbed by a nurse's aide or by one of the civilian volunteers, and put to bed. The most seriously injured children had been identified in the emergency room and taken straight into surgery.

Mrs. Jones was supervising a staff of increasingly overburdened nurses and nurse's aides, and so the civilian volunteers were welcome and appreciated. Among the volunteer helpers were several members of the Junior League, ladies belonging to what was, in 1953, still known as "society". One lady was assigned to the job of bottle-feeding an infant. Although obviously anxious to be of service, the woman confessed to Mrs. Jones in a low, anxious voice that she had never given a bottle to a baby before, and wasn't sure how to go about it.

"Just hold the baby on your lap," Mrs. Jones told her, "hold the nipple of the bottle in front of the baby's face, and he'll do the rest." The woman did so, the infant responded as expected and Mrs. Jones went quickly about her myriad duties.

Spontaneously, people who lived in the neighborhood of Memorial Hospital began making sandwiches and bringing them in by the boxful. Some of the welcome sandwiches found their way up to the children's ward where Mrs. Jones oversaw their distribution.

+++

Doctor Richard Hunter, a Memorial staff physician, was en route to a restaurant with his wife when he heard the disaster reports on his car radio. A report of devastation in the Great Brook Valley housing project was followed by a request that all physicians who were able, report to the projects as soon as possible. Hunter did so, but found little need of his services, so he drove to Memorial without delay where he immediately shouldered his share of the surgical cases.

+++

One of the most unusual cases treated by Dr. Dunlop involved a man who had been at home with his wife and child. Hearing the characteristic "freight train" noise swelling in intensity, he reached to close the front door. The door was ajar and difficult to close, since it rubbed against the thick rug beneath.

As the man struggled with the heavy wooden door, the tornado struck. According to Dr. Dunlop, the house was largely demolished, and the woman and child were both killed in the collapse of the structure. The man himself was sucked out through the closed aluminum screen door, the top half of which had folded down over the lower portion. The man was on his back, facing upward, when he was pulled across the jagged lower half of the ornamental initial built into the door, like a piece of cheese across a grater.

The jagged metal scraped away skin and muscle tissue right down to the ribs. showing white through the bloody wound. A serious wound, sustained in a most unusual fashion. But one of the myriad medical problems faced by Dr. Dunlop and others on that harrowing evening.

+++

One unusual medical condition in particular was observed in a number of tornado victims, including a half-dozen admitted to

Holden District Hospital. A combination of plummeting atmospheric pressure and the "appalling suction of the tornado", according to Dr. Edward J. Crane, Holden Hospital's chief of staff, caused a sudden, enormous expansion of the lungs of some patients, "exploding human chests the way it pulled the walls of houses outward". Dr. Crane, a cardio-pulmonary specialist, compared the effect to that observed in victims of atomic explosions.

Surprisingly, Dr. John Carmody, chief surgeon at City Hospital, could attribute positively only a single death among the victims in his hospital's morgue to this particular medical trauma. Among the other Worcester hospitals surveyed, the chest injuries among patients did not appear to have been sustained in this manner.

To conclude with Dr. Dunlop's account:

"The cases of shock were segregated and given transfusion. [The collapsed veins typical of persons in shock, coupled with inadequate and improper lighting made this routine medical procedure unusually difficult, according to Dunlop.] The patients with large lacerations and major fractures were moved into the operating room suite. The medical men sewed up minor wounds. The head and chest cases were seen by the proper specialists and by early morning three hundred thirty eight cases had been examined and cared for.

Early the next morning, the staff met, discussed the problems, segregated and assigned the cases. The hospital was closed to all but emergencies."

+++

Dr. John T. B. Carmody had left City Hospital for his Paxton home at around 5:00 p.m. that Tuesday afternoon. Driving west on Chandler Street, he wondered why so many of the cars approaching from the opposite direction were covered with mud. The driver of one of these cars appeared to be terrified, Carmody noted.

Walking into his home a few minutes later, Dr. Carmody was greeted by his ringing telephone. The Hahnemann Hospital switchboard operator was on the line describing a bus accident in Great Brook Valley and requesting that Dr. Carmody come at once. No sooner had he agreed to return to the city and hung up the phone then the phone was ringing again. This time it was City Hospital. The caller told him that a major tornado had plowed across northern Worcester, leaving an unknown number of casualties in its wake. The doctor headed back to City Hospital without delay, arriving before all but the earliest victims.

Doctor Carmody called his neurological counterpart at Hahnemann, Dr. Johnson, and the two agreed that Johnson, after initially dressing the head wounds, would mark the dressing to indicate the type of injury; compound fracture, brain laceration, or whatever designation was applicable. Many of these cases were dispatched by ambulance to Carmody at City where he undertook surgical procedures.

City's neurological facilities were far better than any other Worcester Hospital, having been steadily upgraded over the course of the preceding fifteen years by Dr. Carmody, in response to the fact that the victims of accidents or assaults who had sustained head injuries were routinely brought to City by local police.

Someone in authority at City, possibly the chief of surgery, had, upon learning of the tornado, ordered that all doctors affiliated with the hospital report for duty. As a consequence, numerous obstetricians, gynecologists and pediatricians, as well as ear, nose and throat specialists, among others, were on hand, when the influx of patients began.

The collective confusion resulting from the arrival of the injured, their relatives, friends, and the morbidly curious, reminded Dr. Carmody of the accounts he had read of the original Bedlam, London's medieval hospital for the insane.

Carmody recalls operating on a dozen delicate and complicated neurosurgical cases, working through the night and most of the following day. Over half of the ninety seven admissions to City Hospital were cases of this type. Almost all of the most serious cases fell into this category or orthopedic. As a neurosurgeon, Dr. Carmody was particularly struck by the manner in which a half dozen of the persons who were dead when brought to City had succumbed. In Dr. Carmody's own words, reported shortly thereafter in the American Journal of Surgery:

"... it was noted that the entire intracranial contents had been entirely removed. On lifting the scalp flaps, I was amazed to note that the skull vault contained no cerebral tissue, similar to what one would expect on viewing the intracranial cavity following a postmortem removal of the brain. The exact mechanism of this type of injury is, of course, open to much speculation. It would seem that following crushing injuries to the skull, a tremendous suction had suddenly removed the entire cranial contents."

+++

In an effort to balance compassion against efforts to give the best patient care possible under extremely trying conditions,

Worcester's hospitals on that confusion-filled evening were forced to strictly regulate visits by relatives to those patients receiving treatment for tornado- related injuries. Although not deluged with victims to the extent of Hahnemann or Memorial, City Hospital found it expedient to make efforts at visitor control. At least one woman unintentionally circumvented this policy in an unusual manner.

George Logee, who worked in the construction trades, had been hurt in a construction site on Chino Avenue, on the southern edge of Great Brook Valley. He had suffered an injury to an arm which was serious enough to warrant admission to City Hospital.

Mrs. Logee was driven to the hospital that evening by a close female friend of hers and the woman's husband. When the three entered the hospital, and before they had a chance to state their business, an admitting official noticed that Mrs. Logee's friend was in an advanced state of pregnancy and appeared about to deliver.

In reality she was just beginning her ninth month, but before she could correct the erroneous assumption, she and her two companions were hurriedly passed into the hospital proper, whereupon they managed, after making an inquiry or two, to locate Mr. Logee. Patient and visitors enjoyed the recounting of the incident. The harried nurses, once the mistake was realized, allowed to visit to continue.

11

The Guardsmen

National Guard Lieutenant Colonel John J. Pakula, in civilian life, the administrator of the Veteran's Administration hospital in Brockton, Massachusetts, arrived at his Worcester home between 5:45 and 6:00 p.m. that Tuesday evening. Upon arrival there, his wife told him that there had been an urgent phone call from his battalion operations officer, Major Deignan.

Returning Deignan's call immediately, Pakula was told that there were confirmed reports of extensive and severe damage in the Great Brook Valley area, and that there was a distinct possibility that the assistance of the National Guard might be required. The colonel then told his S-3 to send troops, as they arrived at the armory for that evening's drill, to the affected area without delay. He then hurriedly changed into his uniform, jumped back into his car and headed for the Wheaton Square armory.

His route took him down Belmont Street toward Lincoln Square. In front of Memorial Hospital, at which casualty-laden vehicles were beginning to arrive at an increasing rate, two Civil Defense workers were stopping through traffic to make the hospital's main entrance more readily accessible to these emergency vehicles. While one of them scolded the colonel for trying to get through, the other planted himself directly in front of Pakula's automobile.

Giving up his futile efforts to convince the pair of this own urgent need to proceed, the colonel merely shifted into gear and told the man blocking him to move if he wished to avoid being run over. The man hastily sidestepped, and Pakula drove the last three-quarters of a mile to the armory.

Pakula in 1953 commanded the Worcester-based First Battalion of the 181st Infantry Regiment, which in turn was a component of the 26th Infantry "Yankee" Division. At about the beginning of that year, the colonel had managed to obtain authorization for the majority of the battalion's companies to drill on the same evening - Tuesday. Although the battalion's service company had met the previous night, and Company D normally drilled on Thursday evenings, the headquarters company and the three rifle companies - A, B and C, a total of about two hundred men, were scheduled to report to the armory within two hours.

Standard procedure only required drilling Guardsmen to report in time to be ready to fall-in for personnel inspection in the uniform of the day by about 7:45 p.m. Many men, however, would arrive early, others were coming sooner than planned, having received a telephone call alerting them to the need for early reporting. The commanding officers of the first two battalion companies not scheduled to drill that night were also directed to institute emergency call-up procedures. The 181st Infantry Regiment staff officers were being alerted by majors Paul Forhan and Walter Whitney.

Major Forhan, the regiment's plans and training officer (S-2) had decided a couple of hours earlier, not to try to squeeze in a late-afternoon round of golf at the Pakachoag Golf Club, since possible showers threatened and the sky off to the northwest was ominously dark. At about 5:30 he received a call from fellow Guard member Tom Deedy, who told Forhan that he'd just heard a radio news bulletin which told of a tornado having struck the northern part of the city.

Major Forhan went immediately to the armory and with the magnitude of the disaster becoming clearer by the minute, placed a call to the commanding officer of the 181st, Colonel Bigelow, at his home in Natick, urging him to authorize an emergency activation of the entire regiment without delay.

Bigelow immediately agreed, calling his own subordinate on the regimental staff, as well as Colonel Murphy, assistant adjutant general of the state. Murphy was contacted at Holy Cross College, where he was enjoying his alma mater's homecoming festivities. Colonel Murphy also gave his official blessing to the emergency mobilization.

As the call-up was getting underway, an amusing incident occurred at the Wheaton Square armory. Witnessed by several of the author's sources. A dapper, well-dressed, middle-aged gentleman, sporting an old-fashioned straw boater, strolled into the armory and began trying to buttonhole one or another of the busy guardsmen, asking for information about the disaster. Perhaps assuming the man was either a newspaper reporter whom they did not recognize or merely a curious civilian, no one bothered with him.

Some time later the man reappeared, this time in the uniform of a brigadier general, establishing his identity as Otis Whitney, assistant commander of the 26th Division. One young enlisted guardsman who had been posted outside the armory and who had been unable to prevent the unauthorized civilian from entering the building was especially chagrined.

+++

George Bilodeau was enjoying an afternoon of relaxation on the shores of Solomon Pond in Northboro, ten miles east of Worcester. His employer, the Clinton Buick Company, was holding its annual outing. Late in the afternoon as the function was drawing to a close, he saw in the distance a black cloud sliding along. It was miles away to the southwest, and if Bilodeau gave it any thought, it was the assumption that it was merely an unusually concentrated and fast-moving thunderstorm.

Arriving in Clinton in the early evening, Bilodeau, a corporal in Clinton's Company M of the 181st, soon received a phone call alerting him to the unit's emergency call-up. Even when learning that a tornado had cut across the county, including populous Worcester, he did not immediately connect the disaster with what he had seen from the beach in Northboro.

+++

Private Ronald Davidson was one of Company M's newest and youngest members, having been sworn-in exactly one year earlier, on June 9, 1952, shortly before being graduated from Clinton High School. He and three friends drove from Clinton to Worcester as soon as they heard what had happened.

Stopped at the northern fringe of the tornado's path, near the Curtis Apartment complex, the young men saw a cow, head down, painfully making its way along the side of the road, a two-by-four plank protruding from its rib cage. The cow was almost certainly one of the Home Farm herd, and when the young men came upon a police officer a few moments later, they pointed out the suffering animal to him. Drawing his service revolver, the officer ended the animal's suffering.

Self-consciously helpless in the face of the calamity, the quartet drove the dozen miles back to Clinton. Receiving a phone call directing him to report to the armory on Chestnut Street, Davidson would soon be returning to the devastated area, along with fifty other members of Company M.

+++

Grover "Buddy" Wittig, a Clinton plumber in his early twenties had been working in Worcester that afternoon, helping to complete construction of the Lincoln Plaza shopping center, first of its kind in the city. He headed down Lincoln Street around 4:30 in the afternoon, curving left onto Boylston Street and passing the Curtis Apartments where he had worked as a plumber in 1951 and '52 while the large apartment complex was being constructed.

At home in Clinton, Wittig saw some bits of debris sifting down to the earth, as though from a distant fire. Very soon thereafter, Wittig, a Sergeant First Class in Company M, acting more on a hunch than anything else, headed for the Clinton armory, although it was not the company's drill night.

By the time he arrived, he had heard the first news broadcast describing the tornado and quickly got on the phone, "rounding up" ten or twelve unit members and telling them to get to the armory without delay.

In a single army two-and-a-half ton truck and without formal orders or authorization of any kind, Wittig and his men headed for Worcester via Route 110, through West Boylston. They were passed through the police cordon at the Summit, just north of the tornado's path across West Boylston Street. The devastation which greeted them was appalling; most people in the affected area had emerged from an initial state of benumbed disbelief, but there was little apparent organization or direction.

So far as the sergeant and the other Guardsmen could tell, all casualties in the immediate area, other than the numerous slightly injured, had been removed to hospitals. Feeling that he had perhaps acted in haste, but certain that Guard presence in force would soon be occurring, Sergeant Wittig and his little force headed back to the Clinton armory, to become part of a large-scale response, later the same evening.

+++

Major Walter Whitney had arrived at his Holden Street home in Shrewsbury, just down the road and across the city line from Worcester's Great Brook Valley. He had just returned from Ft. Devens, where he had gone with other members of the 181st Infantry Regiment. The major had driven out and back in his own automobile and had arrived home at about 5:00 p.m.

About fifteen minutes later, Whitney heard the freight-train roar of the approaching tornado, saw the huge black clouds in the sky to the southwest and ran for his movie camera. The camera was empty of film, and by the time Major Whitney found some and loaded the camera, the tornado had brushed past a quarter-mile to the south, crossed the northern tip of Lake Quinsigamond and had begun its climb toward Shrewsbury center.

Whitney had a fairly good idea of what it was that had barrelled past. He walked up sloping Holden Street to its intersection with Route 70. Looking across at the two Great Brook Valley housing projects brought confirmation. Double-timing it back to his driveway, the major jumped into his car and turned left onto Route 70, which, as Lincoln Street, would take him to the armory.

The impeded flow of traffic was already backing up toward him, and a quick look told Whitney that Lincoln Street was impassable in both directions opposite the Curtis Apartments. He thereupon headed up East Mountain Street towards the intersection of West Boylston Street at the Summit.

There was a huge tree across the road near that intersection, with an army truck pulled up to it, its passage also prevented by the massive roadblock. The truck was a National Guard vehicle, one of several in a small medical company convoy which had made a run from the Wheaton Square armory to Fort Devens under Major Whitney's direction and which had left the fort for Worcester a few minutes after the officer.

Fortunately there was a power saw aboard the truck, with which the tree was cut into several huge sections. Then, using the strong braided wire cable on the drum which was mounted on the truck's bumper, the heavy sections were lifted out of the truck's path sufficiently far to allow the truck and Major Whitney to continue toward the armory.

By a circuitous route over Norton Company's private streets, Whitney bypassed the carnage on West Boylston Street where the funnel had sucked up a good part of the Diamond Match lumberyard, spewing it against Assumption College and taking several lives in the process. Whitney reached the Wheaton Square armory at about 6:30 p.m.

Many First Battalion members customarily arrived early, to play cards or socialize, to sharpen military skills or in the case of some others, to get up an impromptu basketball game. Tonight there would be no personnel inspection nor any classroom instruction in military subjects, and the men who arrived early had heard of the disaster either through a radio bulletin or through a telephone call directing them to report without delay.

+++

Norman Atterstrom, who had been brushed by the tornado moments after leaving Reed Rolled Thread Company in Holden, was one such individual. As Lieutenant Atterstrom, executive officer of Company B, he knew how important it was to assume his military duties as quickly as possible. He had made it to the Summit, where he encountered the stalled National Guardsmen at about the same time as Major Whitney, although approaching the choke point from the opposite direction.

He joined the medical company in its efforts at finding an accessible route to the armory and recalls the incident of the tree across the road, with the truck winching huge sections of log out of the way, like an elephant, half-lifting, half-dragging a large teak log.

It was after six when Atterstrom and the others reached the armory. As soon as Atterstrom changed into fatigues, Major Whitney, who had already begun pushing people out to the damaged areas, put the lieutenant in charge of the first truckload of men headed for the Clark Street section of the storm-wracked Burncoat neighborhood.

+++

Classical High School senior Jack Ronayne had finished class day activities by late afternoon and walked down to Harrington Corner with his girlfriend, who would take a bus home. Long noted as one of the windiest spots in Worcester, gusts of wind on what had been an airless, sultry afternoon had caused Judy to struggle briefly to keep her fashionably full skirt from billowing up around her shoulders.

With Judy safely aboard the bus, Jack, who lived in the Pleasant Street/Newton Square neighborhood, headed for home. He had not been home long when he received a phone call from a cousin, Eleanor Lang, on Norrback Avenue, four miles to the north.

"Roofs are flying over my house," Eleanor announced, much to Jack's consternation.

Able to offer Eleanor little in the way of enlightenment, the conversation was soon terminated. When Jack hung up, he decided he might as well get an early start for the armory, where his National Guard unit, Company B, would be drilling in a little more than two hours.

As Jack headed down Pleasant Street on foot, Corporal Frederick Daly, also a member of Company B and headed for the armory, picked Jack up and the two arrived at their destination a few minutes after six.

As soon as Jack entered the armory he was buttonholed by Major Deignan, First Battalion operations officer, and told to change into his uniform, requisition a jeep and report back to Deignan - on the double - when this had been done. Minutes later, Private Ronayne at the wheel, he and Major Deignan set out to personally evaluate the tornado damage in northern Worcester.

It is entirely possible, even probable that Ronayne and Deignan were the first two Guardsmen to tour the major damage swath from West Boylston Street and Assumption College across Burncoat Hill down Clark Street, past hard-hit Uncatena and into Great Brook Valley. The pair returned to the armory, where Deignan made a full report to Colonel Pakula, already busy with battalion and regimental staffs in planning efforts to commit maximum manpower to the field at the earliest possible moment.

Meanwhile, Private Ronayne and Sergeant Richard Herbst, also of Company B, returned to the devastated area once again, in Ronayne's jeep. There, for the rest of the evening and far into the night they drove around the Burncoat-Clark Street neighborhood, seeking to offer what humanitarian assistance they could, to anyone in need. While so employed they were under minimal operational control of higher authority and virtually free to decide for themselves how best to carry out their mission.

+++

Arthur Belair, a National Guard lieutenant attached to Company C of the First Battalion, was amazed at the fall of what seemed like golfball-sized hailstones at around 4:45 that afternoon, as he drove home from the downtown area. Little more than a half-hour later, automobiles with horns blaring began speeding south on West Boylston Street from the direction of Greendale, passing not far from his Tower Street home and headed toward the center of the city. The cacaphony of auto horns and wailing sirens alerted Belair to the occurrence of catastrophe of some kind. Behind these first vehicles came word that a tornado had plowed across Greendale, news of which prompted Belair to jump back into his car and drive to the Wheaton Square armory.

Belair, who was the executive officer of Company C, found some of his NCOs, who had reported for a noncommissioned officer's course to be held later that evening. With the assistance of these sergeants, the company's disaster emergency plan was implemented, with Belair calling the commanding officer, Captain Gleason and the other two company officers, while the noncoms notified squad leaders, who in turn were to alert individual Guardsmen.

Verbal orders to report immediately were passed; such was the response that the company was nearly at full strength when it convoyed to Great Brook Valley at about 7:00 p.m.

Art Quitadamo was driving a panel truck through Worcester making deliveries for Moreschi Florists of Shrewsbury when he saw the black cloud passing above the northern part of the city. Curious, he headed the truck in that direction.

Swerving around downed trees and the myriad fallen and hanging utility wires, he arrived in the neighborhood of Clark Street. He saw two bodies being carried from the wreckage, with house doors being used as stretchers. Having the nearest suitable vehicle, he volunteered to take the two corpses to a hospital morgue and they were carefully loaded into the back of his truck.

Art had not traveled more than a few blocks before he encountered a real ambulance, which he flagged down. The transfer of the two bodies was quickly accomplished.

A second lieutenant in the 181st's medical company, Quitadamo had been scheduled for an administrative drill at the Wheaton Square armory that night. Appreciating how badly he would be needed there in a medical capacity, he headed directly for the armory.

+++

Another member of the medical company, Sergeant Rudy Cortesi, was a pharmacist at City Hospital. On this Tuesday afternoon, he was filling in for a friend in the prescription department of Bergwall's Pharmacy on Main Street. Beginning at about 5:30, he saw and heard several ambulances, sirens wailing, race up Main Street en route to City Hospital. Several private cars, horns honking, went racing by, in apparent disregard of the traffic signals on the busy, congested thoroughfare.

Curious as to whether there had been some sort of catastrophic accident in the vicinity, and that he'd be needed at City, Rudy closed the pharmacy and drove the mile-and-a-half to the hospital.

There, with dead and injured streaming in, Rudy learned of the tornado. Hardly had he begun working in the hospital pharmacy than he got word that all National Guardsmen in the city were being ordered to report to the armory without delay. Since his role of pharmacist as Sergeant Cortesi of the regimental medical company was the same as his civilian one and as likely to be of use in the emergency, and finally, because orders were orders, the sergeant went straight for the armory.

Frank Slesinski, a physician on the City Hospital staff, was in essentially the same position as Cortesi. Dr. Slesinski was a National Guard captain, and the commanding officer of Cortesi's unit. He, too, left the busy hospital in response to the sudden mobilization.

Paul Doherty, age twenty-three, was crossing Lincoln Square at about 6:00 p.m. He had enlisted in the 181st Infantry Regiment shortly after turning seventeen, and had recently been commissioned a second lieutenant. He was scheduled to drill this Tuesday evening, and his curiosity was aroused when he saw a couple of First Battalion trucks roll by. None of the battalion's companies whose members were to drill that night should have been on the move so early, so Doherty headed for the Wheaton Square armory a quarter-mile away, to see what was afoot.

He walked into a crisis atmosphere, with word flying around that the northern part of the city had been savaged by a bad storm; some were already calling it a tornado.

+++

It seemed to Lieutenant Doherty that there was no disaster contingency plan capable of swift and efficient implementation as men rushed around the armory that hectic evening. Improvisation seemed to be the order of the day, coupled with the resolve that it was better to get going now with disaster relief and that the details, such as logistical support and coordination with municipal and state agencies could be ironed out later.

Major Walt Whitney was busily dispatching men in jeeps which, in adapted form, were capable of use as ambulances. Each jeep could accommodate one litter across its flat hood and another across its rear deck, both securely lashed down and with the patients strapped in as well.

These vehicles were directed to proceed to the devastated Greendale and Great Brook Valley areas, there to be employed in assisting the civil authorities with casualty evacuation. This operation would initially exceed the capabilities of locally-available hospital and police ambulances.

Later that evening, Sergeant Edwin Larson, driver of one of the "deuce-and-a-half" trucks that had been returning from Ft. Devens that afternoon, told Whitney of his own near-tragic brush with the tornado. The vehicles had been heading south on West Boylston Street as the tornado slammed across the highway from right to left, only a hundred yards or so ahead of the slow-moving vehicles.

Lumber from the Diamond Match yard had gone whirling through the air, and Major Whitney was told by the sergeant how a stud or plank had lanced through the center of the truck's windshield , grazed his cheek as it flew by, missing Warrant Officer Henry Wolosz sitting next to Larson, and lancing through the canvas canopy which enclosed the rear of the truck.

+++

The commander of the 181st's Second Battalion was Lt. Colonel William Samborski, in civilian life the chief of Norton Company's facilities engineering. A member of a four-man car pool in the engineering department, Samborski and two others were delayed a few minutes at quitting time when the driver for that day was unable to leave at five o'clock. Leaving at about quarter-past the hour, they drove up C Street toward Ararat where they would turn left and head for their homes in Holden. They were stunned to see boxcars lying on their sides on the company's spur track which ran beside the company street.

Because of the numerous fallen trees, the usual twelve or fifteen minute ride home stretched into nearly an hour of trying first one main road, then another, and finally following a series of back roads which skirted the southern edge of the tornado's devastation.

Because of the nature of his responsibilities at the Norton Company, he had to return to the plant that evening, another slow and circuitous trip. All security personnel had been recalled, and Samborski, a civil engineer, was in charge of the entire complex. The area was swarming with maintenance personnel, insurance adjusters and supervisors, many of them heading in the direction of the hard-hit machine tool division.

Several hours later, homeward bound for the second time that day, Colonel Samborski found that a National Guard checkpoint had been set up on Shrewsbury Street, just over the Holden line from Worcester. The Guardsmen were part of the 181st's Third Battalion, which was under the command of Lt. Colonel Francis White. While Samborski had been involved in damage assessment work at the Norton plant, the Third Battalion as well as his own had been mobilized, with the Second Battalion under the temporary command of its executive officer, Major Russell Vinton.

+++

George Welch, a National Guard captain and Col. Pakula's personnel officer in the First Battalion, had a day off from his civilian Post Office job that hot Tuesday. Welch lived south of the center of the city, and at about 5:00 p.m., a brief rain shower was followed by an equally short-lived fall of hail.

Like thousands of other city and area residents, the Welches were alerted to the disaster by the radio appeal for the services of off-duty doctors and nurses. This news was followed immediately by a telephone call from Mrs. Welch's agitated sister, who lived in Great Brook Valley.

The highly agitated woman indicated that there had been a very destructive storm and she requested that her father - or someone - come and take them to the family three-decker on Clarendon Street, in which George and his wife had their apartment. Her own apartment had been so wind-damaged, she claimed, that it was unlivable for the time being.

Her brother-in-law, George, volunteered to make the run, and was able to approach near enough, via Lincoln Street and Pasadena Parkway, to make contact. He also got his first look at the tornado-damaged apartment complex, curtains waving through windows devoid of glass. As soon as he delivered Peg to her parents' home, he hurried down to the Wheaton Square armory and reported in.

Even as he arrived at 6:30 or shortly thereafter, Captain Welch heard soon afterward that blankets and folding cots were arriving at the nearby Memorial Auditorium, having been airlifted in from Westover Air Force Base, only forty-five miles west of Worcester.

+++

Harvey Ball, a first lieutenant and commanding officer of First Battalion's Headquarters Company, arrived at the armory at about the same time as George Welch. He recognized Major Whitney's mud-spattered white car as he hurried inside. Meeting the major, he saw that his face and uniform were similarly bespattered, but Whitney was oblivious to everything but the need to make a maximum response to the emergency.

Lt. Ball had been alerted by Supply Sergeant Lasser, a full-time NCO, whose convoy of trucks, returning to the city from Fort Devens, had so narrowly missed disaster on West Boylston Street. As soon as Ball received the sergeant's call, he called his executive officer and the company's other two lieutenants, telling them to report to the armory as quickly as possible and to have the company's noncoms contact the rest of the unit's enlisted men for the same purpose.

+++

The 181st Infantry Regiment's Service Company (as distinct from Lt. Harvey Ball's First Battalion Service Company) was under the command of Captain Frederick L. King. The bulk of his company's strength was quickly ordered to the grounds of Assumption College by the regimental commander, Colonel Bigelow.

In addition to his primary duty as company commander, Captain King had a collateral duty, that of regimental logistics officer. In this capacity he would remain at the armory, tasked with supervising the setting up and operation of a mess hall facilities which would soon comprise nineteen field kitchens set up and grouped together in a paved armory parking lot.

By 6:00 p.m., it was becoming clear to the National Guard that hundreds, perhaps thousands of people had been rendered temporarily homeless. In response to the disaster, hundreds of Guardsmen would be mobilized for an indefinite period - hence Captain King's emergency assignment.

King's executive officer, First Lieutenant Arthur Arakelian, would be on-scene commander of the unit during its activation on the grounds of the battered Assumption College, with support to be furnished as needed to other Guard units on duty in the adjacent residential neighborhood.

The Service Company, numbering about fifty men at full strength, convoyed to the college in two-and-a-half ton trucks long before sunset that evening. Private William Ormond, who had been sworn into the Guard just eleven weeks earlier, was one of those who made up the convoy.

While still two-thirds of a mile from Assumption, Private Ormond began to notice bits of scattered debris. Within another two blocks, the debris, in Ormond's own words "...quickly gave way to rubble; rooftops and other pieces of houses all over the place; whole houses caved in; glass galore all over, uprooted trees, overturned cars".

Private Ormond, who had just finished his freshman year at Assumption the previous Friday, beheld the "barracks-like building" in which he had taken most of his courses during his freshman year. Parts of the flimsy structure had been blown downwind several hundred yards, toward the baseball field abutting Burncoat Street. The chicken coop which Assumptionist Brothers kept was likewise totally demolished and most of the birds killed. A couple of dogs which belonged to one or another of the Assumptionists lay nearby.

Also demolished by the tornado were two science buildings, two dormitories, three private homes on the college grounds, the large garage and the college workshop. This in addition to the ruined convent and devastated main building. A preliminary damage estimate of $3 million would shortly be established.

+++

At about 7:30 p.m., Sergeant Wittig, who had earlier led a handful of other Clinton Guardsmen on a reconnaissance visit to the point, near Assumption, where the tornado had crossed West Boylston Street, returned. With him was the entire strength of Company M, nearly fifty officers and men under the command of Second Lieutenant Joseph Baird.

Alongside West Boylston Street, downslope from battered Assumption College, state police had stopped a northbound trailer truck and had unloaded from it what was believed to be looted merchandise. The stuff had been piled at the side of the highway. Up toward the college on the littered lawn, Private Edmond Goguen saw a battered automobile lying on its roof. The small convoy carrying the men of Company M slowly made its way up the long driveway to the ruins of the college.

+++

The incremental dispatch of men northward from the armory that began as a trickle shortly after 6:00 p.m. became a flood within an hour thereafter. By 7:00 p.m. all available First Battalion troops, under the command of Lt. Col. Pakula, were at Great Brook Valley, where Pakula took over on-scene command from Major Deignan.

Already at the housing projects, a civil defense operation had begun to be established under the city's director of civil defense and former National Guardsman, Lieutenant Fred Maloney of the Worcester Police Department. When the Guard presence began to expand in the area of the housing projects, Maloney conferred with the commander of the 181st Regiment, Colonel Bigelow, upon the latter's arrival, asking him what the Guard expected of the Civil Defense by way of coordinating its disaster relief efforts with that of the military. The colonel assured him the Civil Defense authorities would supervise the recovery efforts as best it saw fit, with the Guard providing the necessary manpower to implement those policies.

When Colonel Pakula arrived on the scene, probably before his superior, Colonel Bigelow, he was immediately approached by City Manager Francis McGrath and the Worcester Housing Authority's executive secretary, Joseph P. Benedict. The two municipal officials were relieved and grateful for the swiftness and scale of the First Battalion's response. They were willing, even eager, to vest the supreme authority for directing the recovery efforts in Great Brook Valley in National Guard hands for the duration of the emergency.

This act of vesting authority in military hands by municipal authorities, and the circumstances under which it may occur, such as in the case of a natural disaster, are carefully spelled out in the Military Laws of Massachusetts, Section 42, of Chapter 33 of the Massachusetts General Laws. In case of a "public catastrophe" or "natural disaster" of such enormity that the state police and police departments are simply inadequate to meet the emergency, then the sheriff of a county, or the mayor, city manager or board of select-men of a city or town may issue a "precept" to the commanding officer of a military unit within that county, city or town directing him to order his command to mobilize at a time and place speci-fied in the precept, to "aid the civil authority in preserving order, affording... protection and supporting the laws".

The precept shall be in writing, according to these laws, and must be signed by the appropriate civil authority. The regulations further state that the precept shall clearly set forth the reason for which the mobilization is being directed. How the command may best carry out the task at hand, and whatever orders may have to be given or "military measures...be used", are strictly within the purview of the senior military commander. A copy of such precept must also be sent by the initiating civil official(s) to the President.

+++

Lieutenant Colonel Pakula, already regarded by members of the battalion as a taskmaster who expected and got the best from his command, pushed his people hard that evening, with the result that, long before the sun set on the devastation in Great Brook Valley a fully operational battalion command post had been set up in the maintenance building there. More then two hundred Guardsmen were visibly present in the Great Brook Valley Gardens and Curtis Apartments projects, an around-the-clock presence that would last for more than a week and that was initially, and simultaneously, engaged in the search for trapped or buried survivors, discour-agement of potential looters who might already be in the area, and the establishment of a cordon of security around the perimeter of the shattered housing projects, to regulate and restrict all vehicu-lar and pedestrian traffic.

This establishment of security checkpoints was somewhat sim-plified by the fact that a single main through street runs for more than a mile completely through the developments. George Welch, now a retired lieutenant colonel, recalls that the Worcester Police Department was initially in charge of the roadblock at the eastern end, where Tacoma Street joins Route 70. Worcester's police chief, William Finneran, supervised the operation personally. At the opposite end of the development, where Tacoma joins Clark Street, the National Guard set up a checkpoint.

Lieutenant Ball's Service Company sector of the perimeter estab-lished by Pakula was along the south side of Curtis Apartments, with the badly- damaged apartments to his rear and the wrecked private homes on Pasadena Parkway and Yukon Avenue upslope on his company's front. It was in the ruins of one of those homes on that first evening of tragic confusion that the officer saw neighbors energetically searching for the occupant, elderly Mr. Skog, whose body had already been removed and brought to a hospital morgue.

After posting his men at designated points within his sector of responsibility, Mr. Ball returned to the battalion command post and to the unexpected pleasure of large quantities of hot food. Captain Welch told him that the food, which included scrambled eggs, had been given by the Red Cross.

+++

The commanding officer of First Battalion's Company B, Captain John Tangney, had remained at the armory to intercept those of his men arriving late and send them along to Great Brook Valley. Tangney's executive officer, Norm Atterstrom, headed out in a two-and-a-half ton truck, only to find Clark Street, which led to the Valley from Burncoat Street, impeded not only by parts of wrecked homes and splintered trees, but to an even greater degree by automobiles. Some were carelessly parked on both sides of the street, others were filled with curious sightseers.

Atterstrom ordered his driver to push aside any parked vehicle which impeded progress, which was done in a far-from-gentle fashion. A mild- mannered man by nature, he also found himself curtly telling the car-borne sightseers to leave the area, thus becoming part of a joint effort by police and Guardsmen which would continue for many days; an increasingly successful attempt to rid the congested streets of curiosity-seekers whose presence in numbers was already slowing early evacuation efforts to a crawl.

At the housing projects, Atterstrom and his people helped in the enormous task of evacuating the more than two thousand residents of the two projects, since the Worcester Housing Authority had decided to empty all apartment buildings, even those with little or no apparent structural damage, until they could be carefully checked for cracks or other signs of having been weakened by the tornado.

When Atterstrom arrived, injured residents were still being evacuated to hospitals; those appearing uninjured were loaded into all types of emergency rescue vehicles, private automobiles and National Guard trucks for the drive to the city's Memorial Auditorium. There, the Red Cross was preparing to receive them, drawing heavily on its own resources of folding cots and blankets, which would soon be augmented by more of the same.

One of the Red Cross volunteers working in Great Brook Valley that evening was Beverly Jellison, who lived on Millbrook Street, a mile or more to the south of the tornado's path and not far from where Lieutenant Belair had been alerted to the disaster by the cacophony of car horns and sirens.

Mrs. Jellison had recently returned from an extended stay in Texas and the oppressive heat and stillness of that day had prompted her to tell her sister in the early afternoon that she thought a tornado was in the offing.

At about the time the funnel was crossing West Boylston Street, Mrs. Jellison happened to glance down into the backyard of another three-decker, which faced on Ruthven Avenue and backed up to hers. A wooden kitchen chair was sitting in the yard, having been used by someone earlier who had gone inside. As Beverly watched disbelievingly, the chair rose straight up in the air, as though being lifted by an invisible elevator. It came to rest on the roof of the three-decker, nearly forty feet above the ground.

+++

In Great Brook Valley, the Salvation Army was already on the scene distributing coffee, sandwiches and other light refreshments to the busy Guardsmen, and to those dazed and homeless survivors who did not require medical attention. The same organization was also distributing flashlights, the most valuable item imaginable as nightfall approached.

Lieutenant Ball approached an unmarked car from which he had seen members of his company procuring coffee and doughnuts. Annoyed at what he took to be someone attempting to turn a quick dollar, the lieutenant walked over and asked, "How much?"

The somewhat puzzled reply came that the food was not being sold, it was being given away. The vehicle contained two Salvation Army volunteers. Moved by the generosity, the Headquarters Company later "passed the hat", collecting a total of twenty-seven dollars, which in check form was sent to the local Salvation Army office in appreciation.

+++

The First Battalion staff, from Colonel Pakula on down, would have been busy enough in undertaking to carry out their purely military duties, but public relations, specifically the public information of the Guard's sudden mobilization could not be ignored. Captain Welch recalls dealing with reporters from every local radio station as well as a Providence, Rhode Island television station, each of whom was given a quick briefing and assigned a Guardsman as a guide. Worcester Telegram and Evening Gazette staff reporters were extended the same basic courtesy.

Sometime in the evening, General Sirois, commanding general of the 26th Infantry Division, arrived along with the adjutant general, Major General William H. Harrison, and the governor, Christian Herter. The party stopped briefly at the battalion command post while making a tour of inspection of the damaged area. The area, the officials now learned, stretched for miles east and west.

Shortly after arriving in Great Brook Valley, Norm Atterstrom's Company B was involved in the search of several of the battered apartment buildings for bodies or for injured or trapped occupants. He remembers that the Guardsmen located a number of children, wide-eyed with fright but uninjured, whose parents had hastily pushed them into closets with orders to remain there. They had obediently stayed put until discovered by the searchers.

While Lieutenant Atterstrom and Sergeant Donald Langille were searching through the top floor of one of the three-story buildings, part of the roof directly overhead gave way and fell onto them. The steel helmets worn by both men averted concussions or skull fractures and, Lieutenant Atterstrom believes quite possibly saved their lives.

Another Guard officer looked into the kitchen of a second-floor Curtis Apartments dwelling unit where the kitchen table had been set for supper just before the tornado struck. Most of the roof had peeled away, as had the greater part of the north and west walls. The occupants had been hastily evacuated, as had all other residents of the project, leaving their uneaten meal behind them. The officer noted with surprise that the winds which had blasted away walls and roof had left the three glasses of milk on the table completely undisturbed.

+++

Lieutenant Paul Doherty of the 181st Regiment's Headquarters and Headquarters Company, whose initial impression had been that disorganization was the order of the day, spent several hours in Great Brook Valley with his platoon when they were suddenly recalled to the armory and reassigned to Ararat Street-Mount Avenue section of Greendale, not far from the roofless Norton grinding machine plant.

In neither place, the former officer recalled, did the platoon do much in the way of rendering direct assistance to the civilian population. Rather, the platoon seemed to be expected to keep order in general terms, and by their presence to discourage the ubiquitous sightseers from becoming a part of the problem by getting underfoot, and finally, to act as a deterrent to potential looters.

+++

Scarcely had the men from Clinton's Company M debarked from their vehicles and begun to absorb some idea of the enormous damage inflicted on the Assumption campus, when a man came running up to them. He excitedly told the soldiers that he believed his mother was trapped in her collapsed home on Randall Street, several hundred yards due south of where they stood.

Sergeant Charles Locke and several other men ran back with him to the house. No sound came from within, nor was the woman visible from any angle. Efforts had already begun at reaching her, and she was known to have been on the first floor when the down-thrusting tornado winds compressed roof and second story into the first floor, which in turn buckled downward into the basement.

One of the Guardsmen with Locke wriggled between layers of the demolished house, inching his way inward and downward. Finally, in his flashlight's glow, he saw the legs of the trapped woman. Crawling back out again, he described the woman's location, and a man with a portable power saw took a position atop the telescoped house above the trapped woman. He began cutting through timbers, shingles, lathes and whatever else was in his way.

Willing hands tossed the stuff aside and after about an hour and a half of the effort, rescuers reached the trapped woman. The body of Mrs. Sigrid Johnson was removed from its place of entombment, some five hours after she had been killed in the collapse of her home.

+++

At 7:30 p.m., General Harrison, the adjutant general, formally ordered the activation of the 181st Infantry and numerous other units. National Guard records indicate that Colonel Bigelow, commander of the 181st, assumed operational control of all mobilized forces, of which Pakula's 1st Battalion was but one element. Simple geography dictated in a general way the deployment of the 181st's three battalions.

Since the First had already "occupied" Great Brook Valley, the Third Battalion, Lt. Col. Francis White, Sr., commanding, drawn from towns in an eastern semicircle around Worcester, gravitated to Shrewsbury on the first night, setting up a command post in the Walter J. Paton elementary school near the center of town. Present in strength, with individuals continuing to report in, were Guardsmen from infantry, tank and heavy weapons companies from Clinton, Hudson, Marlboro, Milford, Whitinsville and Webster. The Second Battalion, from towns to the north and northwest of Worcester, Lt. Col. William Samborski commanding, included the Headquarters Company, Companies E and H from Fitchburg, Company F from Orange, (shortly to be released to fight extensive brush fires in and near Orange, a small town in north-central Massachusetts) and Gardner's Company G. The Second Battalion quickly moved into the Burncoat-Greendale neighborhoods, setting up a command post at the Vernon Drug Pharmacy at the corner of Burncoat and Fales Streets. Its original area of responsibility extended westward to include the town of Holden.

From the first hours of the call-up, companies and platoons from the three mobilized battalions were used wherever the needs of the moment seemed to dictate. In response to these emergencies, no attempt was made to confine a unit's activities to its roughly-defined sector of responsibility.

In addition to the 181st, other components of the 26th Infantry Division were being activated on the evening of June 9th. These included the division's Quartermaster and Reconnaissance companies, located in Framingham and Natick respectively. As with the bulk of the First Battalion in Worcester, both of these units were at their weekly drill sites when the alert came.

Also mobilized and soon to follow were three companies of the 726th Ordinance Battalion with huge cranes and other heavy equipment, as well as most of Boston's 101st Field Artillery Battalion, five companies strong. The commander of the "Yankee Division", Major General Edward Sirois, had been about to leave Boston that evening by train for Washington. Instead of a restful overnight trip in a sleeping car, the general got very little rest that night, devoting his time instead to supervising the mobilization of these nearby elements of his large and geographically extensive command.

The Air National Guard, too, entered the picture in Worcester almost as soon as the tornado hit. Staff Sergeant Joseph Angelheart, a member of Major James F. Swann's 212th Communications Construction Squadron, lived in Great Brook Valley. He began alerting other members of the unit to the disaster almost as soon as the deadly funnel had passed through the area. Linemen and other communications specialists were on the scene within a matter of minutes, quite possibly the very first Guardsmen to respond. They set to work immediately and were to operate, in shifts, around the clock for a full week.

From the initial confusion there began to evolve something approaching order, or perhaps "structure" is a more appropriate term. It didn't just happen; it was deliberately - some would say arbitrarily - imposed. It began with the cordoning off of the entire wind-blasted Great Brook Valley, just as was being done to the battered Burncoat section, up the hill to the west. What the city police initiated but lacked the manpower to implement, the National Guard carried out, both in the establishment of roadblocks, and the beginnings of what would evolve into a system of passes to residents and to those others performing essential services.

If this procedure barred entrance to a street by someone frantic with worry over possible injury to a loved one, it permitted a city bus filled with injured to exit Burncoat for the nearest hospital without undue delay. It allowed the evacuation of the seriously injured on Bay State Road, lying on doors being used as stretchers, to be loaded into the back of a dumptruck and permitted the truck to return within minutes for a second load. It enabled the unending stream of ambulances, hearses and private conveyances, both volunteered and commandeered, to evacuate almost every injured person before the last rays of the setting sun edged the beautiful billowing clouds with gold. Perhaps only measures such as these averted what a later generation would come to call "gridlock".

Not only sightseers and the morbidly curious were kept at bay by the military during the confusion and tragedy of these first days. On the first evening, Warren Snow, an Army Reserve lieutenant colonel, was at a National Guard roadblock which had been established close to his home, at the intersection of Brighton and Bay State roads, just off Burncoat Street.

The sergeant with Snow challenged a particularly aggressive motorist and ordered him to stop. The driver arrogantly declared his intention to proceed and started his car forward. As the man did so, Colonel Snow drew his .45-caliber pistol from its holster, pulled back the receiver, and let it slingshot forward, chambering a round. He informed the driver as he did so, that if the car moved forward any further, he would shoot out one of the tires.

At this point the driver evidently reconsidered his determination to proceed and stopped the car. Either Snow or the sergeant noticed a silver chain hanging out of the closed trunk. Successfully persuading the driver to open it, the trunk was found to contain a quantity of jewelry and other valuable items, looted from wrecked homes in Holden and Worcester. The driver was detained, the police were summoned and the man was taken by them for questioning.

As Private Jack Ronayne and Sergeant Richard Herbst continued their roving patrol of the Burncoat-Clark Street area, they were to participate in an incident which demonstrates that confusion and disorientation were as fully present in the tornado's wake as death, injury and property damage. The patrolling pair picked up an uninjured but visibly upset minister from St. Michael's Episcopal Church. The man was clearly distraught as he hurried down Clark Street, half-walking, half-running along the sidewalk.

The minister gave the two Guardsmen an address and Jack drove him there immediately, pulling up before a house which had been quite thoroughly demolished. At the sight of the devastated home, the minister broke down completely, sobbing that a dear friend of his lay under the rubble.

Should this be the case, Ronayne and Herbst could see that nothing less than a crane would suffice to lift the enormous sections of wall and roof away. Attempting to comfort the disconsolate minister, they drove him back to his extensively damaged church.

Still later that night the pair of Guardsmen were on or near Clark Street, near where they had met the minister, when they saw another man picking his way along the littered street. Since part of their job was to keep sightseers and potential looters out of the devastated area they asked him where he lived. He told them, then got in the jeep and they drove him home - to the same address where they had brought the minister. The man, it turned out, was the same one about whom the minister had been so worried earlier. The man was almost speechless at the extent of the damage, but had not been home when the funnel hit, thus escaping the entombment which his friend had been certain had been his fate.

For a part of the night, Herbst and Ronayne were accompanied by another pair of volunteers, both of whom were military reservists residing in the Burncoat area. One was a naval lieutenant or lieutenant commander attired in whites, the other a senior Army reservist. The former's identity will probably never be known; the latter may quite possibly have been Lt. Col. Snow of Brighton Road, whose cooperation with the National Guard was extensive and is described elsewhere in this book.

+++

Like their First Battalion counterparts in Worcester, the men of Lt. Col. Samborski's Second Battalion heard of the disaster in a variety of ways. Located a good number of miles to the north and northwest of the tornado's impact area, the evening shadows were lengthening when the convoys from Fitchburg, Gardner and Orange crawled slowly down Burncoat Street.

Gil Currier, whose appointment as Second Lieutenant in Fitchburg's Company E was one day old, had been appointed the leader of the company's rifle platoon the previous Saturday. That afternoon Currier had looked at the distant sky off to the southward from his home in South Ashburnham and had seen the moving blackness. Someone's getting a pasting, he thought. He was right. He got a phone call from someone in his Guard unit in the early evening.

Ray Fortier, a second lieutenant in the other Fitchburg unit, Company H, had been on his way to the armory earlier than usual that evening. He was scheduled to instruct a class of Guardsmen that night. Now, three hours later, with classroom training indefinitely suspended, these men would put into practice whatever training and discipline they had already acquired.

Company command posts and checkpoints to be established, patrol routes and schedules to be worked out - all necessary logistical steps. Yet some of the most vivid memories of the north county citizen-soldiers from the first night involve, not military routine but the sight and sound of distraught mothers walking along the wind-scoured stretch of Burncoat Street calling out the name of a missing child and pressing anyone they chanced to encounter for news of the youngster. Only a few hours later some of the young couples along the same half-mile stretch were hosting impromptu house parties and joking about missing roofs and walls, while hiding their relief at their deliverance under a facade of nonchalance.

Gil Currier finally bedded down for the night on the lawn of a home across Burncoat Street from his company's command post. Other, more fortunate members of Company E were invited by some neighborhood residents whose houses had been spared, to use the family's extra bedroom.

The men of Clinton's Company M, Third Battalion, joined the north county men in providing escort into and out of the damage field that evening and some of the Clintonians, especially some of the more senior ones, got no sleep at all that first night. One of these was Sergeant Locke, who was the company's motor pool officer. Locke, with the cooperation of a nearby civilian homeowner, established a motor pool in the man's extra-wide driveway. Here the vehicles would be parked under 24-hour guard, when not actually operating.

Those men of Company M who were able to grab a few hours sleep bedded down for the most part around St. Michael's Church or on the parking lot of Johnson's 1941 House, an ice-cream parlor a quarter-mile up the street. It had begun to turn quite cool, and having neither blankets nor sleeping bags, Sergeant First Class Andrew Munter and some of the other shivering Clinton Guardsmen took tattered drapes from the damaged church and lay down for a few hour's sleep before first light.

+++

Meanwhile, jeep driver Jack Ronayne was experiencing a high level of frustration. His jeep had just sustained two flat tires, almost simultaneously. The mounted spare was substituted for one of the tires, while a few minutes later another jeep driver gave him his own spare, which enabled the exhausted duo to get rolling again. It was now past 4:00 a.m., and with a growing number of patrolling Guardsmen on duty, in addition to a number of civilian rescuers, all who had been injured or entrapped had been removed to hospitals.

For the last time that endless night, Private Ronayne headed down Clark Street, and swung right onto Tacoma Street to reach Company B's bivouac area near the west end of the Curtis Apartments complex. Passing through A Company's assigned area, a sharp-eyed member of that unit noticed that the jeep Ronayne was driving belonged in fact to Company A. Presumably, many hours earlier when Major Deignan had ordered the young Ronayne to grab the first available jeep, the private had done so - literally.

Now, however, it was relinquished without regret. As anyone who has ever driven or ridden in a jeep for any length of time can attest, comfort of driver or passengers was never a factor in the design of the tough and versatile little vehicle. Herbst and Ronayne were only too glad to climb out of the borrowed vehicle and exercise stiff legs for a few minutes in walking the rest of the way to their bivouac area.

+++

C Company spent little time keeping order in the Curtis Apartments area before Captain Gleason received orders to transport his people without delay to the center of nearby Shrewsbury, where they set up a command post at the new Walter Paton elementary school. Captain Gleason and Lieutenant Belair conferred with the chiefs of police and fire departments as well as local Red Cross representatives and the head of the town's civil defense.

Not long after the last of the dazed and bleeding victims of the affected area between Maple Avenue and South Street had been evacuated from their homes and loaded into vehicles for transport to hospitals, C Company checkpoints were going up at strategic spots on the several main roads which had been crossed by the tornado. Through traffic was routed around sections of Maple Avenue, Grafton Street (State Route 140) and South Street. Local access was only permitted to residents known to the chief of police or members of his department.

This type of visual identification, a makeshift expedient evolving in the confusion of the first night would shortly be modified, as in Worcester, to a more workable system. Municipal authorities would issue signed passes to residents of neighborhoods which had sustained major damage.

As in the Burncoat area, these passes would be honored by Guardsmen manning all such checkpoints. Lack of such written authority meant that entry could be flatly denied to any non-authorized individual, as was sometimes done, depending on how assiduous the noncom or officer in charge of the particular checkpoint happened to be in this regard.

One Worcester Telegram reporter, long known for his determination to let no obstacle keep him from getting the close-up information he felt he needed for whatever story he was covering, was told by Guardsmen not to enter or approach storm-wrecked buildings in the Maple Avenue neighborhood.

A heated argument developed, Captain Gleason appeared and reiterated his standing order prohibiting this type of activity in which the reporter was determined to engage. The exchange culminated in a shouting and shoving match - some say Gleason punched the newsmen - in any case the angry and thwarted reporter ceased pressing the issue and went on his way.

+++

Not all of the Guardsmen who were patrolling the streets of the devastated Burncoat neighborhood that first night considered themselves fearless guardians of law and order. After two trips to Memorial Hospital with the dying Dorothea Rice and other tornado casualties, Jack Hildreth, a World War II Navy veteran was walking on Pocasset Avenue near the corner of Ontario Street. From out of the gloom, he heard a rather tremulous command to halt, which he obeyed.

A young and obviously nervous Guardsman stepped closer and Hildreth asked the private if he thought he would be able to frighten away would-be looters. The young man replied frankly that he wasn't sure, as, he added plaintively, "The sergeant didn't give me any bullets."

+++

Spencer resident Gilbert Pervier had been having his car serviced at a station in the southwestern part of the city. While the mechanic was finishing up his work, Pervier noticed the blackness moving across the northern part of Worcester, some five miles away. The storm's appearance was as threatening as any thunderstorm, yet the usual accompanying sound effects were absent.

Just as Pervier was driving away, he picked up one of the earliest radio reports of the disaster. Instead of driving home, the curious young man headed toward the Great Brook Valley housing projects. On Lincoln Street, as he neared the path of the tornado, Pervier encountered a man wearing a Civil Defense armband, who flagged him down.

The man asked if he would help with the evacuation of dead and injured in Great Brook Valley, and Gil immediately agreed. A few minutes later, he found himself among a small but growing group of men and youths from outside the impact area who were arriving to offer whatever help they could to the dazed residents, many of whom were wandering about, some seemingly oblivious to their injuries.

Pervier recalls assisting in the removal of heavy brick and mortar from atop several dead or badly injured Valley residents. Far more numerous were the injured, whom Gil helped into waiting ambulances or private conveyances.

Another young volunteer, who had been driven out to the valley from the Grafton Hill neighborhood by his uncle, was Francis Mahoney, not quite seventeen years of age. After several hours spent helping in the same manner as Gil Pervier, Mahoney recalls the welcome arrival of a Salvation Army mobile kitchen, which was soon dishing out hot beef stew.

+++

A young sailor who lived in the Great Brook Valley complex had been downtown in civilian clothes and minus his Navy identification card when the tornado slashed through the valley. He immediately telephoned First Naval District headquarters in Boston and received verbal authorization for a two-day extension of his leave. He then tried to get through the security cordon around the housing projects, but lacking both ID card and uniform, he was refused admittance.

Returning to the Lincoln Square area downtown, he went into the county courthouse where he chanced to meet a sympathetic court officer. The magistrate drove the young man to Great Brook Valley, explained the youth's predicament to a police officer manning a checkpoint and the sailor was passed through. The youth was then able to retrieve his uniform and identification card and ready himself for the return trip to Boston and his military duties.

12

Scars of Mind and Body

Many of the early news bulletins issued in the first hours after the tornado's passage implied a devastation even greater than that which had actually occurred. Sixty-six Worcesterites in the tornado's path had been killed or fatally injured in a relatively limited swath across the northern part of a city of two hundred thousand. Yet reports of a city being virtually wiped off the map conjured up in the minds of many images like the photographs of Hiroshima and Nagasaki in the wake of the atomic bombings. Particularly concerned were the hundreds of servicemen from Worcester and surrounding county towns serving at bases across the country and around the world.

On the island of Guam in the western Pacific, some nine thousand miles southwest of Worcester, Airman Hank DiLiddo was weary of the unending output of country music coming from his buddy's radio. He suggested to his friend that they switch to an Armed Forces Radio station to try to pick up a news broadcast. The station was changed, and a few minutes later, the two were listening to a summary of world news.

The announcer read an item about a tornado having devastated the Greendale section of Worcester, Massachusetts, at the mention of which the reclining DiLiddo sat bolt upright on his cot. Even though his family lived on Grafton Hill, on the other side of the city, the worried airman headed for the base's Red Cross office, and through its relay system inquired of his family in Worcester.

Arthur Papandrea, twenty-one, a U.S. Army corporal, was strolling through his barracks on the Japanese island of Hokkaido when he happened to spot a copy of the latest issue of the Army's weekly newspaper, Stars and Stripes, lying on someone's footlocker. One of the feature stories on page one led off with a line such as "Massachusetts City Devastated by Tornado." Worcesterite Papandrea grabbed the paper and read every word of the article, which gave a general account of the tornado's havoc.

Apprehensive about the safety of his family, Corporal Papandrea went directly to an on-base Red Cross office. He sent a telegram to his mother reflecting his concern. Three days later he had a re-assuring reply. The tornado had missed their east-side home by several miles; no family members were injured.

One of the scores of stateside servicemen whose first impression was that Worcester had been erased was Navyman Paul Valinski, stationed at Norfolk (Virginia) Naval Base.

Army draftee Francis Carraher had just left his Worcester home the day before and was beginning his basic training at Fort Devens, only twenty miles to the northeast. Hearing the first radio bulletins, Carraher managed to call his mother, at their home in the southern part of the city. Mrs. Carraher quickly put the disaster into perspective for her concerned son by assuring him that their part of the city had been untouched by the deadly funnel.

In an attempt to verify the status of those individuals about whom queries had been received, the Worcester Chapter generally referred to a Red Cross worker in the immediate neighborhood, someone who in many cases would already know the status of the person or family, or at least would be in a good position to ascertain it. This kind of "local knowledge" was employed in the towns of Holden and Shrewsbury as well.

By mid-morning Wednesday, Francis Moy and four other local ham radio operators had gone to the Red Cross Chapter House in downtown Worcester and set up a message center on the top floor of the one hundred fifty year old building. Many hundreds of messages were sent, received or relayed through this expanded civil defense station, W1BIM.

On Wednesday, the 10th, Mr. Edinburg, for whom Francis Moy worked, sent his van, loaded with built-in communications equipment to the Holden District Hospital. Although the tornado had missed the hospital by a scant half-mile, the hospital's telephones, like those at the WTAG transmitter, were knocked out and would require several days to restore. With the availability of this mobile communications center, the hospital could establish and maintain contact with its physicians and nurses, as well as with other hospitals.

Howie Fuller, a/k/a W1JWM, resumed message traffic at 11:00 a.m. the same morning, continuing until 2:20 a.m. the following morning. On Thursday, Mr. Fuller, an employee of radio station WTAG, put in a day's work there before going back on the air with his amateur set. He put in seven hours of this, going off the air at 2:00 a.m. the following morning.

Friday was a repeat of Thursday, with a marked tapering off of traffic on Saturday, during which Fuller monitored the 10-meter band. During his sixty hours on the air, Fuller had used up his car's battery, which had to be replaced, as did the clutch, which was burned-out in the course of the three hundred fifty stop and start miles he covered during the four-day period.

By the end of Wednesday, the first long day of digging out, City Assessor Joseph B. Carney and members of his staff had personally viewed every destroyed or storm damaged home in Worcester, a total of about four hundred buildings. The aggregate damage to these dwellings, according to Carney's estimate, would total in excess of $32 million.

The Assumption College loss was estimated at $3 million; an Army survey team calculated damage to the two Great Brook Valley housing projects at $1.3 million, mostly represented by thousands of blown out windows and extensive deroofing. Municipal building damage was largely represented by the Brookside Home, which was totally demolished at a property loss figure in excess of $750,000. Damage to city streets, trees, and the water system came to $285,000.

Governor Herter, on Wednesday, wired President Eisenhower requesting immediate release of $10 million in emergency federal funds, while identical bills for $25 million in federal aid were introduced in both House and Senate. Also on Wednesday, the tornado damage was viewed by U.S. Representatives from central Massachusetts, Philip Philbin and Harold Donohue. Flying over the entire length of the tornado damage swath and conferring with municipal officials was U.S. Senator John F. Kennedy. The Senator announced that the Federal Housing Authority was authorized to make one hundred percent rebuilding loans. Kennedy also said that the Farmer's Home Administration would be sending field representatives into the area to assess damage to crops and farm buildings. A similar state survey was already underway.

Also on this busy Wednesday, Worcester firemen were stationed throughout the day at a number of points in the tornado-ravaged area. Their presence was thought necessary by Chief Herbert Travers, in case of fire outbreaks caused by ruptured fuel tanks, gas lines, or electrical short circuits. Worcester's firefighting capability was enhanced by equipment from several major industries in the area: Wyman-Gordon Company, American Steel and Wire, Norton Company and U.S. Steel. As noted previously, on Tuesday evening and through the night, firefighting equipment had arrived from communities all over eastern Massachusetts, some up to sixty miles distant. Boston, Lawrence, Haverhill, Melrose and Medford responded, as well as the neighboring towns of Leicester, Auburn, Millbury, Oxford and Sutton. Ambulances came from Webster and Southbridge, twenty miles to the south, and from Clinton, a dozen miles to the north of Worcester.

+++

The initial appeals for whole blood made by all Worcester hospitals on Tuesday evening were answered enthusiastically; so much so that the hospitals reported a surplus of blood on hand twenty-four hours later.

Without wishing to discourage the steady flow of donors, yet in view of the rapidly growing stockpile of whole blood on hand, with its short shelf life, all hospitals on Wednesday morning began to refer donors to the Red Cross Chapter House on Harvard Street. Blood collected there was packed and shipped to Boston, whence had come the emergency allocation only twenty-four hours earlier. In this manner, a normalization of the balance in whole blood stocks throughout eastern Massachusetts was underway within one day.

+++

Four C-54 Air Force transports landed at the Worcester Airport on Wednesday and discharged fifteen tons of bedding and medical supplies, including one hundred pints of plasma and whole blood. The blood, as it turned out, was extraneous; the rest of the cargo, which had been collected from Ground Observer Corps stockpiles at Grenier Field in New Hampshire, and Otis and Westover Air Force bases in Massachusetts, was off-loaded by personnel of the Orange, Massachusetts National Guard Company and trucked to Civil Defense headquarters in Worcester and the two hardest-hit suburbs, Holden and Shrewsbury.

+++

On Thursday, Major Walter Whitney, administrative officer of the 181st, held a briefing for the press. He stated categorically that not a single case of looting had been encountered by the patrolling Guardsmen, or reported to them. Spokesmen for the Worcester and Shrewsbury police departments and for the Holden state police also cited no reports of looting.

The first arrest for the crime to be reported in the Worcester newspapers occurred on the following day. An angry Colonel William Bigelow, commander of the 181st, had already been quoted in a Boston newspaper as saying that looting was widespread in the tornado-ravaged areas. In Thursday morning's Boston Post, Bigelow had been described as "grim...tight-lipped", when he told the Post correspondent that: "...there's been a lot of looting. Just how much, we don't know."

Residents of the Lincolnwood project, which lay just east of the Home Farm, had not had the benefit of heavy Guard protection afforded by Colonel Pakula to the Curtis and Great Brook Valley Gardens projects on Thursday evening. As a consequence, Bigelow described how, "People just drove up in small trucks, beachwagons and other vehicles...telling the civilian (Civil Defense) guards...that they were residents of the project driven out by the tornado." They then proceeded to examine the property of evacuated residents, selecting and carrying away any items they chose, with no one attempting to interfere with their systematic, wholesale plundering. This situation, belatedly discovered, gave impetus to the policy of issuing passes to civilians in devastated areas.

Many Great Brook Valley residents, upon return to their apartments, found that numerous items, valuable or otherwise, had been stolen. Mary Pederson and her two children found their apartment rifled. The motor in her electric sewing machine had been stolen and her son's plastic piggybank, in the shape of a fuel truck, had been split open and the coins removed.

The practice of turning looting suspects over to the civilian police was followed in all cases. In at least one instance, however, a former Guard officer has told the author, a looter caught red-handed was treated rather roughly before being handed over to the police. The Guardsmen on patrol through the ravaged neighborhoods, living as it were for days on end in the midst of devastation, often tended to have as much contempt for those who would steal from the destitute as did the victims themselves. Some Guardsmen experienced occasional difficulty in treating an apprehended looter in a detached and purely professional manner.

Private Curtis Kennedy, also of Company M, was patrolling with another Guardsman in a restricted area when the two came upon a young man of about twenty, approaching the door of a damaged home. The Guardsmen ordered him to stop, whereupon he scornfully said that their authority was unenforceable since he knew they had not been issued ammunition for their rifles. At this, the young Guardsmen drew their .45 caliber service pistols, pulled back the receivers and let them slide forward.

The young man for whose benefit the pair of Guardsmen had done this beat a hasty retreat, not being certain the patrolling Guardsmen had been issued pistol ammunition. They hadn't.

Another of the virtually infinite variations on the general theme of looting is illustrated in a case recalled by Private Goguen. The incident probably occurred very soon after the tornado and before a National Guard restricted access perimeter became completely effective. The Guardsmen saw seven young men loitering in the vicinity of the short block of stores at the corner of Burncoat and Fales.

Goguen and Sergeant First Class Wilfred Baird questioned the men and made them empty their pockets. This action disclosed what appeared to be stolen articles, so the sergeant called on some of the ample Guard manpower nearby to detain the seven suspects while Worcester police were called. The police responded shortly and took the men away for questioning.

One man who lived near the top of Randall Street close to Burncoat had sustained extensive damage to his home. Pilferage on the day following the tornado was already rampant, and the man knew that after nightfall, Guard presence or no, it would probably increase.

Beginning Wednesday night and for several nights thereafter, the man spent the entire period of darkness sitting on his property with a loaded shotgun across his lap. He did not doze or nod, and no one had the slightest doubt of his intention to use the weapon against a nocturnal thief, should one appear. His wary neighbors, while sympathetic, gave him a wide berth after sundown, and would-be looters contented themselves with easier prey.

There is little doubt that the pervasive Guard presense in the Burncoat-Greendale neighborhoods reduced looting, actual and potential, by rigorously limiting admittance to the neighborhoods. Within a few days, however, pilferage on a considerable scale was detected on the part of workmen at the two gutted housing projects in Great Brook Valley, thus prompting the Guard policy of searching each workman upon arrival and again upon departure in the afternoon. This search also included the trunks of workmen's cars.

+++

In the same Thursday press conference in which he minimized the effects of looting, Major Whitney also stated that "...neither is Worcester under or even close to martial law. We are operating under the precept of the city manager and following his orders..."; a statement which on the face of things would appear to be simple and clear-cut, but in point of fact was neither.

Entrance to the two Great Brook Valley housing projects and to the Lincolnwood Project a half-mile to the southeast, was therefore under strict National Guard control, as were movements of persons within those three projects, and the nature of business which brought them there.

The fact that Corporal John McGrail of the Second Battalion, who sat shivering at his post in the Valley, a carbine empty of ammunition slung on his shoulder, wondered what he and other Guardsmen were doing there, is entirely beside the point. They were there in force and would remain there for some days, simply because the city manager had earlier welcomed Col. Pakula and his men of the First Battalion, and in a few informal words expressed the hope that Pakula and his men would remain on duty amidst the gutted apartments.

In one sense this was the extent of the precept so carefully cited in his statement. No written formalization of the city manager's invitation to Col. Pakula ever ensued. "We didn't have time for that legal nicety at the outset of the disaster," former City Manager Francis McGrath told the author in early 1988. "I guess we just forgot about it until later." In a more general sense, though, Major Whitney was correct. Between 7:00 and & 7:30 p.m. on the night of the disaster, Governor Herter's order to the adjutant general of the state National Guard units, met precisely the legal requirement.

+++

On Wednesday evening, June 10th, just over twenty-four hours after the tornado swept through the city, McGrath, together with other high-level municipal and Civil Defense authorities, met in the "Little Theater", the rear section of the Memorial Auditorium. Also present were the commander of the 181st, Col. Bigelow, and Major Whitney.

The city manager felt so comfortable with the National Guard in charge of things in Great Brook Valley, that he offered to extend National Guard authority to the other devastated areas of the city; i.e., Greendale, Burncoat and Ararat Streets. Colonel Bigelow, for a number of reasons was loath to accept this "offer" and he glanced sidelong at Major Whitney, who shook his head almost imperceptibly. Since Whitney, whose judgement Bigelow respected, seemed to have misgivings that confirmed his own, the city manager's offer was politely but firmly declined.

By the same evening, Wednesday, all disabled vehicles belonging to residents of the two Great Brook Valley housing projects had been towed to a holding area in a field below the apartment buildings, and on the edge of the brook from which the valley derives its name. During the night, Captain Welch heard hushed voices and saw flashes of light among the collection of damaged automobiles. He organized an impromptu posse of the few Guardsmen closest at hand and set off at a run down the hill to apprehend the sneak thieves who were looting the damaged autos. Their quarry scattered as the Guardsmen bore down upon them. Hot pursuit continued until Captain Welch and his men found themselves hip-deep in the waters of the mud- bottomed Great Brook.

+++

Early on Wednesday, June 10th, the day after the tornado, Lt. Col. Snow and units of the 413th Ordinance Battalion, which he commanded were ordered to the Assumption campus to reinforce and assist Lt. Arakelian's National Guard Service Company.

With the battalion came several pieces of heavy equipment. One of these machines was used to carefully clear away rubble from the entrance to one of the college chapels so it became possible to retrieve the sacred altar vessels.

On the first day, Wednesday, Snow was asked by an Assumptionist priest if he would allow some college alumni to help in the cleanup of debris. Snow consented, and four trucks loaded with eager volunteers arrived from Rhode Island within a matter of hours.

Charles Bibaud, an Assumption College student and basketball coach at the prep school had left the campus in midafternoon on Tuesday and driven to his home in Amesbury, in the northeastern part of the state about sixty miles from Worcester. When he returned to Assumption the following morning he was appalled at the sight of what a day earlier had been stately, ivy-covered brick buildings fronted by lush green lawn studded with large maple trees.

+++

Under the energetic supervision of the city manager, heads of various departments began assessing the dollar damage of the tornado almost before the last windborne debris had stopped falling. By about 10:00 p.m. on Wednesday night, a scant thirty hours after the disaster's passage, assessors estimated the cost of repair or replacement of homes destroyed or damaged; public works crews gauged replacement cost of hundreds of shade trees planted by the city which had been ruined; water and sewage systems, street lighting, and parks and recreation equipment damaged was also estimated. The initial housing loss of $20 million and other city aggregate damage of $12 million proved later to have been surprisingly accurate, in view of the speed with which the assessment was made.

Utility crews; power, natural gas and telephone began making repairs almost immediately in Worcester and the devastated towns with crews arriving from elsewhere in Massachusetts, New England, and in the case of power crews, from as far distant as the Middle West. On Wednesday, the day following the tornado, a special above-ground telephone line was strung along the sidewalk beside Burncoat Street. Dubbed the "hot line", residents were able to tap into this line with there own telephone sets. So quickly were telephone repairs made in the Burncoat neighborhood that restoration of service was essentially complete by Saturday.

+++

On the night of the disaster, the National Guard's medical company, under the command of Doctor (Captain) Frank Slesinski got set up in the armory and prepared for an anticipated onslaught of casualties. The expected casualties never materialized; persons in need of medical treatment were brought either to one of hospitals in Worcester or Holden, but they were ready.

Even when medical aid stations were set up on Burncoat Street and in Great Brook Valley, all persons in the former area needing treatment or hospitalization had received it; moreover in the case of Great Brook Valley, the entire population had been evicted pending an examination of each building for signs of structural weakness.

What medical treatment was given, for the most part addressed minor cuts and scratches sustained by Guardsmen moving about on a virtual carpet of broken glass, surrounded by jagged pieces of metal and splintered wood. This, and occasional prescriptions when Guardsmen who found themselves sleeping or trying to sleep on the ground, came down with sore throats.

By Friday night, June 12th, according to Captain Slesinski, no fewer than two hundred Guardsmen had received some form of medical treatment by the regiment's medical company. There were numerous sprained ankles sustained in attempts to climb through or over debris, and an even greater number of puncture wounds. Bruises from falling debris were also a factor.

The most serious case involving an injured Guardsman was that of Corporal Edward DiMarzio, who collapsed from exhaustion and was taken to City Hospital. His condition was initially listed as serious and he spent several days of total bed rest before being discharged.

One day early in the medical company's period of activation, Lt. Col. Pakula arrived at the disspensary with a sore throat for which he told Sgt. Rudy Cortesi that he wanted a certain medication. Sergeant Cortesi informed Colonel Pakula that there was none of that particular drug remaining in the medical company's inventory. He offered to do the next best thing, which was to swab the infected throat of the battalion commander.

The annoyed patient, according to Sergeant Ralph Quitadamo, also of the medical company, who related the incident to the author, ordered that an immediate determination be made of what pharmaceuticals were needed for the medical company to function with maximum efficiency. A strongly worded requisition was prepared and pushed through without delay, according to Sergeant Quitadamo, with a marked improvement in the unit's drug inventory taking place very soon thereafter.

On Wednesday, June 10th, a large wall tent was pitched by the National Guard on part of what what had been, until a few days earlier, grazing pasture of the City Farm, until that facility was nearly erased from the landscape by the tornado. The large tent served several purposes; there Civil Defense Director Maloney could be found, passes to residents of the gutted Curtis Apartments just across Route 70 and to the Great Brook Valley Gardens complex behind Curtis could be issued, and there, members of the press could conduct interviews and otherwise attempt to gather information.

+++

On Company M's first day of duty in the Curtis Apartment complex area of Great Brook Valley. one noncom found a pair of ladies' panties. Slipping into them, he did a seductive "hoochy-kootchy" dance to several of the unit's men who were standing with him.

A Guard major happened on the scene and the red-faced sergeant began to hurriedly remove the panties. The annoyed major ordered the sergeant to continue his seductive performance, much to the latter's embarrassment and his friends' amusement.

Members of the Clinton Company recall that after a couple of days of virtual around-the-clock garrison duty on Burncoat Hill and then in Great Brook Valley, they were allowed to go home for a short while to resupply themselves with sets of underwear, clean fatigues and toilet articles. On one such return to the duty site, Corporal Carmen Morabito showed up with a gallon of home-made Italian wine which was passed around and enjoyed by his buddies during off-duty hours, one assumes.

On another occasion, the wife of Company M's Sergeant Daniel Grivakis rode into Worcester with other Guardsmen's wives. The women brought quantities of fresh-brewed coffee and "CARE packages" of sandwiches, snack foods and cigarettes to the men. During the short time Company M spent on Burncoat Hill prior to its week in Great Brook Valley, Sergeant First Class Michael DiGisi saw a Civil Defense worker refuse to allow a couple who lacked an admittance pass to walk around the corner from the upper end of Fales Street to one of the stores in the adjacent business block. DiGisi volunteered to escort them to and from the store; the Civil Defense man consented, and the purchase was accomplished. The former sergeant still recalls the incident as one of the more extreme examples of checkpoint security in this unprecedented situation.

+++

It was nearly noon on Wednesday when Lt. Col. Samborski, commanding officer of the 181st's Second Battalion, reported in to the Wheaton Square armory. He had been Governor Herter's military aide at Holy Cross that morning. Herter, who had spent many hours in Worcester the previous evening assessing damage and issuing orders, had returned to the city the following day, where he was principal speaker at the college's graduation exercises.

Arriving at the armory, Samborski was greeted by an impatient and somewhat angry Bigelow and General Whitney, one of whom asked, curtly where Samborski had been since the activation of his battalion some eighteen hours earlier. This was in reference to the radio announcements the previous evening instructing all National Guardsmen in the area to report immediately, in uniform, for emergency assignment. As previously noted, Samborski had spent the evening at the Norton grinding machine plant as required by his civilian position as chief of the company's facilities engineering department. Major Vinton, battalion executive officer, had taken charge, the bulk of the men had reported, and the Second was fully functional, with its command post at the corner of Burncoat and Fales. Samborski soon succeeded in mollifying the other two officers and quickly joined his command.

+++

Corporal William Atchue, a cook in the First Battalion's Company B, had been married in Worcester on Saturday, the sixth of June. Headed for Niagara Falls, he and his bride were enjoying a leisurely automobile trip across New York State, when on Tuesday, the ninth, their car was pelted by huge hailstones.

That evening when they stopped for the night, they attempted to call home and were told by the long-distance operator that the call couldn't be completed, since Worcester had been devastated by a tornado, putting hundreds, perhaps thousands of telephones out of service. The couple terminated their honeymoon trip and began the nearly four hundred mile return drive to Worcester almost immediately.

Beginning on Wednesday, June 10th, when he reported for duty, Corporal Atchue practiced his military specialty for the next eleven days, assisting in the preparation, serving and distribution of the tons of food consumed by the activated Guardsmen, and especially in the first days, scores of destitute civilians.

+++

Warren Snow, who as an Army Reserve lieutenant colonel, worked so closely with the National Guard on the grounds of ravaged Assumption College, assisted the Guardsmen in other ways as well. He and his wife, who lived on Brighton Road off Burncoat Street, extended an open invitation to Guardsmen who manned a nearby checkpoint to spend off-duty time on the Snows' front porch. Many of them took the opportunity to get out of the sun and relax with a cold drink or a cup of coffee from the pot that Mrs. Snow usually kept on the gas stove. Fortunately for the Snows, although their electric power had been knocked out, the piping from the gas main to their house was unruptured.

An unforeseen and potentially dangerous side effect of the tornado became apparent on the second or third day after its passage. The danger took the form of a number of dogs in the Burncoat area, former house pets all; animals which were no more immune to trauma from having come through the shattering experience of the tornado than were their human owners and as a consequence had reverted to their feral state. Singly, or in small packs, many with eyes bulging from their heads, close to thirty of these animals roamed through the devastated neighborhood.

Colonel Snow was able to obtain the loan of several shotguns from sportsmen friends, as well as coming up with a supply of shotgun shells. With these weapons the Guardsmen were able to stalk the dogs and dispatch them with less risk to the people living in the thickly settled neighborhood than if forced to use .30-caliber rifles or .45-caliber pistols, with the attendant risk of ricocheting bullets.

+++

Less than two hours after the funnel's passage, several enterprising individuals were arrested at gunpoint in Great Brook Valley for attempting to complete a procedure which the tornado had already begun. They were apprehended atop the flat roof of one of the apartment buildings while busily engaged in an attempt to strip the copper flashing from the roof of one of the damaged and temporarily vacant apartment buildings.

More subtle than outright looting, but no less unscrupulous were two "get rich quick" schemes which were in evidence by Thursday and which were quickly reported to the Worcester office of the Better Business Bureau. One scheme was attempted by a number of so-called "building contractors", who suddenly appeared on the local scene, offering home rebuilding or repair contracts to tornado victims at grossly inflated prices. The local Master Builders' spokesman, Wilfred Perrin, was quoted in Friday's Telegram as urging homeowners to employ only builders of known reputation.

Another money-making device was discovered in the form of numerous books of printed lottery tickets, the sale of which allegedly would benefit "a tornado victim". The police vice squad seized one hundred twenty five books of tickets from a single individual. Under questioning it was determined that he, not a tornado victim, would be the principal beneficiary of ticket sales.

+++

After having his cuts cleaned and bandaged at Memorial Hospital, Assumption's Fr. Louis Dion telephoned his parents at their home on Woodland Street in Worcester to let them know he had come through the tornado with minor injuries. His mother, vastly relieved, invited several of her son's temporarily homeless fellow Assumptionists to spend the night at her home.

The following morning, still wearing the bloodstained tee-shirt and torn black clerical trousers he had been wearing while helping to exhume Fr. Devincq's body the previous day, Fr. Dion and his equally ragged clerical companions went to a store in downtown Worcester, Jobber's Outlet, where they bought work clothes, the most practical apparel for the coming days at Assumption.

As the owner, Joseph Casdin, was about to ring up the sale, Fr. Dion asked him to charge the clothing to Assumption College. Realizing the circumstances which had brought Fr. Dion into his store that morning, Joe Casdin shook his head. "No charge," he said.

Attired in his workman's garb, Fr. Dion, securing the assistance of a friend, wasted no time in visiting the college's wooden science building with its caved-in roof. The pair proceeded to examine the microscopes stored there, salvaging a goodly number. Arrangements were soon made to store the undamaged or repairable instruments at Holy Cross College, through the willing cooperation of Father Busam, chairman of the Jesuit college's Biology Department.

Assumption had planned to offer, for the second consecutive year, a summer school in the French language, in which participants, mostly teachers, both lay and religious, could earn a master's degree in the field. Now the summer school's director, Father Devincq, was dead and the Assumption campus looked as though it had been the target of a well-aimed bombing blitz. The language institute was scheduled to begin on Monday, June 15, only five days hence.

Father Dion conferred at length with Assumption's president, Rev. Armand Desautels, on this apparently insurmountable problem. As a result of this urgent meeting, Fr. Dion agreed to assume the summer school's directorship and to make every possible effort to offer the course as promised.

Holy Cross, having already offered rooms to a number of temporarily displaced Assumptionist priests and brothers, came forward once again. Classroom and dormitory space was found and made available to enrollees in the French course, and an office was put at Fr. Dion's disposal. The language school began as scheduled on June 15.

In anticipation of the coming academic year, commencing in September, co-location of Assumption at Holy Cross was logistically impossible. For the coming year, Assumption's administrative offices were to be located in a suite at the Bancroft Hotel, Worcester's largest, located in the downtown area of the city. Classes for both college and prep school would be held in a large rented building at 1010 Main Street, just over a mile south of the Bancroft Hotel.

Edward Kennedy, who had recently opened an insurance office, and whose interest in Assumption College went far beyond having a son in the prep school's freshman class, was asked by college officials to grant himself a couple of weeks leave of absence in order to head a fundraising drive to enable the devastated college to rebuild. Kennedy agreed, never dreaming that the two weeks would stretch into eighteen months, a period during which the college would make fundamental policy and curriculum changes and would relocate to a new campus.

Within a day or so following the tornado, Edward Kennedy called on another Mr. Kennedy to request his financial assistance in helping the stricken college get back on its feet. The newly-appointed fund-raiser had met Joseph P. Kennedy, Sr., former ambassador to the Court of St. James, when he had campaigned for his son Jack the previous year, in the latter's successful bid for the U.S. Senate.

The elder Kennedy, contacted by telephone, immediately agreed "to do something" for Assumption. That "something" took tangible form some days later, when Joseph Kennedy's daughter, Jean, and Jacqueline Bouvier, soon to be his daughter-in-law, presented the grateful Edward Kennedy with a check for $150,000.

Among a host of other donations, large and small, was a gift of $5,000 from the Moscow embassies of several western European nations in appreciation of the Assumptionist chaplain presence which had been available to them since the United States had accorded diplomatic recognition to the Soviet Union nearly two decades earlier.

While continuing to oversee the the ongoing effort to raise money for the college, Ed Kennedy aroused the ire of some members of the Assumption community when he urged that the traditional admissions requirement of fluency in the French language be abolished, and that the teaching of other subjects in French should likewise cease. An advanced biology course, he argued, was challenging enough in English, the language of the general population, without requiring the mastery of an equivalent technical vocabulary in French.

Those who saw Assumption as a bastion of French language and culture were understandably less than enthusiastic about the change, but these traditionalists were not able to prevent its implementation during the 1953-'54 academic year.

Another proposed change, of which Ed Kennedy was a vocal proponent, concerned athletic scholarships, specifically in the sport of basketball. At Kennedy's urging, the college began to aggressively recruit high school seniors who were both high academic achievers and exceptionally talented basketball players.

The players thus recruited that first year, if Ed Kennedy's recollection is correct, numbered three. One of them, a tall young man from New Jersey named Joseph O'Brien would in later years achieve national prominence in the world of college basketball as the manager of the Assumption Greyhounds. Still later, he would be named to head the Basketball Hall of Fame Museum in Springfield, Massachusetts.

By far the most significant change brought to Assumption College by the tornado, and one in which Edward Kennedy, in his capacity as fundraiser was instrumental, concerned the rebuilding of the college's buildings. Only the main building on campus was rebuilt; the convent and other wooden structures were razed. A new campus rose on pasture and wooded land off Salisbury Street on Worcester's west side. The college faculty and students would move to the new campus from their temporary quarters at 1010 Main Street in the fall of 1956, leaving the prep school as sole tenant on the old West Boylston Street site.

+++

Marvin Richmond, who operated his own photographic studio in Worcester and was also on the staff of the Worcester Telegram, toured the devastated areas from Great Brook Valley to Holden on the night of the tornado and the following day. He was equipped with both still and motion picture cameras. The movie film which he shot that evening and the following day was among the most comprehensive footage ever filmed of a natural disaster and would subsequently find use in many disaster training courses across the country.

Some of Mr. Richmond's still photographs were extremely graphic depictions of stunned human beings in the face of sudden destitution. One in particular portrayed Marian D'Agostino, her parents, and her three daughters, bedraggled and clad in borrowed blankets, walking away from their demolished neighborhood. A few days later, a cousin of Marian's, who was on shore leave from his ship in a Turkish seaport would gaze into the plate glass window of a bank and see an enlarged depiction of that photo; with a shock he would recognize his cousin.

+++

One of the busiest people in the city of Worcester the night the tornado struck was Joseph Benedict, assistant director of the Housing Authority. He was a key figure in coordinating the evacuation of all the inhabitants of the roofless and windowless apartments in Great Brook Valley, working closely with the City Manager and National Guard. Yet one of his most vivid memories of that night has no direct relationship to his area of responsibility.

At one point in that hectic evening he was driving past Hahnemann Hospital when a running figure caught his eye. A man was hurrying across the hospital lawn toward the end of a line of would-be blood donors. As he ran, the man was rolling up one of his sleeves. Somehow the hurrying figure seemed to Benedict to embody the spontaneous voluntarism which began immediately and everywhere to manifest itself.

Benedict's major concern, shared by his boss, Raymond Harold, who headed the WHA, was to obtain some sort of temporary housing for as many of the homeless as possible. A large number of government trailers were located in Wichita, Kansas, and Harold soon flew to that midwestern city to arrange for their dispatch to Worcester. This done, Harold flew back to Worcester.

Within four hours of his leaving Wichita, a low-order tornado tore through the area in which the trailers were collected. The funnel destroyed or heavily damaged twenty of the trailers that were earmarked for Worcester.

The first of two hundred and fifty arrived in Worcester on or about the twentieth of June and was set up on the lawn of the James Dixon family, at 152 Uncatena Avenue, being placed beside the slab upon which their home had formerly stood. With Worcester's Mayor Andrew Holmstrom presiding, and Mr. Harold looking on, the trailer was formally presented to the Dixons, to be used as long as it was needed, rent-free.

By early July, a cluster of trailers had been placed near the intersection of Lincoln and Plantation Streets, close to the devastated Lincolnwood project. Others were placed, like that of the Dixons, on the properties of families who were rebuilding. Some of the trailers were large enough to sleep six persons, others only four. All were stuffy and hot during that summer of rebuilding and damp and chilly as fall advanced. However they were infinitely preferable to living in the open air and sleeping on the ground.

Some of the rebuilders were able to move out of the trailers and into their rebuilt homes by late August; most had made the transition by Thanksgiving.

Another source of emergency housing was provided by people who called from outside the stricken area, including persons from Rhode Island and Connecticut, offering spare rooms to homeless people.

A small number of needy persons were provided for by good-hearted city and area residents who owned summer homes. Some had camps or cottages at Worcester County lakes or ponds; a few had summer homes on Cape Cod. A number of temporarily homeless families, especially those with children, gratefully accepted the offer of such facilities, rent-free.

+++

Early on Wednesday morning, the Bonci brothers' milk truck was passed through the National Guard cordon. The brothers' milk route included some of the hardest-hit streets in Greendale. As they struggled to make deliveries to homes which still stood, Art Bonci recalled the previous afternoon, when he had been working in his West Boylston apple orchard.

He had been spraying the trees with their newly formed apples, when a fall of gigantic hailstones forced him to seek shelter, and pulverized the panes of glass in a greenhouse on the adjacent property. Even larger hailstones were falling nearby, several of which were picked up by a young boy, who was then photographed holding them; the largest of which were the size of tangerines.

As the Bonci brothers were struggling to finish the last of their milk route, Alexander Talbot was standing in the middle of his variety store on upper West Boylston Street. He was surveying the havoc wrought by the tornado and trying to calculate what would be required in time, effort and money to restore the business. A determined-looking woman entered the store, which was not open for business, and strode up to him. Annoyed, he recognized the woman as someone who got off the bus from downtown every afternoon and waited in his store for her husband to pick her up. Talbot recalled that she seldom, if ever, made a purchase.

The woman described to Mr. Talbot an experience she had in the store the previous afternoon. In the absence of the owner, a Mr. Roberts had been in charge. During the woman's wait for her husband, the tornado had arrived first. Roberts had urged the woman to accompany him to the comparative safety of the store's basement. Despite the shattering windows and merchandise being tossed about by the wind, she refused.

Roberts wasted no additional words on the woman; instead, he took her firmly by the arm; she resisted, and one or another of the struggling pair nudged a can of paint, which fell from a shelf. The can's cover popped off, and paint splashed on the woman's dress as Roberts practically dragged her to the shelter of the basement.

After describing this heavy-handed treatment at the hands of Talbot's employee, the indignant customer demanded payment for her ruined dress. Mr. Talbot gave the woman no satisfaction, monetary or otherwise. She stormed off, and he turned once again to the task before him.

+++

On the morning after the tornado, Fred Underwood and his father borrowed a truck, secured passes from the National Guard, and were sifting through the ruins of Fred's Brattle Street home, salvaging whatever they could, when a man came up the hill. It was Richard Heald, president of Heald Machine, Mr. Underwood's employer. He had heard on a local radio station the Underwood family listed as fatalities, and had hurried to the Brattle Street homesite hoping the report had been erroneous. Fred assured Mr. Heald that this was the case.

Richard Heald offered whatever assistance he might be able to give, and Fred asked for and received the loan of a company car, to replace his 1950 Ford. The Underwood vehicle had been rendered a total loss when the tornado flung it two hundred yards.

+++

Inevitably, when a disaster of magnitude such as the Central Massachusetts tornado is researched, a number of poignant examples of the "what if..." or the "if only..." type of personal tragedy are uncovered. One such is that involving Harold Erickson, whose death is described earlier in this account.

Mr. Erickson's position at Norton Company was in the experimental laboratories at the western end of New Bond Street. This was the tallest of the buildings in the extensive Norton complex, commanding a good view to the west, in the direction of Holden, the direction from which, on that late afternoon in 1953, the looming funnel made its approach.

Harold Erickson was never able to tell anyone whether he purposely left work some minutes earlier than usual on that fateful afternoon, thus arriving in his driveway at 66 Rowena Street at the moment the tornado struck, causing his fatal injury.

Mr. Erickson's brother, Andrew, has always felt that Harold may have seen the top of the looming tornado above the ridge to the west. Perhaps seeing what he took to be a particularly concentrated and violent thunderstorm, he then abruptly left for home, his brother theorizes, to bring the reassurance of his presence to an elderly mother who would otherwise be alone. Such at least is his brother's premise; whether valid or not will never be known.

What is known, however, with a fair degree of certainty, is that Harold Erickson rode the elevator down from the top floor, with a friend and co-worker in the research and development section, Elmer Hurd, who lived in the Winthrop Oaks development in Holden. Hurd left the parking lot at about 5:07, in all likelihood so did Erickson, heading his car in the opposite direction from his co-worker, and driving directly away from the approaching funnel. Mr. Hurd does not recall having heard his fellow worker express any particular feeling of anxiety or apprehension as the two were leaving for the day.

In any case, traffic would have allowed Mr. Erickson, unaware of the tornado overtaking him, to have covered the two-and-one-half miles to his home in just about seven minutes. The funnel, not constrained, was moving somewhat faster, hence its simultaneous arrival at Mr. Erickson's driveway with such tragic consequences.

+++

In a week filled with stories of misfortune, one of the saddest tornado-related tragedies was concluded Friday morning, when a searcher found the tiny body of two-week-old Charles Oslund, Jr., lying beneath the wreckage of one of several new homes on Colonial Road in Holden.

When the tornado struck, the distraught Mrs. Oslund, infant son in her arms, had been whirled aloft and carried four hundred feet, still clutching her baby. When she was slammed to earth, the baby was spun away from her, sailing another hundred feet before falling to earth, only to be covered by the rain of debris from the sky.

There his tiny body lay like a broken doll, in the midst of countless fragments as searchers combed the neighborhood. Finally, at about 9:00 a.m. on Friday, some sixty hours after the tornado's passage, a neighbor, Melvin Gardephe, who had been searching for the infant through the hours of daylight and darkness, as hope of finding the baby alive began to dwindle, found the small form.

When Mr. Oslund learned that his infant son had been found dead, he murmured, "At last we know...At last we know."

Mrs. Oslund, recovering from her injuries, was not immediately told of this sad discovery. However, a few hours earlier, she had voiced her inner conviction that she would never again see her infant son alive.

+++

The Fisher family of 62 Great Brook Valley Avenue had been almost literally blown out of their apartment. Mrs. Fisher and her daughter Linda were both injured by flying debris and were evacuated to City Hospital. The pregnant Mrs. Fisher had been nearly ready to deliver her child when the tornado struck.. Perhaps precipitated by the injuries she sustained, Mrs. Fisher gave birth to a son in the City Hospital elevator.

Born under these unfortunate circumstances, the little boy fought for his life for about three days. Despite the best efforts of personnel in the maternity ward, on Friday, the newborn lost the unequal battle. The youngest victim of the tornado, and one of the last to succumb, he had never even been given a name.

+++

Worcester Fire Chief Herbert Travers took two steps in the wake of the tornado to minimize the danger of fire breaking out in or near the storm-ravaged areas. He ordered a ban on open fires throughout the devastated areas, except as might be required by governmental agencies. As a further precaution, he ordered a radio-equipped fire engine company to standby duty at the corner of Burncoat and Quinapoxet Lane, This spot was in the midpoint in the swath of destruction across the northern part of the city.

+++

On Wednesday, June 10, the general contractors who had built Great Brook Valley Gardens and Curtis Apartments sent engineers to confer with Raymond P. Harold, chairman of the Worcester Housing Authority. Harold soon gave the go-ahead for temporary repairs to be effected. On Thursday morning, hundreds of workmen reported, called off other jobs all over the East by the contractors.

Working by daylight when possible, under floodlights at night, the mammoth job went quickly forward. In just over four days time, an army of workmen over five hundred strong moved more than 2,500 tons of debris from Great Brook Valley Gardens alone, re-roofed wholly or partially every one of the one hundred fifty nine buildings in both projects, and closed in 4,800 window openings in Great Brook Valley Gardens alone. A grand total of two thousand two hundred rolls of tarpaper was used, along with hundreds of kegs of nails. A survey of the projects disclosed twenty thousand panes of broken glass. An army of one hundred glaziers replaced them in a single day.

By Monday night, June 15, six days after the tornado struck, eight hundred of the nine hundred and ninety apartments in the two complexes had been reoccupied, Through it all, the weather remained rainless, greatly facilitating the round-the-clock repairs.

+++

Many dogs and cats which had survived the tornado and had bolted for cover as the funnel bore down on them came slinking back to their owners during the ensuing days. Some were limping, others were cut, while some appeared to be in a state of shock. The destruction of the Mulhern home on Clark Street, during which Mr. Mulhern was electrocuted, so unnerved Mary's cat, Cooney, that it took many days before he would let any of the family members approach him.

Two blocks away, Ethel Gow had given up all hope of ever seeing her cat alive again. Nearly a week after the tornado, a neighbor across Brandon Road mentioned hearing strange animal noise from his basement. The sounds issued from beneath the platform upon which his washer and dryer stood. Ethel went to the source of the noise and managed to reach far enough under the platform to feel a small animal and carefully draw it forth. She carefully withdrew what proved to be her cat, which had probably been blown across the street and through a cellar window.

Other animals whose owners had been taken to hospitals were brought to the homes of friends or to the Animal Rescue League's kennels for temporary boarding, free of charge to the owners. Injured animals were brought by League personnel to Dr. Masterson, a Worcester veterinarian, who administered necessary treatment, also at no cost to the owners.

One woman, Mary Gagnon, whose dog had disappeared when the funnel wracked her home at 3 Pocasset Avenue, was reading a newspaper several days later and saw a photograph of Animal Rescue League staff caring for stray dogs, whose numbers had dramatically increased as a result of the tornado. She was certain that she recognized her own dog, which she had last seen trying to wedge himself beneath the bathroom washbasin in their home.

She was happily reunited with her pet and learned that he had been found wandering near the Brattle Street Market, three miles from her home. The store's owner had fed the hungry animal before turning it over to the Animal Rescue League.

+++

One young mother, who sustained a deeply gashed knee when her home in Holden's Winthrop Oaks development was flattened, was driven to Worcester City Hospital along with her mother and fifteen-month-old son, each of whom had received a deep scalp cut. Ernest Zottoli, who lived nearby, was trying to bring some semblance of order to the stretch of Route 122 where the tornado had blasted across. In the process, he arranged for a passing motorist from Princeton to drive the injured trio to Worcester City Hospital. With them went their family dog.

The helpful motorist waited at the hospital as long as he was able, but after a couple of hours had passed, he felt compelled to leave for home, taking the dog with him.

After about three weeks, the young mother whom he had assisted finally remembered his name. She called him, was assured that the dog had been well cared for, and the animal was returned to its rightful owners the same evening. It was a joyful reunion.

+++

On Wednesday, June 10, E. Roland Harrison, president of the American Red Cross, announced that the fourteen major natural

disasters occurring since April 18, of which the Worcester tornado was the most recent, had virtually wiped out its natural disaster
relief budget for the entire year.

On the second day following the tornado, Victor C. Passage,
a Red Cross executive, flew to Worcester from the organization's
national headquarters in Washington, D.C. He would personally
direct the Red Cross's massive relief effort, remaining in Worcester
until mid-September.

Stationary canteens operated at the Chapter House, as well at
used clothing and furniture distribution centers. Eight mobile canteens operated on fixed routes through the tornado-ravaged
neighborhoods of the city. These canteens, operating eighteen
hours a day through June 20, and on decreasing schedules and routes
thereafter, served foods and beverages in amounts which soon
reached astronomical proportions. Some eighty thousand cups of
coffee, forty thousand sandwiches, thirty-six thousand doughnuts
and pastries and thirty-seven thousand half-pints of milk were distributed, plus several hundred cases of oranges and apples and lesser
quantities of other foodstuffs. Local and area bakeries and a soft-
drink company gave away quantities of food either directly, through
use of their own trucks, or through the Red Cross.

Food vouchers were given by the Red Cross to needy disaster
victims. These vouchers could be redeemed for staple food items
at local grocery stores. Sometimes, the person redeeming such a
voucher would find that only one or two items on the eligibility
list were still available, yet the entire voucher had to be redeemed
for the recipient to receive even those. One woman, a teenager in
1953, remembers having to surrender a food voucher for a single
can of soup.

The voucher system was laudable in concept, but the redemp-
tion process and inadequate grocer inventories of staple foodstuffs
combined to render this system far less effective than it might
otherwise have been. Flawed or not, the voucher system helped sus-
tain many tornado victims who would otherwise have had to seek
places at the tables of relatives or compassionate friends.

As with blood donations, uncounted tons of completely unso-
licited clothing arrived. The Salvation Army's facility and the two
Catholic Charities stores were recipients of quantities of garments
from Worcester County and beyond. The Red Cross oversaw the clothing collection facility on the main level of the Memorial Auditorium.

As thousands upon thousands of assorted clothing items in all
sizes poured into the Auditorium, the place took on the appearance

of an enormous rummage sale. This influx, plus new shipments of donated merchandise arriving daily needed no fewer than fifty volunteers per shift just to sort it by size and arrange it. The Red Cross estimated that two thousand disaster victims filled "basic needs" from this stockpile.

+++

In March of 1953, Mrs. Elizabeth Berthiaume had been living in a home at 97 Sachem Avenue with her husband and three young sons, when Mr. Berthiaume suddenly died. The young widow was forced to put the home up for sale and she moved with the boys into an apartment in the Great Brook Valley complex.

When her apartment was damaged by the tornado, she applied to the Red Cross for aid. Her modest hopes for financial assistance were far exceeded. The Sachem Avenue home had been seriously damaged by the tornado also, and the Red Cross awarded Mrs. Berthiaume the total of $4,400. This sum covered repair costs to the Sachem Avenue home, basic furnishings, some medical care that had been required, plus the necessities of food and clothing during the weeks when the young family was without a home of its own.

+++

Frank Dakin, a Sutton poultryman, was among the more fortunate of the tornado victims, economically speaking. The Federal Housing Administration made him a loan which partially covered the rebuilding of his poultry house and the Red Cross awarded him the additional money to cover the remaining cost of replacing this structure. The Red Cross also covered replacement of "tools of the trade" for Frank Dakin, which in his case meant the purchase of four hundred laying pullets.

+++

There were many families left homeless by the tornado and living throughout the summer and fall, and into early winter in cramped house trailers parked row on row in the ruins of Lincolnwood. One such included the three surviving members of the Hannah family. As a family of four they had lived at 151 Uncatena Avenue, neighbor of the Steeles, the Sullivans and the Clements. Then the tornado came and Mrs. Hannah had been killed. For her husband, Malcolm, daughter Mary, seventeen, and seven-year-old son David, life could never again be the same.

The Hannahs received the welcome news that their home would be rebuilt through a substantial Red Cross grant. They could look forward to reoccupying it before the worst of winter's cold arrived.

+++

The Red Cross's disaster relief efforts were greater by far in scope than were those of any other single relief organization. If some of those who turned to the Red Cross for aid of one kind or another felt slighted in their personal petitions, this is in part due to an effort at meeting sudden, enormous and varied needs with finite, allocated resources, and in no way detracts from the impressive totality of that organization's work in the tornado disaster.

+++

Jack Tubert, Worcester Telegram sportswriter, wrote movingly on the day following the tornado of the scene in two Catholic Charities distribution centers. Tubert described the groundswell of generosity which caused people to donate cribs, bedding and baby clothing, new and used, in quantity. Both Catholic Charities regular outlets at 70 Green Street, and an emergency relief station set up not far away in the former Glenwood Furniture building on Franklin Street, were deluged with these and other items, to the extent that inventories seemed to grow rather then shrink, despite the heavy demand.

One reason for this, of course, is the generous spirit of those able and willing to give. Another, as Tubert pointed out, is that victims, however destitute, usually sought only the barest necessities, almost always for the children, asking little or nothing for themselves.

Some people, wishing to help, offered cash to be used for the purchase of whatever items were most crucially needed. When Father Timothy Harrington, manager of the Green Street outlet, or another employee informed prospective donors of cash that only merchandise could be accepted, many of these persons rushed out to buy diapers, sheets, even cribs, and returned to the Catholic Charities shop to donate their purchase.

Tubert described the self-consciousness of some of the donors of merchandise, a sort of shy embarrassment. People would set down their bags or boxes where directed, then beat a hasty retreat from the shop. seemingly reluctant to face the flock of mothers, some of whom seemed equally ill at ease, who were trying to fill the basic needs of their children. Seldom, if ever, did a parent leave empty-handed.

Jack Tubert's piece captures the wide-eyed wonder of tots in their parents' arms or held by the hand, to whom the piles of merchandise in the two outlets seemed "like a giant grab-bag". It conveys, too, the sense of selflessness when a mother who had lost every garment she owned, save what she was wearing, smiled at the new pair of shoes her youngster had just tried on, or in some cases let another mother have a particular item for her own child, because she felt theirs was a greater need.

Tubert concluded with a comment on the appropriateness on the city's official seal, which, as befits "the heart of the Commonwealth", features a red heart. The heart, on this day, wrote Tubert, took on an entirely different and deeper meaning, as his short piece depicts so movingly.

The American Supply Company, a department store just across the Worcester Common from Fr. Harrington's busy office, even accepted vouchers for such "big-ticket" items as kitchen ranges, refrigerators, and washers.

One of the more unusual cases recalled by the now-Bishop Harrington involves a woman who came to him one day complaining of soreness of the eyes and blurred vision. Her eyes were red and irritated-looking, so Fr. Harrington arranged for her to see an ophthalmologist who found that tiny particles of fiberglass had been driven under her upper and lower eyelids. The woman received the medical help she needed, gratis. Just as cooperative, the Bishop recalls, were an array of specialists contacted with requests for their assistance in a variety of physical problems, as well as psychological counselling and housing placement.

Bishop Harrington describes Catholic Charities assistance during those days as based on "need, not creed", a moving spirit which was clearly evident in Jack Tubert's description. Thirty-five years after he had issued his last voucher for a tornado victim, Bishop Harrington was in a Worcester store, buying a pair of slacks. A middle-aged woman came up to him and said, "You don't remember me, but I remember you."

He looked at her blankly, and she said, "You helped me in 1953."

"The tornado?" he asked.

"The tornado," she replied. Then she turned and walked away.

+++

On Thursday, June 11, Governor Christian Herter appeared before a joint session of the state's legislature with an appeal for a $5 million bond issue to reimburse Worcester and other tornado-devastated communities for emergency expenditures necessitated by the disaster. In the remarkably short space of five hours and forty minutes, both houses had passed the measure and sent it to Herter who immediately signed it.

Federal help was already being requested by U.S. Senator John F. Kennedy, who had already flown into Worcester, conferred with city officials and toured the damage swath. The senator said he was particularly intent on getting farm loan assistance for county dairymen, orchardists and poultrymen whose means of livelihood had, in a number of cases, been virtually wiped out.

U.S. Representatives Harold Donohue and Philip Philbin had also seen the tornado's legacy firsthand, and were beginning efforts to secure appropriations in the House.

+++

Less than two days after the disaster, the Worcester District Medical Society announced that no person receiving treatment for a tornado-related injury would receive a bill for medical or surgical services, while the County Bar Association pledged the assistance of its member lawyers, free of charge, to any tornado victim in need of legal help arising from the disaster.

+++

On the same day he requested a legislative appropriation, Governor Herter appointed a three-man Central Massachusetts Disaster Relief Committee to receive all donations for tornado relief which were offered or were to be offered by individuals, organizations and businesses. The committee would include George F. Booth, publisher and editor of the Worcester Telegram, John J. Wright, Bishop of the Diocese of Worcester, and former mayor, Everett F. Merrill. In designating the three as members of the committee, the governor named Mr. Booth chairman and Bishop Wright, treasurer.

By late July, contributions to this disaster relief "superfund" totaled over a million dollars. At this point in time the Red Cross had closed six hundred sixteen cases of relief aid to disaster-stricken families, but nearly nine hundred other cases remained open and would be until the families which they represented moved back into their Great Brook Valley apartments.

Although the trio of Herter appointees, Booth, Merrill and Wright - puckishly called by some "the Father, Son and Holy Ghost" - were the nominal overseers of what was often called the "Herter fund" in the early days of its existence, assessing the needs of thousands of potential aid recipients and endeavoring to meet those needs was a monumental task, one that was far beyond the capabilities of any three men.

A broad-based Community Council Disaster Relief Committee was formed, headed by Liscomb Bruce, director of the Community Chest. Other members included Community Chest Assistant

Director Robert Cahill; Walter Olson, Assistant Director of the Family Assistance Organization; Jack Gross of the Jewish Welfare Fund; Monsignor David Sullivan, Director of Catholic Charities; Paul B. Morgan, Jr., of the Red Cross; Rev. George Seale of the Council of Churches; Mildred Wassell, a public-spirited community leader, as well as representatives of organized labor, Worcester industry, and the disaster committees of Holden and Shrewsbury. From this group was chosen a "needs" subcommittee which would review cases of needs and make appropriate allotments. This subcommittee was chaired by Mr. Charles Butler.

On July 22, Morgan and Liscomb Bruce proposed to George Booth that the Morgan Committee be given the responsibility for assessing needs and making appropriate disbursements from the steadily growing relief fund. The offer was accepted, and, at the suggestion of Walter Olson, social workers from every organization represented on the committee were recruited.

+++

Within two days of the tornado's passage, with sightseers seemingly everywhere underfoot, impeding cleanup efforts, the town of Rutland turned this idle curiosity to its collective advantage. Sightseers were pointed in the direction of the Veteran's Administration Hospital and told that the donation of a pint of blood was their ticket of admission to the devastated area.

+++

On Friday, June 12, the city's postmaster, John A. Marshall, received a message from the Postmaster General, Arthur Summerfield, expressing his personal sympathy to all the victims of the tornado. In a concluding sentence, Summerfield said he regretted the wire had not been sent sooner, but he explained that he had just returned to Washington from his home city of Flint, Michigan. Ravaged by a killer tornado the day before Worcester was struck, Flint's death toll had been even greater than the local mortality.

+++

On the same day, a checkbook belonging to a couple residing in the Great Brook Valley Gardens project was received at the Worcester County Trust Company, from a man who had picked it up on his lawn in Dover, thirty-five miles to the southeast. With the checkbook was an offer of financial help if the couple was in particular need of such assistance.

From Dover also came a package containing a pair of woman's panties and a business letter from the files of a Worcester business. The finder had enclosed a brief note. In it, U.S. Senator Leverett

Saltonstall stated that there was probably no connection between the two items.

+++

The Worcester Telegram carried a brief item which indicated that the Wyman-Gordon Company was sending a portable generator to furnish power to Our Lady of the Rosary Church for the Sunday masses scheduled two days hence. The generator would be in place and ready for operation before the end of the day Friday. The church proper had somehow escaped major structural harm, although there was damage to windows, doors and the roof. The parish hall, a solidly-built brick building only two hundred feet to the rear of the church looked as though a bomb had burst at the juncture of roof and back wall.

+++

On Saturday, the thirteenth, the Chaffin's Men's Club of Holden cancelled its meeting which had been scheduled for that evening. This was not surprising, since the tornado had blasted its way across the Chaffin's Village section of the town, before churning through the Winthrop Oaks development. In the same announcement it was mentioned that the homes of seventy-eight of the club's two hundred members had been damaged or destroyed by the tornado.

+++

Emily McNutt of South Weymouth found a wedding gown in her backyard. It was dirty, as would have been expected, but was intact and in surprisingly good condition. A label sewn into the gown read "McDonald, Worcester", indicating that the gown had been blown some fifty miles to its final landing place on the South Shore.

+++

The home of Worcester railway postal clerk Charles Nowlin, who lived on Tara Lane, just off hard-hit Randall Street, had been heavily damaged, like most of those in the neighborhood. Mr. Nowlin had received a paycheck that Tuesday afternoon and had set it down temporarily on the livingroom mantle. During the busy days of cleanup in the tornado's wake, the lost check was forgotten, until one day it was returned in the mail, along with a note from the man who had found it in Weymouth.

+++

Grafton Street Junior High School was closed on the day after the tornado, giving seventh-grade student Kenny Bejune the day off. He and a friend decided to ride their bicycles the four miles to the area of damage.

After the passage of thirty-five years, Ken's most vivid recollection was not so much the incredible battering evident in certain homes which had been reduced to rubble heaps, but instead he was most impressed by the scattering of small, light household articles on a scale he could scarcely comprehend.

For block upon block, the scene was the same. Like pieces of gigantic confetti, articles of clothing, towels, sheets and blankets, whole or in shreds, lay everywhere about them. Trees or their truncated stumps, as well as surviving utility poles and wires, were festooned with these articles or their shredded remnants.

+++

The collection of sheet music accumulated by Ethel Waterfield during her years of professional piano playing had been literally scattered to the winds, as had the evening gowns which she wore during her performances. She had carefully sewn name labels in each of these garments; as a result she was contacted by several individuals who lived along the downwind track of the tornado, from as far east as Westboro, that they had found shredded scraps of some of these once-elegant gowns.

Her pride and joy, the upright piano upon which she had practiced was sent to a company specializing in the restoration and rehabilitation of damaged pianos. Upon close inspection, it was determined that the sounding board was irreparably cracked. The instrument ended its life at Steinert's Music Store in Worcester, serving as a source of parts needed in the repair of other, less severely damaged instruments.

When the initial trauma caused by the destruction of their home had subsided to the point where the Waterfields could attempt an organized inventory of lost possessions, they discovered that their new living room carpet had vanished without leaving the smallest remnant behind. After the passage of several days. they learned that it had blown into the Deedy home which was on the far side of Talbot's store from their own house.

Since the Deedys knew nothing of whence the rug had come, accompanied by numerous other objects from demolished homes upwind, and since the carpet was little the worse for its airborne journey, the Deedys gave it to the local Salvation Army Thrift Store. Upon inquiry, the Waterfields were told by the Salvation Army that it had been sold for a nominal price or simply given away to a needy family.

At this point, the Waterfields resigned themselves to the loss of the carpet. A few days later, however, they received a phone call from the Salvation Army telling them the carpet had been returned for some reason by its new owners. Very shortly thereafter, the Waterfields at last reclaimed it. storing it until their home could be rebuilt.

+++

In Holden, friends and neighbors of Oscar Nygard, whose poultry farm had been obliterated, conducted an all-day search on Thursday, June 11, for the wind-borne birds. Eventually, half of the four thousand hens were located, many hundreds of them dead. Some had been blown up to two miles; many had been thoroughly plucked by the roaring winds.

+++

The carpenter who assumed the job of rebuilding the Phillips home on Worcester's Sachem Avenue didn't think much of the way in which the house had originally been constructed a few years earlier. The term he used for what he felt had been shoddy workmanship was "jerry-built".

Because of this, the carpenter went on, an end wall of the house, the south end, had been torn off by the tornado. Given proper construction techniques, he said this would probably not have happened. However, had it not occurred, he concluded matter-of-factly, the atmospheric pressure differential combined with the power of the tornado's winds would likely have caused the entire house to explode. For the first time, probably, in her life, Helen Phillips was grateful for poor workmanship.

+++

Israel and Sadye Steiman moved away from their Pocasset Avenue duplex very soon after the tornado and have lived for many years on the west side of the city, before Mr. Steiman's death in 1989. Perhaps the only tangible reminder of the tornado in the couple's home is a large pewter tray with a copper inlay in its center. The entire tray is pitted from the high-velocity impact of countless particles of sand, pulverized slate and tiny pebbles.

Mr. Steiman recalled that just below the spot where the tray was displayed in their apartment's living room stood the family's television set. After the tornado, Mr. Steiman took the set, which appeared very little damaged, to a repairman. When that individual removed the tight- fitting back panel from the set, he was surprised to find that a considerable quantity of tiny twigs and shredded leaf matter had somehow filtered through this barrier.

+++

By any standard, Malcolm Hannah was one of the most grievously injured of all the tornado survivors. Hearing his voice on the telephone, the author marvelled that anyone who had been as physically mangled as he, lived for thirty-five minutes after undergoing such an ordeal, never mind thirty-five years.

When his daughter Mary came upon him, he had just suffered serious burns to his lower legs from downed electric wires, through which in his agony he had unthinkingly shuffled. "Shuffled" is the appropriate word, since he had just sustained fractures of both ankles, one so seriously that the joint was destroyed beyond all possibility of surgical restoration. He had an open fracture of the left arm, brain lacerations and a perforated lung. In addition, his left eye had been nearly detached from the optic nerve. Yet somehow he was on his feet when his daughter found him.

Mr. Hannah required blood transfusions totalling ten pints. Lapsing into a coma, he remained in that state for thirty-seven days. Yet a succession of operations restored him to a fair semblance of his former vigor. He walks with a permanent limp, though, due to his shattered ankle joint.

Two or three years after the 1953 tornado, Mr. Hannah and son David were driving through eastern Maryland en route to visit daughter Mary, who had enlisted in the navy not long before and who was stationed at the Norfolk, Virginia naval base. Suddenly, the Hannahs spotted two funnel clouds, in contact with the ground and angling across country, apparently headed in their direction. Worse still, dead ahead, they saw a third funnel cloud coming right at them.

A heavy truck which had just overtaken them from behind speeded up and pulled ahead, then turned sharply off the road and pulled up beside a gas station. At David's urging to "follow the truck", Mr. Hannah pulled in beside the parked truck in such a way that the much larger truck was between their car and the approaching tornado.

Huge hailstones thudded off the car, then the funnel hit. The truck rocked, but remained upright. The car was not overturned either, but was bounced and slammed around so roughly that the two front tires were blown and had to be replaced.

+++

Two blocks west of the spot where the Hannah home had stood until nature's most efficient eraser, a powerful tornado, had moved across the landscape, the Benedicts had reason to count themselves among the more fortunate of the storm's victims. After a three-mile ride in the back of a neighbor's truck to Memorial Hospital, Mrs. Benedict and son Dick had waited with a host of others in the overflowing emergency ward until at length their injuries were examined and the deep gashes sustained by both were sutured.

When Mr. Benedict picked them up later that night, the three stopped and had a long-delayed supper at the Waldorf Restaurant in Lincoln Square, at the foot of Worcester's Main Street. Somehow or other the circumstances of their late arrival came out in the course of conversation. When, at the conclusion of the meal, the Benedicts asked for their check, they were told by the waitress that there would not be one. It was little enough, they were told, after what they had been through during the preceding six hours.

Some days later, Louise Benedict's social security card, which was replaceable, was returned from Orleans, a town on Cape Cod, one hundred air miles to the southeast. Mrs. Benedict's heirloom silver table service, which was not replaceable at any price, was found in the back yard, or at any rate most of the pieces were.

A neighbor of the Benedicts, who was also a member of the Worcester Fire Department, told Scotty Benedict he had seen the front half of their roof, which was of a distinctive and unusual design. It had come to rest atop one of the flat-roofed two-story Curtis Apartments buildings, after sailing a mile and a quarter through the air.

+++

One of the homeowners in nearby Brentwood Estates had taken title to a brand-new home in the development around the first of June. Steve Grant, an insurance agent who lived a few houses up the street, suggested that the man add a wind-damage rider to his homeowner's insurance. After considering the additional cost, the man told Steve he thought instead he'd put the money into shrubbery for his new home.

The tornado did not level the man's home, but caused considerable damage to the exterior, pretty well wrecking the aluminum combination windows. Bill Birge, who lived next door to the Grants, and who made his living selling such windows, supplied replacements to the damaged home - gratis.

+++

The frightened crane operator who bolted from the Norton Grinding Machine plant when the tornado struck, suffered a serious, though non-fatal heart attack that night. He retired on a disability; so far as is known, he never returned to the plant he left so hurriedly, not even to clear out his locker.

About a week after the tornado, Dick Boucher was standing in the damaged plant, with Ed Ledoux and several others, when the subject of the bulky foreman's wriggling between the closely-spaced columns arose. One of the group, who had not seen this feat, asked him to repeat it. Ledoux tried to insinuate himself between the posts, but no matter how hard he pushed or which way he turned, he found it impossible to slide between them.

The new Machine Division plant had been touted by those who had designed it as solid enough to withstand atomic attack. Some days after the tornado struck, a large roof panel from the building was found in Framingham, twenty miles away, giving rise to doubt on the part of many regarding the assertion so recently and confidently made.

A week and a day after he had left the plant to join the other members of Clinton's National Guard company for their emergency mobilization, Andrew Munter returned to work at the machine tool plant. He had left his toolbox unlocked on the afternoon of the ninth and, with some apprehension he went to his workbench and opened the box. Somewhat to his surprise, he found nothing missing; nor had any tool been moved or even touched, so far as he could tell.

With the plant resuming operation, it was found that a grinding machine which a group of mechanics had virtually completed when the tornado hit, was somehow missing an essential part. Then, one of the mechanics remembered he'd been holding the part in his hand when the tornado hit and that he'd continued to hold it when he ran to the parking lot to check on the condition of his car. He was able to remember where he had put it, and when it was located and installed, the new machine worked perfectly.

+++

For many months after the tornado, members of the Bartlett family on Acushnet Avenue would point to a still-visible grease stain on a living room wall, and tell visitors how it had come to be. A can of congealed bacon fat had been standing on a kitchen counter beside the stove when the tornado hit. The can was wafted from the kitchen through the dining room and living room on a curving clockwise trajectory, only being prevented from completing its circuit of the first floor by the intervening interior wall.

+++

To Driane Leland, the noise of the portable National Guard generators set up to furnish emergency power seemed as frightening as the roaring of cyclonic winds. On Wednesday, the day following the tornado, Jim and Driane received a telephone call from his mother in Connecticut. The woman was in a state of near-hysteria, having heard that a Mrs. Leland of Burncoat Street, Worcester, was listed among those known definitely to have died. Driane was able to reassure her distraught mother-in-law, even as the picture of the dead woman's body lying at the feet of her dazed husband came again to her mind's eye.

Jim, who would begin his teaching career in Worcester that September, worked that summer as a carpenter, helping to make habitable again the ravaged apartment units in the Great Brook Valley Gardens and Curtis Avenue housing projects. After working a physically tiring day, Jim was glad to be able to return each evening to the comfort of a full-sized home, in contrast to the hot, cramped house trailers which many homeless families were to live in for up to six months while rebuilding proceeded.

When little Diane DeFosse opened her eyes and looked around her room at Holden District Hospital, the first thing she saw was a tall stuffed animal sitting in one corner, a present from the man who had driven her to the hospital. A tent-like frame lifted the sheet and blank above where her legs had been. No one had to tell her that her legs were gone, and she did not want to peek under the blanket. She remembered everything.

Now, she was treated like a little princess by everyone she met, and she loved it. Even people she didn't know and would never meet sent her dolls and stuffed animals with notes or letters. She even received a watch from someone in Texas. Day after day the get-well cards kept arriving; there were piles of them in her room.

Her surgeon, Doctor Crane, and her nurses were wonderful to her. It seemed that they couldn't do enough for her, even with all the other tornado victims in the hospital who had to be cared for. It was even arranged for her sister Nancy to be transferred to the Holden Hospital from Boylston, so she could spend time with Diane, and continue her own recuperation from a concussion.

At least once a day, nurses would load up a tray with coffee and juices, clamp it onto Diane's wheelchair and off she would go, distributing the refreshments through the men's ward, along with her own special kind of sunshine. She became the pet of many of the patients in the ward; one, John Armand of Hartford, Connecticut, called her "Potato Bug". She found that she was dreading the day when she would have to leave this wonderful world which seemed to revolve around her.

+++

Brian Willett remembers days at Memorial Hospital with his eyes bandaged, then seemingly endless applications of salve. When the nurses weren't looking, there were wheelchair races with his neighborhood playmate, David Hannah. Then, like hundreds of other Worcesterites who had been blown out of their homes, Brian went home to a cramped house trailer that made a normally hot summer seem unbearable.

His eyes had been carefully cleaned of all foreign matter, but physicians were certain that his vision had been impaired to some degree. So, at the age of five, he was fitted to his first pair of glasses. Brian hated glasses; he somehow managed to "lose" or "accidentally" break several pairs in succession, until finally his parents gave up their struggle to keep glasses on their son. Today, having passed forty years of age, Brian Willett does not need glasses.

Brian's sister, Mary Jo, no longer has the brightly-colored sunsuit spotted by a sharp-eyed neighbor on that long-ago afternoon. As Mary Jo Boucher, she lives in an enlarged ranch-style house built on the site of the demolished Willett home. The basement of the present home contains most of the foundation of the original smaller house, largely preventing its effective use.

On a television set sits a black ceramic lamp with a crack in one side. It's the same lamp which struck Mrs. Willett a glancing blow to the head as she huddled in the hall with her children. Her daughter would never part with this grim reminder of a cataclysmic event.

+++

Mrs. Muriel Bailey of Maple Avenue in Shrewsbury for many years kept a ragged pair of trousers that had belonged to one of her sons, as a memento of the tornado. The pants, with identification in one of the pockets, had been blown clear to Westwood, thirty-five miles to the southeast, and had been mailed back by the finder.

An even more surprising item from Shrewsbury that found its way back to its owner, was a waterlogged wedding portrait found floating in the ocean just off the state's eastern coastline. A photograph of the picture was sent to the Worcester Telegram, which published it in the hopes that someone might be able to identify it. Someone did; it proved to be a photograph of Stuart Allen's brother and sister-in-law. The picture was sent to Stuart and Dorothy Allen, from whose home it had been blown.

+++

Simeon Fortin received a prompt insurance settlement for damages to his market; one which he considered eminently fair. He was puzzled, therefore, when the agent covering the claim offered to increase the amount of the settlement by ten percent. When Mr. Fortin asked why this additional settlement was being offered, the agent said that the stresses on the frame building, sturdy as it was, had doubtless been so great that the gradual settling of the structure would cause a major crack to appear across the entire floor in about a year's time. Mr. Fortin was frankly skeptical on this account, yet within a year an extensive fissure, as predicted, did appear.

+++

The Thorndyke Road Elementary School, on a side street just off Burncoat, had been at least five hundred yards south of the tornado's swath of maximum devastation. Yet even so, winds had been strong enough to topple two large trees which had stood in front of the building. As well, many feet of metal flashing had been peeled from the roof by the cyclonic winds.

When the tornado passed that evening, the building had been empty of students. Yet, John McGinn, then a young teacher in the building, recalls that for several years after the tornado, whenever it grew suddenly dark during the school day, often as a prelude to a thunderstorm, many of the younger children would become visibly apprehensive, even fearful. McGinn remembers that a few would sometimes begin to cry. Perhaps they were remembering young Bobby Jackson...or Beverly Clement...or Mike Sullivan...or George Steele...or Dorothea Rice...

+++

The Worcester City Council passed two amendments to the building code which impacted directly on Worcester homeowners trying to decide how to rebuild their damaged homes. One of these stipulated that any residential structure that had been pushed off its foundation to any degree, must be leveled. Exceptions would not be made, even if qualified building inspectors could find no weakening of the structure whatever.

Several homeowners, whose damage was of this sort, were upset at this ruling. Yet these buildings, which the tornado had failed to topple, succumbed to the wrecker's ball. One such example were was the home of Hugh and Christine Dolan. They took grim satisfaction in the difficulty experienced by the professional wrecker, who found that levelling the structure was a far more formidable task than he had anticipated.

The other code amendment concerned the repair or rebuilding of the numerous three-deckers which had suffered major damage or complete destruction in the tornado. These buildings could only be rebuilt or restored to two stories in height.

A far more popular City Council decision was that which exempted homeowners who had suffered tornado damages from payment of municipal property taxes for the ensuing year. In a similar vein, many Worcester banks, which had held the mortgages of tornado victims, allowed deferral of the monthly payment for June, without late charge or penalty of any kind. Many affected persons learned of this generosity only when in a bank or thrift institution, about to make a payment to a teller. Such was the case of the Randall Street homeowner in the Worcester Federal Savings and Loan Association. Pleased and appreciative, he nevertheless elected to make his payment for that month on schedule.

+++

Faced with the problem of trucking away the enormous quantity of rubble strewn across the northern part of the city, the Public Works Department found its own resources unequal to the task at hand, so private rubbish removal contractors were hired to supplement the city's work force and equipment pool.

Day after day, and continuing for several weeks, homeowners in the affected area sifted through the remnants of their wind-ravaged homes and furnishings. That which was salvageable or capable of being reused in repair or rebuilding efforts was put aside. The rest was carried or trundled in wheelbarrows to the front of the property and dumped at curbside.

Each day, large trucks and frontloaders worked their way slowly along the streets in the impact area, scooping up piles of rubbish which had been left since the previous collection and trucking it to be dumped on city-owned land east and north of the Great Brook Valley housing projects.

+++

Tom and Nancy Connor, whose Clark Street home had been half demolished, lived with relatives on the north shore of Massachusetts that summer, while repairs were begun on their Worcester home. At a July 4th fireworks display, the loud fireworks started young Nancy crying hysterically as memories of roaring winds came flooding back. Her mother, recalling the special supper she had begun cooking that ninth of June, ruefully claims it was many months before she could bring herself to undertake the preparation of corned beef again.

+++

"Franny" and Mary Forhan, whose home on 48 Yukon Avenue was blown out of existence on June 9, 1953, built a new home on nearby Carpenter Avenue the following year. In it, and still in daily use, is the only piece of furniture salvaged from their former dwelling - the kitchen table.

+++

Mary Walsh still lives at 90 Randall Street with her husband Francis. Their grown children have long since moved away, to start families and careers of their own. She, too, has a possession which came through the tornado.

When rummaging through the host of broken objects on the floor of her son's bedroom, she came across something given by a friend of hers, a member of the Sisters of Notre Dame, to their son at the time of his birth. The seven-inch-tall white plaster statue of the Infant of Prague, one hand raised in benediction and with its severed head carefully attached, still watches over the household.

+++

One of the controversial medical procedures arising out of the tornado involved the proper treatment of the large number of open soft-tissue wounds, most with considerable amount of dead tissue and nearly always contaminated with foreign matter. Some of these wounds, doubtless because of the makeshift surgical settings or patient overload, had not been thoroughly debrided - cleansed of dead tissue - or irrigated with a weak sterile solution to remove contaminating matter, before being closed. In a number of such cases, the resulting infection necessitated a subsequent return of the patient to the hospital for wound reopening and retreatment. Dr. George Dunlop, commenting on this situation still feels that the actual cases of infection experienced in wounds closed surgically - "Healing by first intention" in medical parlance - was more than offset by the disadvantage of allowing open wounds to heal naturally, "by second intention"; taking weeks to do so, and often resulting in extensive and disfiguring scarring.

In concluding his short paper delivered to the American Medical Society in 1954, Dr. Dunlop stressed the need for a hospital to have designated resident surgeons prepared, when any natural disaster should occur, to do initial screening literally at the door so that patient segregation is done on the way into the hospital, as opposed to a number of physicians attempting to perform triage on an agglomeration of patients with injuries ranging from superficial to mortal.

TORNADO!

+++

At the Rutland VA Hospital on the night of the storm, with the aid of electric power form a generator loaned by a local contractor, a surgical team worked far into the night on Linda Marsh. The branch which impaled her was carefully removed, the massive bleeding was controlled, and the gaping puncture wound was carefully debrided. The enormous amount of internal surgical repair of damaged tissue left Linda Marsh with a long, curving scar from her chest around her side to the middle of her neck. Notwithstanding, Linda made a complete recovery and is today married and the mother of two.

Her mother's fractured spine prevented her from attending her husband's funeral, It was many weeks before she was ambulatory once again, and many months passed before recovery was complete. The Marshes' marriage certificate was found lying on the ground in a Boston suburb.

+++

For five years after the tornado, Catherine Jackson was unable to walk without the aid of crutches. After a dozen years of unaided but painful mobility, in 1970, she was once again unable to walk. A succession of osteopathic specialists confidently attributed this inability to move her legs to arthritis, dismissing the significance of those symptoms which did not seem to support their diagnosis.

Finally, a circulatory specialist sought to explain Mrs. Jackson's persistent complaints of numbness in her legs. Exploratory surgery revealed that the femoral artery in her right leg was constricted due to a buildup of plaque caused by pieces of the wooden bannister which had been embedded in her groin three decades before. With the aid of bypass surgery and the implanting of a section of dacron tubing, Catherine Jackson walks unaided once more.

Because of the confusion at City Hospital on the night of the tornado, her attending physician told her with a smile that she was the only patient he had ever known to leave a hospital morgue alive. More seriously, another doctor told her in 1975, as kindly as he could, that she should expect to live perhaps two years.

"I'm still around," she said in 1988, and considering what this woman has been through since that fateful June day so long ago, she'll probably continue to be around for some time to come. One certainly hopes so.

+++

Two or three days after Bob Harvey's home was spread across South Street, a large side-delivery hay rake which had been in use on Tuesday afternoon, and which had been left behind in the dairy barn was located. It was deeply mired in the muck of Cedar Swamp, about three hundred fifty yards further along the tornado's track.

Even though it lacked surface area which would have enabled the tornado to more easily lift its half-ton weight, the funnel had apparently done just that. After wrenching it out of its new resting place by means of a powerful truck and steel towing cable, Bob cleaned off the machine and examined it. It appeared to be in excellent condition; no parts were bent or broken.

Young Jean Granger was never to forget the pervasive sense of isolation that held Westboro in its grip for several days following the tornado's deadly passage. Telephone communications were of course nonexistent; with electric power cut, radios and television sets stood silent.

The tornado damage had caused West Main Street [state Route 30,] to be closed to traffic in the vicinity of the obliterated Aronson farm. A similar closure of South Street [state Route 135,] was effected when the tornado obliterated the homestead of Emory Harvey, his sons and their neighbors. The police carefully restricted traffic to the eastward from the town's center, in the direction of the spot where Mrs. Cahill had met sudden, violent death. Even on the wholly untouched western part of Route 135 (Milk Street), heading northward from the center of town toward Route 9 and Northboro beyond, traffic was stringently regulated.

The Salvation Army presence in Westboro was actively felt on June 10, the day following the tornado. Salvation Army workers rang the doorbells of many persons whose homes had been untouched, seeking to temporarily place people who were homeless. Jean's father was one of those approached and he immediately agreed to shelter one of the unfortunate.

+++

Walking in a lightly-wooded area near the home he had bought in Shrewsbury in late the 1960s, Jack Flaherty almost literally stumbled across the rusting remnant of the heavy zinc-lined Coca Cola machine which had been heavily patronized on the hot summer days at his golf driving range in 1953. It now rested about a third of a mile from the site of the original shanty in which it had originally stood. Flaherty, however, never saw his brand-new pair of Florsheim shoes again.

+++

A scant thirty seconds before the tornado plowed across the Cosgrove-Flaherty driving range, it had swerved a few degrees to its left, sparing Joe Krilovich's ranch home on Old Mill Road its full brunt.

In preparation for some extensive landscaping work, Joe had recently purchased a truckload of loam - ten cubic yards - which had been dumped in the yard near his house. After he got back from his dash to the shore of Lake Quinsigamond to assist those unfortunates directly in the tornado's path, he returned to his own home - and did a double take.

His home, which had recently been painted pink, was now, almost completely, a muddy brown. The large loam pile, every last particle of it, had vanished. Although Mr. Krilovich hired a crew of professional cleaners, who conscientiously scrubbed and steamed the cedar shake siding of his home, the original color and finish could not be restored. The particles of dirt, moving at about three hundred miles an hour, had abraded the finish and been pressure-driven into the wood itself. It took careful priming and complete repainting to finally cure the problem.

+++

Ten years or thereabouts after the tornado, John Personis, whose car had been spun aloft on Route 9 in Westboro and which had landed atop his lower body, received a letter form the New York motorist who had rescued him. In 1953 the two had not exchanged addresses, but the man had somehow remembered the victim's name. Encountering the name by chance a decade later, the man wrote to inquire whether it was the same man. John wrote to assure him it was, and that he had recovered fully.

+++

Returning from a long trans-Pacfic flight in 1984, Arthur Quitadamo and his wife changed planes in Anchorage, Alaska. In the process, the couple presented their tickets for validation to a young agent behind the counter.

Noting the Worcester home address on the tickets, the agent remarked, half to himself: "Worcester- the twister city."

Asked by a curious Quitadamo why he'd made the remark, the young man told them that in the early 1950s his father had been in the Navy, stationed at the First Naval District headquarters in Boston and living with his family at the South Weymouth Naval Air Station, some fifteen miles to the southeast. The man recalled that as a very small boy he had found a number of windborne "souvenirs" on the NAS grounds, many of them of Worcester origin.

+++

That the tornado's trauma had lasting effect on many of its victims would be difficult to dispute. However, with the passage of years, the nightmares for many seemed to be fewer and less vivid, and it became easier to suppress the panic felt at the onrushing blackness which heralds a severe thunderstorm.

One rather unusual experience was that of Jane Hildreth McKeon. As Janie Hildreth, she had been a year-and-a-half-old toddler in June of 1953. For more than thirty years thereafter Janie had frequently experienced the same disturbing nightmare, never knowing the genesis of the troubling dream.

She imagined herself in darkness with flashes and sparks of light flickering in the gloom around her. As she stared at the strange sight before her, an unseen force would press down upon her, until she felt she was suffocating - or drowning - she could not be certain which. Then she would awaken, and the disturbing dream would fade from her consciousness - until the next time.

Probably because of the death and suffering which the tornado had brought to their old neighborhood, the Hildreths, who had moved immediately thereafter to Coventry Road, five blocks nearer Burncoat Street, never discussed the storm with either of their daughters. However, one day in 1985 or 1986, the subject somehow arose.

As Janie began recounting the dream which had troubled her for a third of a century, her parents were dumbfounded. This woman, now in her middle thirties, who had been little more than a baby in the summer of 1953, was describing the huddling of her family on the basement stairs, while windborne pebbles, like ricocheting bullets, struck sparks form the furnace and cellar walls.

In turn, Janie learned that she and her older sister had been wrapped in protective blankets. The older girl, Paula, had kept her head well covered to shut out the eerie sight and sounds, but the inquisitive Janie kept lifting her head to get a better look at the weird goings-on. In reaction, one of her parents would gently push the curious child's head down and pull the blanket over it once again.

Recounting her recollections proved to be a catharsis for Janie. The recurrent nightmares, which the woman had come to accept as part of her life, did not return to trouble her sleep, ever again.

+++

Three years after the devastating tornado which is the subject of this book, a disaster study published by the National Academy of Sciences - National Research Council in Washington, D.C. appeared. Little more than a booklet of double-spaced typewritten pages, it bore the impressive title Tornado in Worcester: An Exploratory Study of Individual and Community Behavior in an Extreme Situation. The study approached the tornado and the city's reaction to it from a civil defense disaster recovery point of view, treating the subject as analogous to a community trying to recover from a sudden enemy attack.

The study raises a number of interesting and highly debatable points, some of which, at such a remove in time, will never be conclusively settled. There were, the study claims, no fewer than three tornado warnings from various sources before the deadly funnel cloud descended on Worcester from the hills to the west. First was a warning to the New England Telephone Company's main office in Worcester prior to 3:45 p.m. on June 9. The telephone company notified the Telegram and Gazette office immediately and the newspaper city editor asked for, and received, confirmation. However, the phone company refused to divulge the source of its information. The city editor then called the Associated Press's regional office in Boston, which checked with the U.S. Weather Bureau at Logan Airport. The weather office replied that it had received no tornado reports, and the city editor in Worcester was so informed.

A second pseudo-warning involved a weather reconnaissance aircraft from a "military airbase nearby", which allegedly spotted a tornado and reported it. This report is so vague that it explains nothing, while raising several important questions. Why was an Air Force plane making a weather recon flight, such as were conducted in pre-satellite days over the Caribbean in hurricane season, over central Massachusetts in June? Was it out of Westover AFB in Chicopee, then a major bomber base of the Strategic Air Command, or had it taken off from the smaller Hanscom AFB, located about fifteen miles northwest of Boston - or perhaps from Grenier Field, just south of Manchester, New Hampshire?

A third warning is reported in the study. This one took the form of a tornado warning during the afternoon broadcast on an unidentified radio station somewhere in central or western Massachusetts. Whether based on an actual sighting or not is unclear, nor is the time of such report or by whom received.

There was no U.S. Weather Bureau presence in Worcester in 1953, despite the city's population of two hundred thousand. Only a Federal Aviation Administration "observer", Sy Griesdorff, was assigned to the Worcester Airport, which rests on a hilltop high above the rest of the city.

Griesdorff made routine meteorological observations and recorded them in a logbook. An entry for June 9, 1953 is cryptic, but to the point" "Tornado, 10 mi. E of Worc", at about 5:30 p.m. This means that the tornado had entered the city from the west about twenty-two minutes previously, had finished its course across northern Worcester ten minutes later, and was crossing Route 20 in Shrewsbury when Greisdorff logged his report.

This report, from the Worcester police, was sent when the tornado had completed nearly nine-tenths of its deadly journey. With this in mind, it is possible to understand why some of the more cynically-minded saw the establishment of a Weather Bureau office at Worcester Airport soon afterward as an example of padlocking the barn after the horse had been stolen.

The federal study does not attempt to evaluate the veracity of the several quasi-reports, only the first of which seems to have any potential value in serving to alert the city about what might be heading its way. What the study does mention, though, as a frequent cue to an impending tornado, was the fall of enormous - nor merely large - hailstones throughout areas that within a few minutes would comprise the tornado's area of greatest impact, at least in Holden and the northern part of Worcester.

The federal study also published what is believed to be the third of four known photographs taken of this particular tornado. Snapped by a Worcester Telegram photographer who noted the time as 5:08 p.m., it looks in a northwesterly direction across Indian Lake and shows a rather loosely-defined funnel cloud just as it was crossing into Worcester from adjacent Holden.

A number of persons who sighted the rough funnel and recognized it for what it was, had time, the study claims, to take cover. A man in Curtis Apartments saw the funnel "in the distance" and warned the other residents of the apartment building to seek shelter in the basement, which they hastily did. Given the topography to the west of Great Brook Valley in which Curtis Apartments are located, there could have been little more than a minute between the tornado's looming above Burncoat Hill and its ripping into the apartment house at fourteen minutes after five. For the quick-acting residents of this particular building, it was enough.

A fourteen-year-old paperboy in the Burncoat area also correctly evaluated the roaring noise and funnel cloud according to the study, and ran into the nearest house, yelling that a tornado was approaching. The family took the warning at face value and ran immediately to the cellar. The house above them was totally wrecked; the family escaped unscathed. Unfortunately, the name of the paperboy, to whom the family members possibly owed their lives, went unrecorded.

The tornado crossed into Worcester at 5:08 p.m., followed a three and one half mile path across northern Worcester and exited into Shrewsbury eight minutes later, the federal study notes. The diameter of the funnel was one-half mile during its passage through Worcester, which limited the area of so-called "total impact", though not total destruction. The study uses data gathered from tornadoes of similar magnitude in estimating the velocity of the rotating winds at five hundred miles per hour. That estimate proved to be an overstatement of about one-third. Moreover, the funnel crossed into Worcester at 5:04 p.m. and was fourteen minutes in transit across the city.

The atmospheric pressure differential, with the abnormally low pressure associated with the tornado's inner ring caused tightly-closed buildings, such as the Donohue home to explode outward. Even a two pound per square inch drop in atmospheric pressure would cause outward pressure on a wall of nearly three hundred pounds per square foot. The inner ring atmospheric pressure exerted on buildings by this particular tornado may have been considerably lower than a two-pound per square inch differential, with a proportionately higher "explosion" potential.

A bizarre effect of the extreme pressure differential was a phenomenon akin to the weightlessness experienced by astronauts during this last quarter-century, a condition virtually without precedent in 1953 (except for a ski jumper or someone in free-fall). The federal study gives numerous examples of homes wherein windows and doors stood open as a result of oppressive heat which lasted until shortly before the tornado struck. As the normal pressure was rapidly sucked from such a building by the tornado's inner ring, some peculiar things happened. In one instance a pane of glass popped from its frame, fell inward but floated gently down to land unbroken on a concrete floor.

In a second instance, a little girl watched her mother's oven door drop and some potatoes which had begun to bake for supper float across the room and "hit my daddy on the head". In still another apparent deviation from the law of gravity, some eggs popped out of a farmer's crate and began floating away. In a few instances also, the study asserts that very small children "floated" at least partway across a room.

Because of the time of day, many people who lived inside but worked outside the northern Worcester impact area, and who were on the job until 5:00 p.m., had not yet arrived home. Thus, while the population in this area of maximum damage was computed by the federal study at nine thousand, perhaps fewer than 7,500 were in the impact area when the tornado hit. The same would hold true for Holden and Rutland to the west and Shrewsbury and Westboro to the east, especially for those working in Worcester and returning in the evening to those "bedroom" towns.

Perhaps reflective of the 1953 workforce, in which the ratio of men to women was higher than at present, there were about half again as many deaths of adult females as males.

Even in the impact area across Worcester, the total casualties were just a shade over ten percent of those estimated to have been in the impact area when the tornado struck. Of this total of eight hundred and four, sixty-six were killed or died soon thereafter, three hundred twenty-seven suffered major injuries, while four hundred eleven were cases of less severe injury which were reported, through having received treatment at an aid station or hospital. If one assumes, as is likely, that there were as many unreported minor injuries, those treated by a passing doctor, a neighbor, family member or the victim himself, or simply left untreated, then the minor casualty rate doubles, but still would only represent a little more than three percent of the potential victims in the devastated swath.

Hardest hit, from a fatality viewpoint, was Great Brook Valley. Most of the fifteen deaths, however, occurred not in the two projects, but rather in the neighborhood of single-family homes along the streets just to the south. Other sections of the impacted area and their fatality totals according to the survey were Greendale (9), the Uncatena-St. Nicholas area (8) and the Burncoat and Home Farm areas, which sustained five deaths apiece.

Four thousand dwellings were destroyed or damaged to some extent by the tornado, with an aggregate property loss calculated in 1953 dollars at $53 million or more.

Almost unnoticed in the enormity of what has generally come to be known as the "Worcester" tornado, was the fact that at about the same time the huge funnel rolled into being, the same frontal convergence cell sliding northeastward gave birth almost simultaneously to a second tornado, far smaller in size and of a far lower destructive magnitude.

Seeming to come out of nowhere, the small tornado alighted in Exeter, New Hampshire. There it deroofed the Exeter Country

Club, carrying a heavy roof beam almost half a mile. It pounced on six cars parked in a supermarket lot and flung them together, damaging all beyond repair. People in the town saw it looming in the sky and were able to take shelter. Persons walking downtown fell flat as the small funnel spent its brief life. No one in the town was injured, while total damage was estimated at two hundred thousand dollars.

When applying for federal disaster relief funds, the town secured the testimony of professional meteorologists who indicated that this small tornado was almost certainly spawned by the same turbulent cell of frontal convergences as the larger one. With the storm's origin thus attested to, Exeter was eligible for Federal Housing Administration assistance.

+++

The prevailing public belief in central Massachusetts in 1953 relative to the likelihood of a tornado was: "It can't happen here." Meteorological records, however, indicate that it does "happen here" in Massachusetts about five times a year, on average, generally in the spring or early summer. Granted that most of these tornadoes are of low order of magnitude, in which deaths and serious injuries are infrequent, the fact that twenty-seven such storms were authenticated in the Bay State in 1958 by the U.S. Weather Bureau, means that this type of disturbance is far from the kind of anomaly that, for example, a heavy snowfall in Death Valley would constitute.

The enormously powerful hurricane which devastated southern New England in September of 1938 with its attendant damage to roofs and chimneys, caused many Central Massachusetts homeowners to add an extended coverage wind damage rider to their [property] insurance policies. The wisdom of this precaution was amply demonstrated fifteen years later.

As David Ludlum pointed out in his work The American Weather Book, it was not merely public indifference which permitted a hugely powerful tornado to reach such a heavily populated area so unexpectedly, but also the absence of a real capacity for early detection. A photograph of a radar screen at Massachusetts Institute of Technology taken at about five minutes to five, when the tornado was between Rutland and Holden, shows the funnel as an amorphous disturbance, indistinguishable from small thunderstorms. In 1953, radar capable of such discrimination lay years in the future.

Still, meteorologists were well aware that the tornadoes in Flint, Michigan, and in Northern Ohio which had taken a total of about one hundred fifty lives the previous day, had been spawned from cells of the same storm system; an area of instability which was sliding almost due east.

Even with adequate warning, and a consequent reduction in the loss of life which almost certainly would have occurred, property damage in all likelihood would have been undiminished. This, due to the simple fact that this gigantic funnel was one of the most powerful ever known anywhere. In the Fujita classification, devised some years after 1953 to measure the magnitude of tornadoes by estimating wind velocity from a study of debris field configuration, this immense storm ranks as an F-5, at the top of the most powerful of the five strength levels.

Its wind velocity was estimated with reasonable accuracy at three hundred twenty eight to three hundred thirty eight miles per hour; no higher wind speed has ever been gauged for a tornado. Of the thousands of tornadoes studied and ranked between 1950 and 1977, only about two percent rank in this top category.

Of the more than eighteen thousand tornadoes recorded during this period, the average duration of a funnel is fifteen minutes, with a track about six miles long. For the central Massachusetts behemoth, the funnel was in existence for nearly eighty minutes. Its total track, including six or seven miles of above-the-ground skips or bounces, was at least forty-two miles.

The average width of a tornado funnel was computed in the same study to be about one hundred forty yards. At its widest, the tornado which clawed its way across Greendale and Burncoat Hill that afternoon was about seven hundred yards in breadth, exclusive of the damaging fringe winds which extended outward at least five hundred yards from the south or right-hand side of the eastward-moving funnel.

+++

June 9, 1973 was the twentieth anniversary of the tornado's march across Worcester County. At a few minutes after four that afternoon, something occurred that was highly improbable; in fact the odds against it were astronomical. From a churning black cloud above the Kendrick Field baseball diamond on the southernmost edge of the '53 tornado's track, another funnel was born.

Accompanied by a conglomeration of thunder, lightning and a shower of hailstones, the storm moved across West Boylston Street and climbed the west slope of Burncoat Hill, moving along Kendrick Avenue. The storm was a low-order tornado, perhaps an F-2 or possibly an F-3, not deserving comparison with the destructive monster of 1953, yet coming on the fateful ninth of June, it re-awakened painful memories in scores of neighborhood residents.

The small tornado left numerous fallen trees, downed wires and even a few toppled chimneys in its wake as it climbed the hill. Just before reaching Burncoat Street, it turned right and headed south-ward, paralleling the thoroughfare.

Early in its meandering course this small funnel uprooted a fair-sized tree in the backyard of Raymond Rebert and his wife at 110 Kendrick Avenue. Twenty years earlier the couple had been living on Hyde Street, a third of a mile to the north when the tornado destroyed their home.

Mrs. William Harnois of 33 Greendale Avenue experienced a chilling sense of deja' vu when the black cloud enveloped her home and the wind rose. She was upstairs when the blackness descended and her home began to shudder. She forced herself to think of her mother, who had died three weeks earlier. She drew comfort from the memories and from the heartfelt prayer she mur-mured. Soon the trembling ceased and daylight returned.

Modest though the damage was in comparison with its pre-decessor, it took thirty Massachusetts Electric workers some four hours to restore electric power to some three hundred affected households. City workers needed several days to clear away top-pled trees and fallen limbs. Fortunately, no one had been injured in the little storm's mischievous ramble.

It was as though a powerful animal had flicked its tail in the quiet streets of Greendale, causing pulses to quicken and dormant memories to race back two decades to an unforgettable day, when, through the same tree-lined streets, a roaring beast had raged.

* * * * * * *

Addendum

Tornado fatalities by community. Communities are listed in sequence corresponding to the progress of the tornado. Parentheses indicate an individual killed or sustaining fatal injury while in, or passing through an affected community, whose actual place of residence is thus indicated.

BARRE
Beverly Strong
Edward White

RUTLAND
Robert Harding
Donald Marsh

HOLDEN
Alice Beek
Edward Butler
Florence Butler
Lawrence Faucher
Arne Hakala

Liisa Hakala
Frank Hatstat (of Paxton)
Virginia Martilla
Charles Oslund Jr.
Elsie Regan

WORCESTER
Anna Anderson
Nancy Aslanian
James Benoit
Joseph Blouin
Joseph Brunelle
Ruth Burns (of Sterling)
Beverly Clement
Lillis Cleveland
Catherine Dagostino
James DeMarco
Rev. Engelbert Devincq
Grace Dixon
Harold Erickson
Joseph Falcone
Lillian Falcone
Robert Fisher
Abbie Gleason
Susan Gurry
Eleazer Hamilton
Lillian Hannah
Virginia Harrison
Littleton Hayden
William Heyde
Annie Hutton
Barbara Ann Hutton
Robert Jackson
Clarence Johnson
Sigrid Johnson
Anna Karagosian

Joan Karras (of W. Boylston)
Agnes Leland
Blanche Lesage
Ann Lovell (of W. Boylston)
Katherine Marcinkus
Victor Marcinkus
Jacqueline Martel**
Mary Milano
Michael Milano
Jane Montgomery
John Mulhern Sr.
John O'Malley
Philip Osterberg
Mary Pederson
Tillie Pettigrew
Dorothea Rice
Eben Rich
Sheila Riley (of Pittsburgh)
William Riley (of Pittsburgh)
Elliott Santon
Helen Santon
Marie Alice Simard***
Oscar Skog Sr.
May Slack
Lettie May Smalley
George Steele Jr.
Michael Sullivan
Frank Traupis
John Turbidy

TORNADO!

SHREWSBURY
Ruth Carlson (of Northboro)
Lawrence Daly
Nora Daly
Marlene Fisher
Barbara Heitin
Cecilia Howe (of Worcester)

WESTBORO
Charles Aronson
Sadie Aronson
Sheila Aronson
Henry Bailey
Harriet Cahill
Clarence Stantiel (of Melrose)

William Howe (of Worcester)
Ethel McDonald
Stanley Manning (of Worcester)
Nora Mason (of Stoneham)
Jean Paul Niquette (of Worcester)
Catherine O'Hearn

SOUTHBORO
Irmgard Noberini
Robert Noberini
Florence Trioli

*A power company lineman, Frank Hatstat was not killed or fatally injured   by the tornado itself, but was electrocuted two days later in Holden when working to restore power to that town. Including him as a tornado fatality raises the total to 94.

** Known in religion as Sister St. John of God

***Known in religion as Sister Marie St. Helen

INDEX